PROFESSIONALISM
Real Skills for Workplace Success

Lydia E. Anderson

Sandra B. Bolt

PEARSON

Prentice
Hall

Upper Saddle River, New Jersey

Library of Congress Cataloging-in-Publication Data

Anderson, Lydia E. (Lydia Elaine)
  Professionalism : real skills for workplace success / Lydia E. Anderson, Sandra B. Bolt.
    p. cm.
  Includes bibliographical references.
  ISBN 0-13-171439-2
  1. Vocational qualifications. 2. Employability 3. Performance 4. Life skills. I. Bolt, Sandra
B. II. Title.

HF5381.6.A53 2008
650.1—dc22   2006019850

Editor in Chief: Vernon R. Anthony
Senior Acquisitions Editor: Gary Bauer
Editorial Assistant: Dan Trudden
Marketing Manager: Leigh Ann Sims
Marketing Coordinator: Alicia Dysert
Managing Editor—Production: Mary Carnis
Manufacturing Buyer: Ilene Sanford
Production Liaison: Denise Brown
Full-Service Production and Composition: Carlisle Editorial Services
Manager of Media Production: Amy Peltier
Media Production Project Manager: Lisa Rinaldi
Director, Image Resource Center: Melinda Patelli
Manager, Rights and Permissions: Zina Arabia
Manager, Visual Research: Beth Brenzel
Manager, Cover Visual Research and Permissions: Karen Sanatar
Image Permission Coordinator: Kathy Gavilanes
Senior Design Coordinator/Cover Design: Christopher Weigand
Cover Image: Getty Images/Digital Vision
Printer/Binder: Banta Harrisonburg
Cover Printer: Phoenix Color

Chapter opening photos (with the exception of Chapter 8) are from StockByte Royalty Free CD/Getty Images. Chapter 8
chapter opening photo is from Getty Images, Inc./Photodisc/Spike Mafford.

Pearson Education Ltd.
Pearson Education Singapore, Pte. Ltd.
Pearson Education Canada, Ltd.
Pearson Education-Japan

Pearson Education Australia PTY, Limited
Pearson Education North Asia Ltd
Pearson Educación de Mexico, S.A. de C.V.
Pearson Education Malaysia, Pte. Ltd

PEARSON
Prentice
Hall

10 9 8 7 6 5 4 3 2 1
ISBN: 0-13-171439-2

BRIEF CONTENTS

CONTENTS

Over the past few years, college educators have been bombarded with employer concerns regarding graduates' lack of ability to demonstrate appropriate workplace behavior. Few students are able to make the link between their self-esteem and personal financial management and their workplace performance. Many are unaware of expectations regarding business etiquette, appropriate use of technology, and proper attire. In an increasingly competitive work environment, students need to know how to appropriately communicate and deal with conflict, teamwork, and accountability in a fair and ethical manner. Educators have an obligation to employers to teach students these soft but vital skills regarding workplace behavior. This text addresses these issues and provides readers the practical skills necessary to maintain success on the job. Information is complete yet presented in a concise, easy-to-read format.

Professionalism: Real Skills for Workplace Success is written to address employer concerns and provide basic skills for success on the job. This text prepares students for their first professional workplace experience. However, the content is applicable to any individual who works within a traditional business environment. The book is designed not as a textbook but as a workbook that can be kept and referred to throughout one's career.

Presented in a simple, highly interactive format, the text assists individuals in understanding the foundation of effective workplace relationships and how to appropriately manage these relationships. Based on the basic business principle of how performance affects success and profitability, readers are able to integrate soft skills within the framework of a formal business structure. The topics and principles presented will benefit every individual, no matter their career goal. Utilizing a gender-neutral character named Cory, individuals will gain valuable insights based upon Cory's real workplace dilemmas presented as case studies. Additionally, throughout the text are exercises and activities designed to improve the reader's written and oral communication skills.

This book is written for professors, instructors, teachers, and workshop trainers to motivate individuals toward success in the workplace. Attitude, communication, and human relations are the keys to surviving in today's ever-changing workplace. This book teaches realistic survival skills and motivates individuals toward improving both their personal and professional performance.

▶ ORGANIZATION OF TEXT

The text is divided into four modules and sixteen chapters that are arranged to accommodate quarter-, half-, or full-semester courses. Module and chapter topics include:

Module 1: Self-Management

Your Attitude and Personality
Goal Setting and Life Management
Personal Financial Management
Time and Stress Management/Organization Skills

Module 2: Workplace Basics

Ethics and Politics
Etiquette/Dress
Diversity
Customer Service/Quality

Module 3: Relationships

Accountability and Workplace Relationships
Communication
Teamwork, Motivation, and Leadership
Conflict and Negotiation

Module 4: Quality and the Future

Human Resource Management
Networking and Resumés
Job Search and Interview Techniques
Changes in Employment Status

▶ UNIQUE APPROACH OF THE BOOK

This text provides basic information found in working relations guides but accomplishes this task by integrating traditional workplace skills and practical technical topics typically not covered in working relations texts. Unique topics covered in this text include personal finance, human resource management, basic policies/procedures, basic business structures, conflict management, and technology applications.

The overall goal of the text is to provide readers with realistic workplace expectations and experiences. Each chapter challenges readers to apply their newfound knowledge to situations from the boss's perspective in an effort to begin preparing readers for future leadership and management positions. Throughout the chapters are Cory stories and interactive exercises designed to assist the student in applying the topic at hand. At the close of each chapter are a number of activities that reinforce the topics learned. Included are a summary of key concepts; key terms; "if you were the boss" discussion questions; Web links; workplace do's and don'ts; activities; and sample exam questions.

▶ INSTRUCTOR SUPPORT

INSTRUCTOR'S RESOURCE GUIDE

This resource provides instructors an easy-to-follow teaching format for each chapter. Each chapter guide contains an outline of the chapter, suggestions for potential guest speakers and field studies, comprehensive writing activities, and answers to textbook exercises and activities.

TEST BANK

The test bank is presented chapter by chapter with true/false, multiple choice, and short-answer questions.

POWERPOINT SLIDES

Detailed PowerPoint slides are provided for each chapter.

ACKNOWLEDGMENTS

As educators, we are blessed to have jobs we love and families that love us even more. This text was a result of a great friendship between the coauthors and was inspired during a shopping trip when we were discussing how to better prepare our students for the real world. This book is written for our students, current and future, to provide them a competitive advantage in successfully realizing and achieving their career goals.

We are indebted to members of the Fresno, CA area business community who openly shared their expertise and concerns regarding necessary workplace skills. We are also thankful for Prentice Hall Publishing and its wonderful staff who have assisted us throughout the project.

Our grateful appreciation goes to the reviewers of this text for their valued insight: Nancy Porretto, Katharine Gibbs School, Melville, NY; Bob Boutell, National College of Business and Technology, Louisville, KY; Bonnie Heimlich, Fox Valley Technical College, Appleton, WI.

We dedicate this book to our sons Timmy Anderson and Brandon Bolt, two active teens who always manage to surprise and amaze us; and, of course, to our cherished husbands, Randy Anderson and Bret Bolt, who consistently provide us unconditional love, support, and laughter.

AUTHOR PROFILES

Sandra B. Bolt has a Masters in Business Administration with an emphasis in human resource management. She has been teaching in the college setting for over seventeen years. She is currently a tenured faculty member and past Chair of the Business and Technology Department at Fresno City College in Fresno, California. Her teaching areas of expertise include workplace relationships, office occupations, office technology, resumé/interview, and document formatting. She has extensive secretarial and leadership experience, and has served as a computer applications trainer. She is a certified Crown Financial Leader and Trainer and has led many personal financial management sessions for community groups.

Lydia E. Anderson has a Masters in Business Administration with an emphasis in marketing. In addition to years of corporate marketing and strategic planning experience, she has been teaching for over ten years in a community college setting. She is currently a tenured faculty member and past Chair of the Business Administration and Marketing Department at Fresno City College in Fresno, California. Her teaching areas of expertise include human relations in business, management/supervision, human resource management, and marketing. Ms. Anderson regularly consults with corporations and serves as a guest columnist for a business periodical, writing on topics relating to human relations and management.

Both authors have used their professional, educational, and personal experiences to provide readers with realistic stories and challenges experienced in a typical workplace.

YOUR ATTITUDE AND PERSONALITY

OBJECTIVES

▶ Define and describe personality and *attitude* and their influence in the workplace

▶ Identify individual *personality* traits and *values*

▶ State the difference between *self-esteem* and *self-image*

▶ Identify and develop a strategy to deal with past, negative experiences

▶ Define *locus of control*

▶ Identify your primary and secondary *learning styles*

▶ Create a personal handbook

*We
sometimes from
dreams pick up
some hint worth
improving by reflection.*

**Thomas Jefferson
(1743–1826)**

► ALL ABOUT YOU

Congratulations! Whether you know it or not, this is a book about you. And because this text is about you, we need you to first perform a simple exercise. Look in a mirror and write the first three words that immediately come to your mind.

1. _____

2. _____

3. _____

These three words are your "mirror words." Believe it or not, these words describe the foundation of how you view yourself, how you view others, and how you will perform in the workplace.

Reading this text is the first step toward experiencing a more fulfilling and productive career. The secret to healthy relationships at work is to first understand you. Once you understand your personal needs, motivators, and irritants, it becomes easier to begin to understand and successfully work with others. This is why chapter 1 focuses on you, including your personality, your values, and your self-esteem.

Personality and attitude dictate how one responds to conflict, crisis, and other typical workplace situations. Each of these typical workplace situations involves working with and through people. Once you begin to understand your own personality and attitude, it makes it much easier to understand your reactions to others' personalities and attitudes.

The workplace is comprised of people. **Human relations** are the interactions that occur with and through people. For an organization to be profitable, its employees must be productive. It is difficult to be productive if you cannot work with your colleagues. Therefore, workplace productivity is a result of positive workplace interactions and relationships.

Because your personality is a result of influences, it is important to note that there are many outside influences that affect workplace relationships. These influences may include immediate family, friends, extended family, church, and even society as a whole. This means that your experiences and influences outside of work affect your professional behavior. It also means the inverse: your experiences and influences at work affect your personal life. Therefore, to understand workplace relationships, you must first understand yourself.

► PERSONALITY AND VALUES

Your behavior is a reflection of your personality. **Personality** is a stable set of traits that assist in explaining and predicting an individual's behavior. For example, if you are typically organized at work and suddenly become disorganized, others may believe something is wrong. This is because your disorganized behavior was not in sync with your typical stable set of organized traits. In the total person approach, an individual's personality is shaped by many variables including past experience, family, friends, religion, and society influences. Perhaps a family member was incredibly organized and passed this trait on to you. Maybe someone in your sphere of influence was incredibly unorganized, which influenced you to always be organized. These experiences (positive or not) shape your values. **Values** are ideas that are important to you as an individual. Note that your values are only good or bad based upon your personal experiences and influences. For example, one individual may not value money because he or she has been told "money is the root of all evil." Contrast this with an individual who values money because he or she has been taught that it is a valuable resource used to ensure a safe, secure future.

Here is an example of how one's past experience shapes one's values. Cory has worked hard to secure a new job. None of Cory's friends attended college, and many in Cory's sphere of influence have a hard time securing and/or maintaining employment. For this reason, Cory gets no support from friends regarding Cory's goals toward education and securing employment. Unfortunately, as long as Cory maintains the same set of friends, it will be difficult for Cory to achieve success at work because the influences from these friends heavily impact Cory's values and beliefs in the ability to perform successfully at work.

► ATTITUDES

As explained in the preceding example, Cory's lifestyle and behavior are heavily influenced by Cory's peer group (family and friends). If Cory is not careful, over time, Cory will develop the same attitude as Cory's friends regarding education.

An **attitude** is a strong belief toward people, things, and situations. Your past success and failures affect your attitude. That attitude, in turn, affects your performance. An individual's performance significantly influences a group's performance. The group's performance, in turn, impacts an organization's performance. Think about a barrel of juicy, red apples. Place one bad apple in the barrel of good apples, and, over time, the entire barrel will be spoiled. That is why it is so important to evaluate your personal influences. That barrel reflects your personal goals and your workplace behavior. Your attitude affects not only your performance but also the performance of those with whom you come in contact.

Does this mean you avoid anyone you believe is a bad influence? Not necessarily. You cannot avoid certain individuals such as relatives and coworkers. However, you should be aware of the impact individuals have on your life. If certain individuals have a negative influence, avoid or limit your exposure to the negative influence (bad apple). If you continue to expose yourself to negative influences, you lose sight of goals, which may result in a poor attitude.

► SELF-ESTEEM, SELF-IMAGE, AND PROJECTION

Let us review your "mirror words" from the beginning of this chapter. What did you see? Are your words positive or negative? Whatever you are feeling is a result of your **self-esteem**. Your self-esteem is your perception of how you view yourself. Thoughts regarding your intelligence, attractiveness, or ability to achieve a dream are examples of self-esteem. **Self-image** is your belief of how others view you. If your self-esteem is positive and strong, you will reflect confidence and not worry about how others view your actions. If you are insecure, you will rely heavily on what others think of you; hence, you will rely heavily on creating a favorable self-image. While it is important to show concern for what others think of you, it is more important to have a positive self-concept—not conceited but self-confident. People are drawn to individuals who display a good attitude, are confident, and are consistently positive. If you believe in yourself, a positive self-image will follow without effort. It is easy to see the tremendous impact both personality and attitude have in the development of your self-esteem and self-image. The way you feel about yourself and your environment is reflected in how you treat others. This is called **projection**.

◄ EXERCISE 1–1: **All about You:** *Write down four words that explain the following personal attributes.*

Personality Traits	Your Personal Values	Your Attitude Toward Working Full-Time
1.	1.	1.
2.	2.	2.
3.	3.	3.
4.	4.	4.

Envision a hand mirror. The handle of the mirror (the foundation) is your personality. The frame of the mirror is your personal values. The mirror itself is your attitude, which is reflected for you and the world to see. The way you view yourself is your self-esteem; the way others see you is your self-image.

► DEALING WITH NEGATIVE "BAGGAGE"

Many individuals have had past experiences that have been traumatic and painful. These past experiences may include rape, incest, an unplanned pregnancy, a criminal offense, or a poor choice. Unfortunately, these experiences are the ones that most heavily impact your personality, values, and self-esteem.

Consider the following example concerning Cory. In high school, Cory made a poor choice and stole a car. Although Cory paid the dues, Cory is still embarrassed for what was done and feels unworthy of a brighter future. Cory is trying to climb the mountain of success carrying a hundred-pound suitcase. The suitcase is filled with Cory's past poor choice and embarrassment. From others' perspective, Cory does not need to carry this unnecessary baggage. In fact, the majority of those who know Cory are unaware of Cory's past mistake.

If you are one of these individuals, you must recognize the impact your past has on your future. Although you cannot change yesterday, you can most certainly improve your today and your future. Begin taking these steps toward a more productive future:

1. *Confront your past.* Whatever skeleton is in your past, admit that it occurred. Do not try to hide or deny that it happened. This does not mean that you have to share the episode with everyone with whom you come in contact, but it may help to confidentially share the experience with one individual (close friend, family member, religious leader, or trained professional) who had no involvement with the negative experience. Verbally talking through your feelings is the first step toward healing.

2. *Practice forgiveness.* Your past negative experience created hurt. A very important process in healing is to forgive whoever hurt you. This does not justify that what was done was OK. The act of forgiveness does, however, reconcile in your heart that you are dealing with the experience head-on and are beginning to heal. The major question in this step is to identify who needs forgiveness. Maybe it was a family member, perhaps it was a friend or neighbor, or maybe it was you. Your act of forgiveness may involve a conversation with someone, or it may just involve a conversation with yourself. Practice forgiveness. In doing so, you will begin to feel a huge burden being lifted.

3. *Move forward.* Let go of the guilt and/or embarrassment. Once you have begun dealing with your past, move forward. Do not keep dwelling on the past and using it as an excuse or barrier to achieving your goals. If you are caught in this step, physically write the experience down on a piece of paper and the words "I forgive XXXXX" (include the name of the individual that harmed you). Then take the paper and destroy it. This physical act puts you in control and allows you to visualize the negative experience being diminished. As you become more confident with yourself, your negative experience becomes enveloped with the rest of your past and frees you to create a positive future.

This sometimes painful process is necessary if your goal is to become the best individual you can be. It is not something that happens overnight. As mentioned earlier, some individuals may need professional assistance to help them through the process. There is no shame in seeking help. In fact, there is great freedom when you have finally let go of the "baggage" and are able to climb to the top of the mountain unencumbered.

► LOCUS OF CONTROL

The reality is that you will not be 100 percent surrounded by positive influences. You cannot control everything that happens in your life. Your attitude is affected by who you believe has control over situations that occur in your life. The **locus of control** identifies who you believe controls your future. An individual with an *internal* locus of control believes that he or she controls his or her own future. An individual with an *external* locus of control believes that others control his or her future.

Extremes on either end of the locus of control are not healthy. You must realize that individual effort and a belief in the ability to perform well translate to individual success. However, external factors also influence your ability to achieve personal goals. You must take responsibility for your actions and try your best. You must also realize that you cannot totally control the environment and future. Power, politics, and other factors discussed later in the text play an important part in the attainment of goals.

► LEARNING STYLES

Another important element of your personality is your **learning style**. Learning styles define the method of how you best take in information and/or learn new ideas. There are three primary learning styles: visual, auditory, and tactile/kinesthetic.

To determine what your dominant learning style is, do this common exercise: Imagine you are lost and need directions. Do you:

a. want to see a map,
b. want someone to tell you the directions, or
c. need to draw or write down the directions yourself?

If you prefer answer *a,* you are a visual learner. You prefer learning by seeing. If you selected *b,* you are an auditory learner. This means you learn best by hearing. If you selected *c,* you are a tactile/kinesthetic learner, which means you learn best by feeling, touching, or holding. No one learning style is better than the other. However, it is important to recognize your primary and secondary learning styles so that you can get the most out of your world (in and out of the classroom or on the job). As a visual learner, you may digest material best by reading and researching. Auditory learners pay close attention to course lectures and class discussions. Tactile/kinesthetic learners will learn best by performing application exercises and physically writing down course notes. Recognize what works best for you and implement that method to maximize your learning experience. Also recognize that not everyone learns the same way you do. With that recognition, you can become a better classmate, team member, and coworker.

► YOUR PERSONAL HANDBOOK

Many new terms and concepts are defined in this chapter. The main idea of this discussion is that your personality and attitude affect your performance both personally and professionally. If you can say with confidence that you have no doubts regarding your external influences (friends and family) *and* your internal confidence and attitude, congratulations! You have just crossed the first big hurdle toward workplace success. If you are like the majority of the population and need a little improvement with either your internal or external influences, a bigger congratulation is extended to you! Identifying areas for improvement is by far one of the most difficult hurdles to jump but certainly the most rewarding.

This book, which is about you, is designed to be a personal handbook. This handbook is going to take you on an exciting path toward creating both personal and career plans and developing a respect and understanding for personal financial management. Self-management skills including time, stress, and organization will be addressed, as well as professional etiquette and dress. Workplace politics, their implications on performance, and how to successfully use these politics in your favor will be discussed, as will your rights as an employee. These newfound workplace skills will improve your ability to lead, motivate, and successfully work with others in a team setting. Finally, you will learn how to handle conflict and work with difficult coworkers.

As we move through key concepts in this text, begin developing a positive attitude; believe in yourself and your abilities. Equally as important is that you learn from your past. Little by little, you will make lifestyle changes that will make you a better individual, which will make you an even better employee. It all translates to success at work and success in life!

◀ SUMMARY OF KEY CONCEPTS

▶ How you view yourself dictates how you treat others and what type of employee you will be

▶ Your views of yourself, your environment, and your past experiences comprise your personality, values, attitude, and self-esteem

▶ Negative past experiences create unnecessary baggage that either delays or prevents you from reaching your goals. It is important that you acknowledge and begin dealing with these negative experiences

▶ There are three primary learning styles: visual, auditory, and tactile/kinesthetic (sight, sound, and touch). Individuals must recognize how they best learn and also be aware that others may or may not share their same learning style

◀ KEY TERMS

attitude	locus of control	self-esteem
human relations	personality	self-image
learning style	projection	values

◀ REFERENCE

Rotter, J. B. "Generalized Expectancies for Internal versus External Control of Reinforcement." *Psychological Monographs* 80, (1966).

◀ IF YOU WERE THE BOSS

1. How would you deal with an employee who displays poor self-esteem?
2. How would recognizing different learning styles help you be a better boss?

◀ WEB LINKS

http://www.humanmetrics.com/cgi-win/JTypes1.htm

http://www.colorquiz.com

http://personality-project.org/personality.html

http://www.ncrel.org/sdrs/areas/issues/students/learning/lr2locus.htm

◀ WORKPLACE DO'S AND DON'TS

Do realize the impact your personality has on overall workplace performance	*Don't* assume that everyone thinks and behaves like you
Do believe that you are a talented, capable human being. Project self-confidence	*Don't* become obsessed with how others view you. Be and do your best
Do let go of past baggage	*Don't* keep telling everyone about your past negative experience

ACTIVITY 1–1

Apply the learning styles discussed in this chapter and complete the following statements.

In the classroom, I learn best by

_____

In the classroom, I have difficulty learning when

_____

How will you use this information to perform better?

_____

ACTIVITY 1–2

Write down four words to describe your ideal self-image.

1. _____

2. _____

3. _____

4. _____

What steps are necessary to make your ideal self-image a reality?

_____

_____

ACTIVITY 1–3

What outside experiences and influences affect your educational behavior?

OUTSIDE EXPERIENCES	OUTSIDE INFLUENCES
1.	1.
2.	2.
3.	3.
4.	4.

1. The _____ identifies who you believe controls your future.

2. _____ is an individual's perception of how he or she views himself or herself, while _____ is one's belief of how others view him or her.

3. When one understands his or her own _____ and _____, it is much easier to understand reactions to others' actions.

4. A/An _____ affects group performance, which, in turn, impacts organizational performance.

5. Dealing with negative baggage involves _____ your past, _____, and moving _____.

6. Past influences shape our _____.

CHAPTER 2

GOAL SETTING AND LIFE MANAGEMENT

OBJECTIVES

▶ Describe the importance of goal setting

▶ Identify the impact setting *goals* will have on your life plan

▶ Set realistic goals to help you reach your full potential in life

▶ Define goal-setting techniques

▶ Create *short-term* and *long-term goals*

▶ Describe the importance of setting *priorities*

▶ State the advantages of having a *mentor*

The future belongs to those who believe in the beauty of their dreams.

Eleanor Roosevelt (1884–1962)

▶ THE IMPORTANCE OF PERSONAL GOAL SETTING

To realize the importance of a goal, you must first know what a goal is. A **goal** is a long-term target. You need to think of a goal as a reward at the top of a ladder. To reach that reward, you need to progress up each step of the ladder. The degree of your goal will determine how long it will take to get there. Each step on your ladder has to contribute to your achievement of the final reward and support your personal values.

Goals will help you become more focused; help you increase your self-esteem; and help you overcome procrastination, fear, and failure. Setting goals will help you become more successful in your career. Your career focus will become more clear and meaningful.

▶ INFLUENCES OF GOALS

Goals will help you keep focused on where you want to be in your future. They keep you motivated to continue working to better yourself. Goals help you achieve, not just hope for, what you want in life.

Take a look at Cory. When Cory was twenty-two years old, Cory had only a high-school education. After working as a service clerk since graduating from high school, Cory decided to go to college. Cory was self-supporting and had to work, so Cory set a realistic goal to obtain an associate degree in accounting within three years. Since Cory reached that goal, Cory has found a good job, has a good income, and has more self-confidence. Cory has now decided to become a CPA. Cory needs to get a bachelor's degree and has set a goal to do that within two years. This is motivating Cory to perform well.

As in the example with Cory, as one goal is reached, you will be motivated and self-confident enough to set a higher goal. You will continually strive for improvement.

Goals can and should be set in major areas of your life including personal, career, financial, educational, physical, social, and mental. These goals will help you maintain a positive outlook in all aspects of your life. They will help you maintain a more positive perception of yourself and will result in improved human relations with others. If you perceive yourself as doing well and being positive, others will feel your positive attitude.

▶ HOW TO SET GOALS

Achieving short- and long-term goals is like climbing a ladder. Imagine that there is a major prize (what you value most) at the top of the ladder. The prize can be considered your long-term goal, and each step on the ladder is a progressive short-term goal that helps you reach the major prize.

You need to set short-term and long-term goals, and they need to be put into writing. **Long-term goals** can be for anywhere from five to ten years, although you should reevaluate your goals each year.

Think of what you want to accomplish in your life. Write down everything you can think of, including personal, career, and education. Now go through the list and choose what items you most value. Choose the realistic ones and list those first. Break this list into long- and short-term goals.

In reviewing your list, ask yourself where you want to be in five to ten years. Make sure that it is realistic and something that you want. It should be challenging enough that you will work toward it, but it should also be attainable. There must be a reason to reach this goal. Why is it important to you? This is important; you are setting yourself up for success, so you must be realistic in identifying both opportunities and potential barriers. For example, remember Cory's goal to be a CPA? Cory has a reason to be a CPA: it represents success. It is important to Cory, and it is a realistic goal that can be reached within the two years that Cory set for this goal.

◀ EXERCISE 2–1: **Long-Term Career Goal:** *Fill in the star with your long-term career goal. What do you want to achieve in five years?*

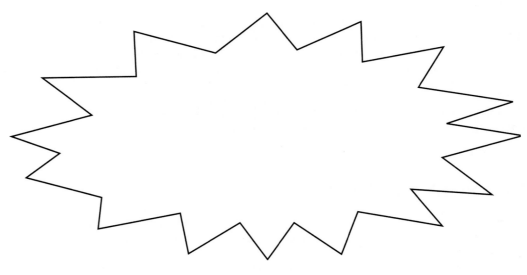

Exercise 2–1 Goal

Short-term goals should be goals that can be reached within a year's time. Short-term goals are set to help reach long-term goals. Businesses often refer to short-term goals as objectives because they are short-term, measurable, and have specific time lines. When creating personal goals, several short-term goals need to be set. These goals can be achieved in one day, a week, a month, or even several months. However, they should be achieved within a year's time and support the long-term goals.

Remember that these must also be realistic, achievable, and important to you. They need to be measurable so you know that you actually have reached them.

An example of a long-term goal for Cory is to buy a car a year after graduation. Cory has set several short-term goals, one being to save a specific amount of money each month. Another supporting goal would be to work a specific amount of hours each week. Cory needs to be specific on the kind of car to buy, whether to buy used or new, and whether Cory needs to take out a loan. The answers to these questions will determine if the time frame is realistic and how much Cory needs to save per month.

◀ EXERCISE 2–2: **Short-Term Goals:** *Using your long-term career goal from the previous exercise (the star), identify short-term goals for each step on the ladder.*

Now that you have a good list of goals, there are a few more important aspects of goal setting to consider. These include owning the goals, being in control of the goals, making the goals measurable, and setting a time frame to achieve these goals.

Owning the goal is important to being successful in reaching a goal. Make sure the goal belongs to you. You should be the one to decide your goals, not your parents, friends, relatives, or anyone else who may have influence over you. For example, if Cory goes to college because it is how to reach the dream of being a CPA, it will be accomplished. However, if Cory goes to college to become a CPA because it

Year 5
Year 4
Year 3
Year 2
Year 1

Exercise 2–2 Short-Term Goals

was Cory's parents' idea to be a CPA, this would not be Cory's goal, and it could be hard to accomplish this goal.

Know who is in *control of the goal*. Make sure you have the right information to create these goals. This includes knowing what resources and constraints are involved. Drawing on the concept of locus of control from chapter 1, not every factor is within your control. Therefore, it is important that you be flexible and maintain a realistic control of your goal.

Set a time frame for reaching the goal. This will make sure it is measurable. In other words, you will know that your goal has been reached. Make sure you write down details. For example, instead of writing "I will become a manager in the future," you should write "I will become a manager in the X Company accounting firm by the beginning of the year 2010."

Write goals positively and in detail. Make sure you include: what you want, when you want to accomplish it, where you will be when you reach the goal, who is involved in helping you reach the goal, and how you will get there. It is important to know what it will take to meet goals. Make sure the goals are realistic so they are achievable.

▶ CREATING A LIFE PLAN

Creating goals will help you with your life plan. At the end of this chapter, you will be completing activities that will assist you in developing a life plan. You need to create goals in all areas of your life, including your personal life, career, and education. Some of your goals may blend in two or more of these areas. What should you look for in your personal life? Consider all areas of your life, including:

- ▶ *Social and spiritual:* Marriage, family, friends, religion
- ▶ *Financial:* Home, car, ownership
- ▶ *Activities:* Travel, hobbies, life experiences

What do you look for in personal relationships? Think about the type of people you want to be a part of your life in the future.

Consider where you want to be financially. Many people dream of becoming a millionaire, but you need to be realistic. What will you be comfortable with? Think about what kind of house you want to live in and what kind of car you want to drive. If a spouse and children are in your future, you must account for their financial needs as well. Also, what outside activities do you like? Your personal financial plan will determine your ability to achieve these goals. This will be discussed in more detail in the next chapter. All these areas of your personal life should be considered.

Think about what results will come from your goals. Make sure you know what rewards will come from achieving your goals. Make sure you look at both intrinsic and extrinsic rewards. **Intrinsic rewards** include such things as self-satisfaction and pride of accomplishment. These come from within you. **Extrinsic rewards** include such things as money and praise. These rewards come from external sources. Both intrinsic and extrinsic rewards are needed to achieve satisfaction in your future. Both are equally important and need to be recognized. They help motivate and can help you keep a positive outlook when working toward goals.

Planning a career is equally as important as planning your personal life. When planning your career you should consider:

- ▶ Why your selected career is important
- ▶ How you will know you have achieved success
- ▶ What resources are needed

Choosing the right career is important. How can this be done? People choose careers for different reasons, including earning power, status, intellect, and self-satisfaction. If there is a career center available at your college, make sure you take time to visit and see what it offers. Talk to friends and family members about what you do well. There are several personality and career interest tests you can take that will help you determine your potential career. These career assessments are offered at many college career centers or online. They will help you identify interests, abilities, and personality traits to help determine what career will suit you best. Use all resources available and gather information to help you make the best career decision. Do some Internet searching and interview people who are already working in your prospective field.

To be successful in your career, it is important to enjoy what you do. Make sure you select a career that supports your goals.

Education is an important key to achieving your life plan. Just as your personal life goals and career goals are important, education is another factor to reaching your life plan. You need to consider:

- ► Degrees/certificates needed
- ► Time frame
- ► Financial resources
- ► Support network

No one can ever take your knowledge away from you! Course choices are important. It is important to know what courses to take depending on what outcome you desire. Choose courses that will benefit you and help you explore new concepts.

Take a trip to your college career center or talk to a counselor. One way to explore potential careers is through job shadowing or internships.

► PRIORITIES

Priorities help you decide what needs to be done and in what order. Juggling priorities will be the key to reaching goals. Not only is it important in your personal life, but it will be necessary at work as well.

You may need to adjust priorities to reach your goals. Before priorities can be put in order, you need to determine what they are. It is important to remember that sometimes your first priority is not necessarily what is most important in life; it is just that a particular activity demands the most attention at that point in time. For example, if Cory has a young child, that child would be most important to Cory. However, if Cory is attending college to become a CPA and needs an evening to study for a big exam, the priority would be to study for that test. That does not mean the exam is more important than the child. However, the test is a step to a better future for Cory and that child.

Cory's decision is called a **trade-off**. A trade-off means giving up something to do something else. Another example involving Cory is the decision to purchase a car in one year; Cory needs to save a certain amount of money each month. In order to do this, Cory may have to give up going to the coffeehouse each morning and, instead, make coffee at home in order to save enough money to meet the savings goal to purchase the car.

Be prepared to be flexible in all areas of your life plan. When working toward goals, flexibility is needed. Times change, technology changes, and you will change. Make sure to reevaluate your goals at least once a year. At times, you may need to update or revise your goals and/or time lines; do not just give them up.

► MENTORING

Another opportunity to improve your job skills and increase your potential for career advancement is to find a mentor. A **mentor** is someone who can help you learn more about your present position, provide support, and help you to develop in your career. In addition, the mentor will help you learn about the culture of the company. The **corporate culture** includes the values, expectations, and behaviors of people at work. Knowing the culture of the company will help you succeed. You will learn about the policies and how people expect you to act on the job.

A mentor is different than a coach. Although a mentor could be a coach, a coach is not a mentor. A mentor is someone who will help you focus and work toward your career goals. A coach is someone who serves as an advisor in your current job.

Finding a mentor can be a formal or informal process. Some companies have a *formal mentor program*. In this instance, you will be assigned a mentor that is able to help you succeed on the job. In addition, he or she will be able to help you to identify and reach your career goals. This mentor may be paid to help you. This allows more time for the mentor to work with you.

If your company does not offer a formal mentor program, you should try to establish a mentoring relationship with someone who can help you while you are learning about your new job and career. This person may choose you, or you may choose that person. This person should be someone who can trust, someone who knows the company and industry, and someone who is willing to spend time to help you succeed.

◀ EXERCISE 2–3: **Finding a Mentor:** *Name at least three qualities you would look for in a person that you would want to be a mentor to you.*

1. _____

2. _____

3. _____

What would you say to that person (how would you ask that person to be your mentor)?

_____

_____

_____

◀ SUMMARY OF KEY CONCEPTS

▶ Goal setting is important in helping you keep focused. It will increase your self-esteem and help you become more successful in all areas of your life

▶ As goals are reached, motivation and self-confidence will increase

▶ Goals need to be put into writing. They need to be realistic and measurable. It is important to know who owns the goals and who controls the goals. A time frame is needed to know when you plan on reaching these goals

▶ Long-term goals are set to be achieved in five to ten years

▶ Short-term goals can usually be achieved within a year's time and are needed to reach long-term goals

▶ When creating a life plan, you must consider all aspects of your life, including personal, career, and education

▶ Flexibility and juggling priorities are needed to achieve goals

▶ As you begin your new job, it is important that you establish a relationship with a mentor

▶ A good mentor will help you learn more about your position and the company

◀ KEY TERMS

corporate culture	intrinsic rewards	priorities
extrinsic rewards	long-term goals	short-term goals
goal	mentor	trade-off

◄ IF YOU WERE THE BOSS

1. Why does an employer need to set goals?
2. Why is it important that an employer ensure that employees set personal and career goals?
3. Why would you establish a mentoring program for your employees? What specific advantages would it provide your department?

◄ WEB LINKS

http://www.mindtools.com/pages/article/newHTE_06.htm

http://www.topachievement.com/goalsetting.html

http://www.mygoals.com/helpGoalsettingTips.html

http://www.gems4friends.com/goals/index.html

http://www.management-mentors.com

◄ WORKPLACE DO'S AND DON'TS

Do set goals in writing	*Don't* set goals that are difficult to reach due to lack of control
Do set long-term and short-term goals	*Don't* give up on goals that are not completely in your control
Do make sure your goals are attainable	*Don't* wait to create goals
Do have measurable goals	*Don't* create unrealistic goals
Do set priorities. Include trade-offs and being flexible when creating goals	*Don't* ever give up when working to reach your goals
Do try to establish a mentor relationship	*Don't* try to learn about the company culture on your own

ACTIVITY 2–1

Think of all you want to accomplish in your life. List your personal, career, and education dreams.

PERSONAL	CAREER	EDUCATION
1.	1.	1.
2.	2.	2.
3.	3.	3.
4.	4.	4.
5.	5.	5.
6.	6.	6.

ACTIVITY 2–2

From your Activity 2–1 list, create three long-term goals in each section. Make sure they are realistic and measurable.

PERSONAL	CAREER	EDUCATION
1.	1.	1.
2.	2.	2.
3.	3.	3.

ACTIVITY 2–3

From Activity 2–2, prioritize the goals you set.

PERSONAL	CAREER	EDUCATION
1.	1.	1.
2.	2.	2.
3.	3.	3.

ACTIVITY 2–4

Using the previous activities in this chapter, set long- and short-term goals. The star is your long-term goal. The steps are your short-term goals. Write positively and in detail. Set one personal goal and one career goal. Make sure they are specific. They need to be measurable and realistic. Include what (the goal), when (specific time you plan to achieve it), and how to get there (be specific). *Hint:* Refer back to Cory's goal to obtain a car.

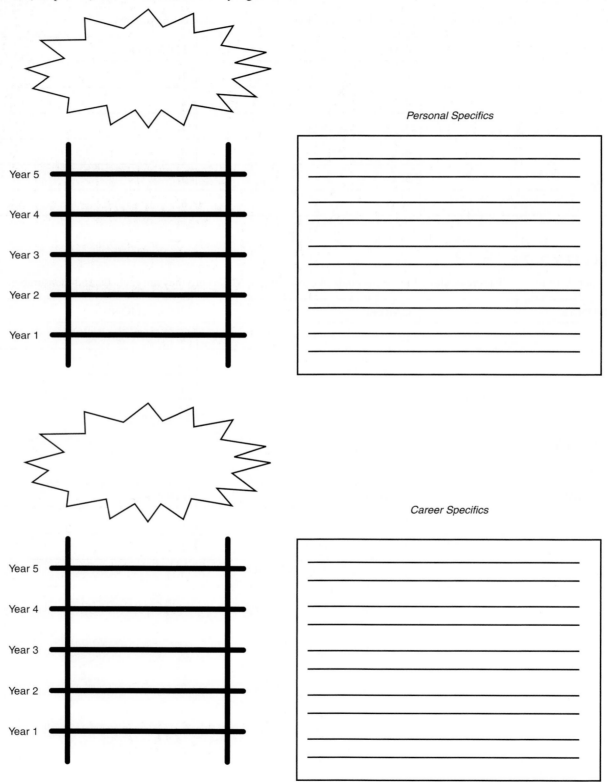

Personal Specifics

Career Specifics

ACTIVITY 2–5

Write a letter to someone you would like as a mentor. Explain your position and formally ask him or her to become your mentor.

_____

_____

_____

_____

1. Goals need to be set so you can become _____.

2. Long-term goals are set to be reached after _____.

3. Short-term goals should usually be reached _____.

4. _____ help you reach long-term goals.

5. When setting a goal, there must be a time frame; it must be _____ and _____.

6. _____ will help you decide what needs to be done and in what order.

7. To give up one thing for another is known as a/an _____.

8. Goals should be challenging but _____.

9. It is important to put goals into _____.

10. When creating a life plan, you should consider the following three areas: _____, _____, and _____.

11. A/An _____ is someone who can help you to develop in your career.

CAREER GOAL SETTING

By (Student Name)

This writing assignment guides you through the process of creating goals. Remember that these goals must be realistic, attainable, important to you, and measurable. Be as specific as possible in every paragraph.

TEN-YEAR GOAL

Paragraph 1:
In ten years, I want to be . . .

Identify and write your ten-year career goal here. Be specific: Identify what kind of job and what title you want, in what city you want to work, whom you want to work for, and why you chose this goal.

FIVE-YEAR GOAL

Paragraph 2:
In five years, I want to be . . .

Identify and write your five-year career goal here. Be specific: Identify what kind of job and what title you want, in what city you want to work, whom you want to work for, and why you chose this goal.

ONE-YEAR GOAL(S)

Paragraph 3:
In order to reach my five-year goal, I need to set the following short-term goals . . .

Identify necessary steps to reach your five-year goal. Be specific with activities, resources, and time frames.

Paragraph 4:
I am currently . . .

What are you currently doing to reach these short-term goals? Be specific with activities, resources, and time frames.

Paragraph 5:
I will know I have reached these goals when . . .

Goals must be measurable. How will you know when you have reached each short-term goal? Be specific with activities, resources, and time frames.

Paragraph 6:
I need the following resources to reach my goal . . .

Identify physical, financial, emotional, and social resources and where they will come from.

Paragraph 7:
My priorities for reaching my goals are . . . . My trade-offs include . . . . I must be flexible . . .

Make sure you have priorities set for reaching your goals. This should include your trade-offs and the areas where you may need to be flexible.

PERSONAL FINANCIAL MANAGEMENT

OBJECTIVES

▶ Describe the importance of *personal financial management*

▶ Identify the significance of money management and budgeting

▶ Create a personal *budget*

▶ Recognize *money wasters*

▶ Identify *debt* and debt management resources

▶ Identify wise use of credit

▶ Describe the importance of savings and investments

▶ Protect yourself from identity theft

The entire essence of America is the hope to first make money—then make money with money—then make lots of money with lots of money.

Paul Erdman (1932–)

► FINANCIAL MANAGEMENT

Personal financial management is the process of controlling your income (money coming in) and your expenses (money going out). Your **income** is money coming in. This money may come from your parents, grants, student loans, and/or some kind of job. While you are a student, your income may be minimal. However, after finishing college, you will start your new career and your income most likely will increase. Although you need to be careful handling your money presently, this becomes even more important later in your career.

An **expense** is money going out. This is money being spent. Some examples of expenses associated with being a student include tuition, textbooks, school supplies, housing, and transportation. Expenses you have because of life needs include food, shelter, and clothes. Then there are other expenses such as hobbies, entertainment, and other activities.

As you achieve your career goal and your income increases, your expenses will also increase. This is where personal financial management becomes extremely important. You need to learn healthy financial management by creating good spending and saving habits.

► HOW PERSONAL FINANCIAL MANAGEMENT AFFECTS YOUR PERFORMANCE

It is important to be aware of how finances impact all areas of your life. Finances are important in helping you reach the goals that you identified in chapter 2. Personal financial management does not have to restrict your activities. Instead, it is a way to make your financial resources help you reach goals while ensuring a healthy financial future. Now is the time to start working on controlling your finances.

You need to manage your money and keep your debt under control. It is important to maintain positive credit reports by using credit wisely. It is important to begin savings and investment plans now. In addition, you need to be aware of how to protect yourself from identity theft.

You are probably wondering how personal financial management can affect your work situation. If you are not properly managing your finances, you will eventually have difficulty paying your bills or not be able to make purchases. Eventually you will experience considerable strain and stress. In turn, this stress will flow into the workplace and your performance will start to deteriorate. This will then cause stress within the workplace. Many employers now require that you submit references and/or agree to a credit check prior to hiring, especially if your job requires working with money. Employers rationalize that if you cannot manage your personal finances, you may not be a responsible employee.

For example, a coworker has been asking to borrow money for lunch from Cory. Cory has noticed that this coworker buys lunch every day and comes into work with a specialty coffee each morning. This is causing a strain on the relationship between Cory and this coworker. Cory has been on a strict budget since starting this job. Cory brings lunch from home instead of buying it and only goes to the coffeehouse on special occasions. After loaning money to the coworker several times, Cory decided to confront the coworker. Cory shared with the coworker the importance of budgeting and helped the coworker to create a budget of her own. The coworker apologized to Cory and stopped asking Cory and others for money. The coworker started bringing lunch from home and treated herself to a specialty coffee only once in a while. This coworker thanked Cory because now she is beginning to save money.

► YOUR FIRST PAYCHECK

If you are like most students, you have probably been struggling to try to keep up with expenses. You have been low on cash and have had just enough money to get you through school. But, you made it, you graduated, and now you have a career job. With that job comes your first paycheck.

What should you do with it? You now have money to spend on something you have wanted for so long but could not afford until now. Why not do it now? Although you deserve a treat, do not overdo it. Now is the time to start managing that money.

Chapter 2 explained how to create goals. These goals are supported by your finances. You need to work with your finances and create a budget to reach the goals you created in chapter 2. Many goals take time and money to achieve. Therefore, it is important to create both long-term and short-term financial goals. If you recall, Cory had a goal to get a car. Cory has to stay on a budget and put away a specific amount of money to get that car when planned. It is important to start that budget with your first paycheck, if not before. Sometimes it is tempting to go and spend money just because you have it. Do not give in to that temptation. Financial success begins with discipline and planning.

▶ MONEY MANAGEMENT

The best way to manage your money and still be able to buy some of the extras you want is to create a budget. A **budget** is a detailed financial plan for a specific time period. A budget reflects your goals and specifies where your money goes in order to reach these goals. You need to control and prioritize your spending to match these goals. You also need to be as precise and honest as you can when you are creating and working with a budget.

Cash management is the key to good budgeting. Carry only a small amount of cash. It is too easy to use cash, and you will usually spend more when you have cash readily available. To practice good cash management, you should write checks but make sure you record every transaction. Reduce your trips to the ATM for cash. Do not use a debit card unless you are disciplined enough to use it appropriately and immediately record every transaction. These tips will help you realize when and where you are spending money.

The first step in creating a budget is to identify goals. That is why in chapter 2 you were taught how to create goals and started identifying goals for the future. Remember, these goals must be in writing and should provide direction for setting up your budget. You should have some of these goals identified from chapter 2. Now you need to attach financial goals to these personal goals. Exercises throughout this chapter will assist you in creating your financial goals.

The next step in creating a budget is to determine your income and expenses. Remember, your income is money coming in and your expenses are money going out. It is best to set up a budget on a month-to-month basis.

Determine your income by including all money that you receive on an annual (yearly) basis. Then divide by 12 to determine your monthly income. Technically, when creating a budget, you should use your **gross total income** and then deduct your taxes and/or other deductions. Gross total income is the amount of money on your paycheck before taxes or other deductions are made. However, to make it easier to set up the budget, you just need to know your net income. The net income from your paycheck is what you get after your employer takes out all taxes and deductions.

◀ EXERCISE 3–1: **Determine Your Annual Income:** *Fill in the following information the best you can.*

Salary(s)/wage(s) per year $_____
    (Make sure you use net income—after taxes.)

Interest income per year
    (Savings, checking, other)   _____

Other income per year   _____
    Total annual income   _____
    Total monthly income   _____
    (Divide annual income by 12 to get total monthly income.)

Now determine your expenses. This is where you need to keep track of your spending. At this time, you can estimate what you spend in each category. If you spend money in an area that is not listed, just add another category to the list. Although you may use a miscellaneous category, be careful not to overuse it. The idea here is to know exactly where your money is being spent. To do this, you will need to keep track of all your spending for the next few months—every penny. This will give you an estimated amount of what you spend in each category. You will find a worksheet at the end of the chapter for keeping track of your spending.

Fixed expenses are more easily identified. These are expenses that do not change from month to month, such as your monthly mortgage or rent payment. Your **flexible expenses** are those that change from month to month, such food or utilities. It is better to average these flexible expenses than to try to determine which months may be more or less.

◄ EXERCISE 3–2: **Determine Your Annual Expenses:** *Fill in the following information as accurately as you can. You determine what amount goes in each category. This will be an estimate. In time, you should put in actual amounts as you become aware of them.*

Category	Annual	Monthly (Divide Annual by 12)
Housing	$	$
Food		
Transportation		
Education		
Health		
Clothing		
Entertainment		
Loans (debts)		
Utilities		
Daycare		
Investments/savings		
Insurance		
Donations		
Miscellaneous		
Total	$	$

Your first budget will not be perfect. Adjust it monthly as you identify specific income and expenses. Your budget will identify where you are spending unnecessary money and will allow you to modify your spending while developing good personal financial management. You will be able to determine **money wasters**, which are those small expenditures that you do not realize are actually using up a portion of your income.

Here is a common example of a money waster: Think about how many times you have gone to a coffeehouse. On average, a specialty cup of coffee is about $3 (depending on where you go). If you buy a cup of coffee five days a week, over a year's time you have spent $780 ($3 × 5 days × 52 weeks) on coffee. You may have been buying coffee because you do not have a coffeemaker and think you cannot afford to purchase one. Assume a coffeemaker costs about $25 and, on average, flavored coffee runs about $8.99 a pound. This will last one person about two to three months. So the total spent for coffee for the year would be under $100 ($8.99 × 5 + $25). If you purchased the supplies and made your own coffee, you could save $680. Just think about what you could do with an extra $680.

◀ **EXERCISE 3–3: Determine Money Wasters:** *Working with a partner, list at least five ways people waste money on small expenditures. What is the estimated cost? What can be done to save that money? Refer to the preceding coffee example.*

Small Expenditure Waste (Money Wasters)	Estimated Cost	Behavior Change
1.		
2.		
3.		
4.		
5.		

▶ WISE USE OF CREDIT

The best way to stay out of the debt hole is to manage your credit. As you begin your career, you will receive many offers from credit card companies. You need to realize that you should not accept every offer. Although credit can buy you a lot of things, do not abuse the privilege. You do need to build your credit and maintain that credit. Good credit helps you to buy large items (such as a car or house) at a lower interest rate. If you have a credit card, use it as a tool for gaining good credit. Spend wisely and pay off the balance each month. This will assure you good credit and keep you out of debt. If you know you cannot pay it off each month, then do not use a credit card for costly items. Make sure you only use the credit card for items you can afford. Always make credit payments on time.

If you find yourself in a credit hole, do not get in the habit of only making a minimum payment. Pay as much of the balance as you can. Do not skip making a payment, and do not make a late payment as this will show on your credit report.

As for loans, you should try to stay away from taking out any loans. The only exception to this rule is for education and a home. Even then, make sure you use the money wisely and do not overspend on these items. Make sure when you do purchase a home that it is one that you can afford.

When applying for credit, lenders consider your character, capacity, collateral, and condition. Your character reflects your past attitude toward any previous credit and/or that you pay your bills on time. This is displayed in your credit history, thus telling the lender if you will repay the loan. Capacity is how you are able to repay the loan; your salary will play an important role here. Collateral is used by comparing your assets and liabilities to determine your net worth, which shows your ability to repay the loan. Other issues you need to be aware of when applying for a loan are interest rates, hidden costs, the purpose of the loan or credit card, what your payments will be, and how long you will be paying on the loan.

For example, Cory has been getting preapproved credit cards and is undecided what to do. Cory knows credit cards can be dangerous and can cause financial trouble. However, Cory also realizes that good credit is needed in order to get a car loan. Cory decided that getting a credit card would not be a bad idea as long as it was not used on frivolous items. Cory read all the details on each credit card application, including annual fees, minimum payments, and annual percentage rates. After researching the fine print on the credit offers, Cory identified all hidden fees. Cory secured a good credit card but uses it only for establishing credit. Cory rarely uses the credit card, and each time it is used it is paid in full each month.

▶ DEBT MANAGEMENT

Debt is money you owe. What is the difference between *expense* and *debt*? Expenses are bills that come regularly and are paid on time. Debt is usually a larger amount of money that is paid over a period of time and usually has interest added to the payment. **Interest** is the cost of borrowing money; it is extra money you pay to the loan company. Debt includes all types of loans (car, home, school) and credit cards. You may already have some debt such as a student loan or a credit card that is not paid in full.

With the ease of credit card use, it is no wonder so many people are in deep debt. Many end up filing bankruptcy, which causes long-term bad credit. Do not let yourself fall into the debt trap. The best way to avoid this is to only purchase what you can afford.

Make sure your net worth is positive. Your **net worth** is the amount of money that is yours after paying off debt. This is determined by looking at your assets and liabilities. Your net worth may not be high now, but in the future you want to build it up. If your net worth is low or is negative, you need to decrease your liabilities and increase your assets.

Total assets − total liabilities = *total net worth.*

Assets are what you own. These are tangible items that are worth money—for example, a car, home, and furniture. A **liability** is what you owe. If you have a car loan, it is a liability.

If you get (or already are) in debt, now is the time to start working on getting yourself out of debt. Seek advice and support from a parent, school counselor, or financial counselor. Talk with your creditor; you may be able to work out a reduced payment or lower interest plan. Cancel your credit and destroy the card. There are some national, nonprofit credit counseling services that can help such as *The National Foundation for Consumer Credit* or *Myvesta Foundation* that can help.

Steps to get out of debt follow:

1. Do not create additional debt. Do not use your existing credit card (cut it up if necessary) or take on additional debt.
2. Prioritize what you owe. Pay off the smallest amount or the amount with the largest interest.
3. After you have paid off one loan, take the extra cash and apply to the next debt on your priority list.

◀ **EXERCISE 3–4: Debt Repayment Goals:** *Write down each loan you currently have. Then put the amount you pay each month and the total amount you owe. Include the amount of interest you pay annually. Identify which creditor should be paid first.*

Creditor (Whom You Have the Loan With)	Amount Paid per Month	Total Amount Still Owed	Interest Percentage	Order of Payoff
1.	$	$	%	
2.				

(Continued)

Creditor (Whom You Have the Loan With)	Amount Paid per Month	Total Amount Still Owed	Interest Percentage	Order of Payoff
3.				
4.				
5.				
6.				
7.				
8.				

▶ CREDIT REPORTS

A **credit report** is a detailed credit history on an individual. Most creditors will want to look at this report before deciding if you are a good candidate for credit. It will detail how many credit cards and loans you have along with their balances. It will also show if you have paid these debts on time or are late on payments.

The credit report will include all personal identification information. This includes any previous names, addresses, and employers. If you have had any liens, foreclosures, or bankruptcies, they will show up on this report. If you are denied credit because of information on your credit report, the financial institution is required by law to provide you a copy of your credit report. You should check that copy thoroughly and notify the credit report company of any errors.

▶ SAVINGS AND INVESTMENTS

Do not wait until you have acquired your career job to start a savings plan. Now is the time to start saving. A good rule of thumb is to have at least three months' income saved for emergencies or major expenses that you did not expect. How do you do this? You have to spend less than you earn. You should take a certain percentage, about 5 percent, from your paycheck and put it in the bank. This may mean that you will need to sacrifice spending so you have this money for saving. When you complete your budget, you will need to determine what you can realistically give up.

You need to make sure your savings is in a bank. This way you can earn interest. You can take the money to the bank each payday or have an **automatic deduction plan**. If your company provides this service, the automatic deduction plan usually works best because the funds are automatically deducted from your paycheck and placed into your bank account so you do not get the chance to have it in your hands for spending. As for earning interest, you need to decide if you need the money to be readily available or if it can be left in the bank to collect interest. This will help you determine if you should use just a regular savings account or a certificate of deposit (CD). The younger you are when you start saving, the better.

Investments for the future are important to start now. If invested properly, money grows over time. There are many ways to invest money, all of which you need to research to decide what level of risk you want to take. Remember, do not invest all of your money and do not invest it all in one place. You still need to keep an emergency fund available, so investments should be in addition to your savings.

▶ IDENTITY THEFT

Protecting yourself from identity theft has become increasingly important over the last few years. Identity theft is when another individual uses your personal information to obtain credit in your name. To prevent this, you need to dispose of junk mail properly, including credit card offers. Make sure anything thrown in the garbage does not have personal information listed. This includes your social security number, date of birth, credit card numbers, and so on. To prevent this, cut up or shred junk mail. Keep track of all your credit card numbers and other important information. Make a copy of your license, social security number, and all credit information. Make sure to keep it in a safe place. Do not share your social security number, birthplace, birthday, or mother's maiden name unless you have verified that this individual works for the company from whom you want to secure credit. This private information is used to verify your identity and credit history. If this information gets in the wrong hands, it can give someone access to stealing your identity.

Following are some tips to remember:

- ▶ Do not give out your social security number over the telephone or Internet without verifying for whom that individual works.
- ▶ Document all important numbers, such as license, credit cards, savings account, and others, and keep them in a private and safe place.
- ▶ Practice good personal financial management by reviewing detailed charges on your credit card bills and other documents.
- ▶ Delete your name from credit card lists and marketing lists.

If you become a victim of identity theft, the first thing you need to do is file a police report. Immediately contact your bank, all credit card companies, and your cell phone provider. Do not change your social security number, but do call the Social Security Administration Fraud Department and at least one of the three credit report agency fraud lines. Make sure you document, in writing, everyone you talk to and everything you do.

▶ IMPORTANT TELEPHONE NUMBERS AND WEB SITES

The following is a list of important resources to assist you with credit and fraud issues.

Consumer Counseling Services:

- ▶ The National Foundation for Consumer Credit:1-800-388-2227 or http://www.nfcc.org
- ▶ Myvesta Foundation: http://www.myvesta.org
- ▶ Social Security Administration Fraud Department:1-877-438-4338 or http://www.ssa.gov/oig/ifyou.htm

Credit Report Agencies:

- ▶ Equifax credit report:1-800-685-1111; fraud:1-800-525-6285
- ▶ Experian credit report:1-800-397-3742; fraud:1-800-397-3742
- ▶ TransUnion credit report:1-800-916-8800; fraud:1-800-680-7289

◀ SUMMARY OF KEY CONCEPTS

- ▶ Personal financial management is the process of controlling your income and expenses
- ▶ Income is money coming in
- ▶ Expense is money going out

- A budget is a detailed plan for finances
- The first step to creating a budget is to identify goals
- Debt (liability) is the money you owe
- Net worth is assets minus liabilities
- A credit report is a detailed credit history
- Identity theft is when another individual uses your personal information

◀ KEY TERMS

assets	fixed expenses	money wasters
automatic deduction plan	flexible expenses	net worth
budget	gross total income	personal financial
credit report	income	management
debt	interest	
expense	liability	

◀ IF YOU WERE THE BOSS

1. You need to hire a receptionist that will be handling cash. What steps would you take to make sure you hire the right person?
2. Why should you teach your employees the importance of personal financial management? What are some creative ways of doing this?

◀ WEB LINKS

http://www.betterbudgeting.com

http://www.personal-budget-planning-saving-money.com

http://financialplan.about.com/cs/budgeting/a/Budgeting101.htm

http://www.moneyadvise.com

http://www.rightonthemoney.org/indexes/budgeting.shtml

◀ WORKPLACE DO'S AND DON'TS

Do create good financial goals	*Don't* use credit cards unwisely
Do keep a budget	*Don't* waste money
Do start saving and investing now	*Don't* ignore credit reports
Do learn to protect yourself from identity theft	*Don't* use cash for all spending

ACTIVITY 3–1

Create a personal financial statement. Put the net worth of all your *assets* (what they would be worth today if you sold them). Under *liabilities,* put the total amount you owe (not just monthly payments) to any creditors. For your *net worth*, take your total amount of assets minus your total amount of liabilities.

	AMOUNT	
Assets (Present Value)		
Cash (savings/checking)	$	
Investments		
Life insurance		
House		
Automobile		
Furniture		
Jewelry		
Other assets		
Total assets		$
Liabilities		
Home loan	$	
Automobile loan		
Credit card debt		
Educational loan		
Other loans		
Total liabilities		$
Net Worth (Total Assets Minus Liabilities)		$

ACTIVITY 3–2

Create financial goals and a budget to support these goals. Write the specific goal you want to reach. Then put the amount of money needed to reach that goal. In the last column, add when you want to reach that goal.

GOALS	AMOUNT	TIME
Debt payoffs	$	
Education		
Personal (car, home)		
Miscellaneous		
Savings		
Starting a business		

ACTIVITY 3–3

Use these sheets to record all income and spending for two weeks. Make sure you record all spending. Even minor expenses (every penny) should be recorded. Make sure you include the date, amount spent, what you bought (service or product), and how you paid for the item (means).

	SPENDING RECORD SHEET, WEEK 1		
DATE	AMOUNT SPENT	ITEM BOUGHT	MEANS (CASH, CREDIT CARD, ATM, CHECK)
	$		

(Continued)

		SPENDING RECORD SHEET, WEEK 2	
DATE	AMOUNT SPENT	ITEM BOUGHT	MEANS (CASH, CREDIT CARD, ATM, CHECK)
	$		

ACTIVITY 3–4

Create a personal budget.

MONTHLY PAYMENT CATEGORY	ESTIMATED BUDGET	ACTUAL BUDGET	DIFFERENCE + OR −	BALANCED BUDGET
BUDGET FOR MONTH OF _____				
Net Spendable Income per Month	$	$	$	$
Housing				
Food				
Insurance				
Debts				
Clothing				
Medical				
Donations				
Entertainment				
Miscellaneous				
Investments				

► SAMPLE EXAM QUESTIONS

1. _____ is the process of controlling your income and your expenses.

2. A/An _____ is a detailed plan for a specific time period for specifying your financial goals.

3. The small expenditures that add up to larger amounts are referred to as _____.

4. When considering applications for credit, lenders consider _____, _____, _____, and _____.

5. _____ is money you owe.

6. Your _____ is the amount of money that is yours after paying off debts.

7. A detailed credit history on an individual is called a/an _____.

CHAPTER 4

TIME AND STRESS MANAGEMENT/ ORGANIZATION SKILLS

OBJECTIVES

► Describe how *stress* impacts workplace performance

► Identify the causes of stress and name methods of dealing with stress

► Apply *time management* techniques in the workplace

► Define the importance of organizing for optimal performance

► Apply organizational techniques in the workplace

We must use time as a tool, not as a crutch.

John F. Kennedy (1917–1963)

37

► THE IMPACT OF STRESS ON PERFORMANCE

Stress is the body's reaction to tense situations. Stress can cause more than just a bad day. Constant stress can result in permanent mental and/or physical harm to you.

Although some forms of stress are beneficial and keep you mentally challenged, continued stress will eventually harm you in one way or another. It will start to affect your work performance and will carry on to your personal life. It is important to maintain a low and controlled stress level. Stress-related losses are high and are costing organizations billions of dollars annually.

This chapter addresses the many areas where stress can impact workplace productivity including time management, being organized, working with others, and common workplace stressors. Keep in mind that personal stress can harm your performance at work. You need to take the ideas learned in this chapter and apply them to both the work environment and your personal life.

► TYPES OF STRESS

Stress is a fact of life. What is important is that you recognize when you are stressed and deal with the stress appropriately. There is positive and negative stress. You will experience stress; there is no avoiding it. However, how you react and deal with stress determines how it will affect you. Some stress is minor and can affect you only at a specific time. This can be **positive stress**. Positive stress is a productive stress that gives you the strength to accomplish a task. However, even positive stress can become negative if it continues and becomes problematic. For example, if you have a rushed deadline for a special project, your adrenalin will increase giving you the mental and/or physical strength to finish the project on time. However, if you consistently have rushed deadlines, your stress level could increase and will eventually start working negatively on your mind and body.

Any stress can become **negative stress**. Becoming emotional or illogical or starting to lose control of your temper is a sign that you are dealing with an unproductive or negative stress. This stress usually continues until it starts affecting your mental and/or physical health. Negative stress can cause headaches, ulcers, heart disease, or mental disturbances. Negative stress commonly results in anger, depression, and/or distrust. Other signs of stress may include fatigue, diminished or increased appetite, and physical weakness.

Cory has been noticing that a coworker, Tammy, has been short-tempered and moody lately. Because Tammy is normally very pleasant to work with, Cory decides to talk to her and see if something is wrong. Talking with Tammy, Cory finds out that Tammy is being harassed by someone at work. She tells Cory how stressful this has been and that it is affecting her work and personal life. Cory encourages Tammy to take steps to stop this harassment (as presented in chapter 12). Cory also gives Tammy some tips to help deal with the stress. After a few weeks, Cory notices there is a positive change in Tammy. Dealing with the problem, along with using stress relievers, is helping to get Tammy back to her pleasant self.

The key is to become aware of what is causing you stress. You cannot just ignore it. Your body will respond to stress; be aware of these responses. By being aware of what causes your stress, you can change how it will affect you.

◄ EXERCISE 4–1: **Recognize Your Stress:** *List at least five things that have happened to you in the last year that have caused you stress. Next to the stressor, include what happened to you mentally and/or physically.*

Stressor	Symptoms of the Stressor (How You Respond Mentally and/or Physically)
1.	
2.	

Stressor	Symptoms of the Stressor (How You Respond Mentally and/or Physically)
3.	
4.	
5.	

▶ DEALING WITH STRESS

Learning to deal with stress is a must. Identify key stressors in your life. Be aware of these stressors and how they affect your attitude and behavior. Although life is not stress free, the following steps will assist you in not allowing stressful situations to get the best of you:

1. Identify the stressor. Find out what is causing you to be stressed.
2. Recognize why and how you are reacting to that stressor.
3. Take steps to better deal with the stress by visualizing and setting a goal to respond in a positive manner.
4. Put into practice some stress relievers.

The following are some ways to relieve stress:

▶ Find an outlet to release tension. This could include daily exercise, a hobby, or some other healthy activity.
▶ Diminish (or ideally eliminate) the use of alcohol and/or drugs. These stimulants will cause mood swings that typically make matters worse.
▶ Do not become emotional. Becoming emotional means you are losing control and may become illogical in your response to the stress.
▶ Get organized! Take control of your work space by eliminating unwanted clutter and prioritizing your projects.
▶ Make time for yourself and learn to relax.
▶ Eat a balanced diet and get plenty of sleep.

◀ **EXERCISE 4–2: Handling Stress:** *How have you handled a stressful situation in the recent past?*

_____

_____

_____

One common way to help manage stress is to control your diet. Make sure your nutritional intake is balanced. A healthy physical body leads to a healthy mental body. Make sure you eat a balanced diet. This includes having breakfast, lunch, and dinner. At these meals, you should balance protein, carbohydrates, vegetables, and fruit. Do not skip meals, especially breakfast.

Along with a balanced diet, exercise is a must. This does not mean you have to join a gym or lift weights; it just means you need to have a consistent exercise plan. Exercising is a good way to clear your mind of troubles. There are other ways to increase your physical activity. You can walk up stairs instead of taking the elevator or park your car a little farther away to increase your walking distance.

◄ **EXERCISE 4–3: What Have You Eaten in the Last Twenty-Four Hours:** *A nutritional diet can make a difference in how you feel during the day and how you react to stressful situations. List what you have eaten in the last twenty-four hours. Decide whether or not it was nutritional.*

What Have You Eaten?	Is It Nutritional?
1.	
2.	
3.	
4.	
5.	
6.	
7.	
8.	
9.	
10.	

You can relieve stress in many other ways. You probably do some of these things without realizing that they relieve stress. A few other methods to relieve stress follow:

► Develop realistic goals
► Maintain relationships with people you can talk to and trust
► Make sure to have some leisure time
► Listen to music
► Relax
► Get enough sleep
► Take time to do some deep breathing
► Use positive visualization
► Take a break
► Meditate

◄ **EXERCISE 4–4: What Do You Do to Relieve Stress?** *Other than what we have listed, what are some of the ways you relieve stress?*

1. _____   4. _____

2. _____   5. _____

3. _____   6. _____

Just remember, you must learn to recognize what situations cause stress. If you recognize these situations, you can better control them. The more organized you are, the better prepared you will be, thus reducing stress.

When at work, if you cannot surround yourself with positive people, then keep some personal space. Find a private place where you can take a few minutes for yourself and relax. Realize that people are not always going to agree with you at the workplace. There will be annoying people, and there will be people with whom you may not have a positive relationship. You may find yourself in situations that become very stressful. Use the stress relief tools mentioned earlier in this chapter.

Take time outside of work to relax. Do not bring your work or troubles home with you. When you recognize your stressors and take care of yourself, you can reduce and/or eliminate the harm stress can do to you both at work and at home.

If your company has an Employee Assistance Program, use it to get professional help. This can include financial, legal, and psychological help.

▶ TIME MANAGEMENT TIPS AND TRICKS

Time management is how you manage time when it seems like you never have enough hours in the day. You want to get out of work on time, but you have not completed what needs to be done. What about that to-do list? Some days, it just seems to get longer and longer. Believe it or not, it takes time to get organized enough to use your time wisely. Taking time to organize your life will be time well spent.

Many times in the workplace, you may get stressed because you do not have enough time to complete a project. However, many of your projects will probably be similar. Prior to starting a project, take time to make a plan. Set priorities and get organized. If you constantly have similar projects, take time out to make a template so you are not constantly starting over. Do not rush through a job and then have it done wrong. It will only take more time to redo. Instead, take a little extra time to complete the job right the first time.

Keep in mind that the ability to use time wisely is a skill in itself. This skill is needed in the workplace. By using your time efficiently, your tasks will get done on time. You can focus on tasks at hand and pay attention to details needed to do the job right. If you are being more efficient and paying attention, your employer sees that you care about your job and are organized. In turn, this could lead to higher pay and/or a promotion.

Without time management, you may spend more time than needed on a project or you may forget to complete an important task or lose an important project. This is why you must take time to get organized and control your time. You can do this by following a few tips:

1. Keep a calendar handy at all times. This calendar should list all appointments, meetings, and tasks for each day. This can be a regular paper calendar or an electronic calendar (handheld or computer application).
2. Make a list of tasks for each day and prioritize that list.
3. Keep a time log to see where your time is spent.
4. Organize your work area. Get file folders and in-boxes to organize and prioritize your projects.
5. Avoid time wasters. These are small activities that take up only a small amount of time but are done more frequently than you may realize. This could include unnecessary visiting and unproductive activities.
6. Practice a one-touch policy. In other words, after you have looked at a project, letter, memo, or so on, file it, put it into a priority pile, pass it on, or throw it away. Do not keep piling papers on your desk.
7. Set a time to address all correspondence at once.
8. Do not be afraid to ask for help.

One way Cory has learned to save time is by answering some memos in writing. When Cory receives a memo from a coworker who needs only a short response, instead of creating a new memo, Cory writes a response on the original memo. After writing the answer and making a copy for record, Cory sends the memo back. This has saved Cory time.

◀ **EXERCISE 4–5: Avoid Time Wasters:** *List some time wasters you have used in the last few weeks. How did these time wasters affect your productivity? What can you do to improve this?*

Time Waster	What Was the Result? (How It Affected Productivity)	What Will You Improve?
1.		
2.		
3.		
4.		
5.		

▶ ORGANIZING AND PERFORMANCE

Getting yourself organized for optimal performance is not difficult. Being organized will not only optimize your performance but will also help you use your time more efficiently and reduce stress. There are many tools for getting organized in the workplace (which can be used at home as well). Technology has made it easier to get organized with electronic devices (handheld or computer). However, there are other common organization tools to use as well, such as shredders, utilizing desk space, and file cabinets.

Obviously, one of the easiest ways to get organized is to use a calendar. Because most of you will use a computer at work, a software application is best. With these computer applications, you can keep track of your appointments, both work related and personal. The calendar can be used to keep track of meetings and deadlines. You can even set it to remind you with an alarm. You can also maintain telephone numbers and e-mail addresses for easy access. Tasks and notes can be monitored and updated. If you choose to utilize a computerized calendar, customize the application to suit your needs.

If a computer is not available, then the use of a desktop calendar can help. These calendars provide enough room to write appointments. Keep a notepad and/or sticky notes with a pen handy for writing important tasks and reminders. An address book or index card organizer should be easily available for finding addresses, telephone numbers, and e-mail addresses. In addition, the use of a small bulletin board for posting important reminders will help you to keep track of tasks and appointments.

Other ways to help you keep organized and improve performance are to return messages at one time; answer e-mails at one time; and break large tasks into simpler, smaller tasks. If you take time out to return each message as it comes in, you end up spending more time answering them. Instead, set aside a time each day to answer your messages. Make sure you do not do this during the lunch hour. The same holds true for answering e-mails. They come in at all times of the day. Instead of answering each one as it comes in, wait until the end of the day and answer them all at one time. The only exception to this is if there is an important message or e-mail that needs to be answered immediately. When you break down tasks, you can space out your projects. This way, you can organize the time needed to complete each task before starting the next. Again, the exception to this would be if you have a priority task that needs to be completed immediately.

You should keep your work space/environment and desk clean and clutter free. Your desk should have no more than two personal pictures to maintain a professional look. Make sure all work tools are handy. These include such items as a stapler, tape, notepad, pens, pencils, Wite-Out®, paper clips, scissors, ruler, calculator, highlighters, and disc (if applicable). Keep extra supplies at hand. Have a trash can close to your desk, and throw away supplies that have been used or do not work anymore.

A shredder is important to have but sometimes is used by more than one person and is generally not located near your desk. Confidential materials should not be thrown away; they should be shredded. Keep a place to put materials that need to be shredded. Do not wait too long to shred these materials. They should be shredded at least daily.

Files should be maintained properly in a file cabinet and kept neatly arranged in clearly labeled file folders. You should keep dated documents in chronological order (most recent first). Other files should be arranged by subject or alphabetically. Make sure you have easy access to files you need. Keep files updated, and be sure to dispose of old files properly. Any files with personal information or identification numbers should be shredded. If they are not important and do not have identification, they can be thrown in the trash.

You need to be organized when handling mail. Your job may include sorting and/or opening mail for your department. Use a letter opener to open all mail at one time. After opening the mail, sort it into piles. Make sure to throw away or shred junk mail immediately after opening. Respond to the sender of the mail if needed, file the document, or forward the mail to the appropriate party within the company. Do not open mail that is marked confidential unless instructed to do so. All mail should be kept private and not shared with coworkers. If you encounter a piece of mail that should be confidential, put it in a separate envelope and mark it confidential. Do not use company letterhead or postage for personal mail.

◀ SUMMARY OF KEY CONCEPTS

▶ Stress is a physical, chemical, or emotional factor that causes bodily or mental tension
▶ Stress can be positive and/or negative
▶ Signs of stress include becoming emotional or illogical or losing control of your temper
▶ The first step in dealing with stress is to identify the stressor
▶ A balanced diet along with exercise will help you to better manage stress
▶ There are many ways to reduce stress, such as setting goals, relaxing, and getting enough sleep
▶ Good time management comes from being organized
▶ Being organized will optimize your performance and reduce stress

◀ KEY TERMS

negative stress   stress
positive stress   time management

◀ IF YOU WERE THE BOSS

1. You have noticed that an employee frequently is calling in sick and appears agitated when at work. What do you do?
2. You have just become the supervisor for a new department. What can you do to make the department and its employees more organized? Discuss appointment tools, necessary equipment, and software.

◀ WEB LINKS

http://www.mindtools.com/smpage.html

http://www.createahappylife.com/7tips_reduce_stress.html

http://www.ivf.com/stress.html

http://www.cdc.gov/niosh/topics/stress

◀ WORKPLACE DO'S AND DON'TS

Do recognize your stressors	*Don't* let stress go until you get mentally or physically sick
Do deal with stress appropriately	*Don't* think that stress will just go away
Do eat a balanced diet and have an exercise plan	*Don't* skip breakfast
Do manage your time by setting priorities and getting organized	*Don't* be afraid of asking for help when getting behind
Do take time to get organized	*Don't* give in to time wasters

► ACTIVITIES

ACTIVITY 4–1

Using the following time log, keep track of how you spend your time for the next week. Make sure you complete it in hourly blocks to know exactly how your time was spent. Make additional copies if needed. At the end of the week, identify specific time wasters.

DATE	TIME FRAME	ACTIVITY

(Continued)

ACTIVITY 4–1 (*Continued*)

CDATE	TIME FRAME	ACTIVITY

Identify time wasters you found in the last week.

1.
2.
3.
4.
5.

ACTIVITY 4–2

In addition to what was mentioned in the chapter, research physical responses generated by prolonged stress. List your findings.

1.	7.
2.	8.
3.	9.
4.	10.
5.	11.
6.	12.

ACTIVITY 4–3

Identify the workplace effects of good and bad time management.

EFFECTS OF GOOD TIME MANAGEMENT	EFFECTS OF BAD TIME MANAGEMENT
1.	1.
2.	2.
3.	3.
4.	4.
5.	5.

ACTIVITY 4–4

Conduct additional research and identify tips for relieving work stress. List them and explain how they help relieve stress.

TIP FOR RELIEVING STRESS AT WORK	HOW DOES IT HELP?
1.	
2.	
3.	
4.	

1. Stress is a physical, chemical, or emotional factor that causes tension and may be a factor in _____.

2. Stress can be positive and/or _____.

3. The first step in dealing with stress is to _____.

4. Some ways to relieve stress include (choose four): _____, _____, _____, or _____.

5. Realizing your stressors and taking care of yourself will reduce or eliminate _____.

6. Managing time when you do not seem to have enough hours in the day is _____.

7. Being organized can _____ your performance.

CHAPTER 5

ETHICS AND POLITICS

OBJECTIVES

▶ Define *ethics* and its impact both personally and professionally

▶ Identify the importance of maintaining *confidentiality*

▶ Define and identify the appropriate use of *power* and power bases

▶ Understand the topics of *politics* and *reciprocity* and their appropriate use in the workplace

▶ Understand the importance of ethical decision making

I hope I shall possess firmness and virtue enough to maintain what I consider the most enviable of all titles, the character of an honest man.

George Washington (1732–1799)

49

► ETHICS DEFINED

Throughout our school days, we are told to behave ethically. In education, ethics typically refers to not cheating on homework and exams. At work, cheating can occur in all areas of a job. From the time we clock in to the time we leave the office—and even extending into the weekend, we must behave in an ethical manner. Ethical behavior is a twenty-four-hour process. Our behavior reflects our ethical values. In turn, our ethical behavior reflects and represents our company.

Ethics is a moral standard of right and wrong. Although the meaning of ethics is a simple statement, it is important to identify who and what determines what is morally right and wrong. Just as your personality is shaped by outside influences, so is your ethical makeup.

Your ethical behavior is a reflection of the influences of coworkers, friends, family, religion, and society. For example, if you associate with people who shoplift, you most likely will not view shoplifting as being unethical. As a result, you may shoplift without remorse. If your family routinely lies about a child's age to pay a lower admission fee to a movie theater or amusement park, the child is being taught that it is okay to cheat. Common religions teach that lying, cheating, and stealing are wrong. Finally, consider the influences our society and culture have on our ethical behavior. Corporate America has been bombarded with ethical scandals, and many of the marketing messages we receive on a daily basis influence our ethical behavior.

Although the preceding factors all have an enormous influence on the makeup of one's ethics, it is important to note that ethical behavior starts with the individual. As we explore the concept of ethics at work, you must remember that ethics begins with you.

► INFLUENCES ON ETHICS AT WORK

At work, you will be confronted with ethical issues. Many issues must be kept **confidential.** These issues include private matters such as client records, employee information, business reports, documentation, and files. Whether you are overtly told or not told to keep information within your department confidential, you have an obligation to not share information with individuals with whom the business is of no concern. This is called **implied confidentiality.** Sometimes, you may be tempted or even asked to share confidential information. Do not fall into that trap. If you are uncertain about sharing confidential information with someone, check with your boss. Doing so will demonstrate to your boss that you want to not only maintain the privacy of your department but also behave in a professional manner.

Your ethical behavior extends beyond the professionalism of how you deal with others. It is also reflected in your dependability and how you conduct yourself on company time. Remember that the company is paying you to work when you are on the job. Although at times it may be necessary to conduct personal business on company time, it is inappropriate to consistently spend your time on noncompany activities. The following activities should not be done during your work time:

- ► Surfing the Internet for personal business
- ► Taking personal telephone calls
- ► Making personal telephone calls (including family, personal appointments)
- ► Routinely exceeding the allotted break and lunch periods
- ► Playing computer games
- ► Using company supplies and equipment for nonbusiness purposes

If you must conduct personal business during work time, only do so during your break or lunch hour. Whenever possible, conduct the business before or after work hours and in a private manner.

Cory is responsible for the department's petty cash box. Cory is planning on going to lunch with friends but does not have time to stop by the ATM until later in the afternoon. Cory struggles with the thought of temporarily borrowing $10 from the petty cash box and returning the money later in the day (after a visit to the ATM). No one would ever know. Technically, it is not stealing. It is just borrowing. Cory decides the behavior is wrong, does not take the petty cash, and skips going out to lunch with friends.

◀ **EXERCISE 5–1: Legal Behavior:** *Based on Cory's dilemma, is Cory borrowing money from the petty cash box legal?*

Yes ☐   No ☐

Is this behavior fair?

Yes ☐   No ☐

Whom could it harm and why?

_____

_____

_____

▶ POWER AND ETHICS

Power is one's ability to influence another's behavior. Whether you recognize it or not, everyone at work has some power. Some people understand this ability to influence others' behavior and use it appropriately. Let us first review the different types of power, what they are, and how you can increase this use of power at work. There are seven bases of power: legitimate, coercive, reward, connection, charismatic, information, and expert.

Legitimate power is the power that is given to you by the company. It includes your title and any other formal authority that comes with your position at work. **Coercive power** is also power that is derived from your formal position. However, the difference between legitimate and coercive power is that coercive power uses threats and punishment. In contrast to coercive power is **reward power.** Reward power is the ability to influence someone with something of value. Those with legitimate power can reward others with promotions, pay increases, and other incentives. You do not have to have legitimate power to reward others in the workplace. **Connection power** is based on using someone else's legitimate power. Consider the department assistant that arranges meetings based on his boss's power. This is because the department assistant has connections to a powerful individual.

◀ **EXERCISE 5–2: Identify What Power Can Do:** *Identify four ways employees without legitimate power can reward others.*

1. _____

2. _____

3. _____

4. _____

The last three types of power come from within. They are often referred to as types of personal power. **Charismatic power** is a type of personal power that makes people attracted to you. We all know someone who walks into a room and immediately people are attracted to her. This is because the individual with charismatic power or charisma shows a sincere interest in others. **Information power** is based upon an individual's ability to obtain and share information. Doing so makes you more valuable to those with whom you interact. **Expert power** is power that is earned by one's knowledge, experience, or expertise. Consider the company's computer repair person. On the company's organization chart, he or she is not very high in the formal chain of command. However, this individual wields a lot of power.

▶ INCREASING YOUR POWER BASES

As mentioned earlier, everyone possesses some power. The trick is to recognize, utilize, and increase your power. The easiest way to increase your legitimate power is to make people aware of your title and responsibilities. Because coercive power utilizes threats and/or punishment, coercive power should only be used when an individual is breaking policy or behaving inappropriately.

Reward power should be used daily. Whenever possible, dispense a sincere word or note of appreciation to a coworker who has assisted you or has performed exceptionally well. Doing so will develop and enhance relationships not only within your department but also outside your immediate work space. Just remember to be sincere. Increase your connection power by strengthening your network. **Networking** means meeting and developing relationships with individuals outside your immediate work area. It is important to network with individuals within and outside of your organization. A more in-depth discussion of the importance of networking is discussed in chapter 15.

Charismatic power is increased when you focus attention on others. Make eye contact, initiate conversation, and focus the conversation on the other individual instead of on yourself. Information power is developed by attending meetings and networking. Whenever possible and without overcommitting, join committees and attend meetings. Doing so exposes you to other people and issues throughout the company. You, in turn, not only learn more about what's going on within the organization but also increase your connection or network power. Increase your expert power by practicing continual learning. Read books and business-related magazine articles and attend workshops and conferences when possible. Whenever you learn something new that can assist others at work, share this information. Coworkers will see you as the expert in the respective area.

▶ POLITICS AND RECIPROCITY

When you begin to obtain and utilize your power, you are practicing politics. **Politics** means to obtain and use power. People generally get a bad taste in their mouth when someone accuses them of being political, but this is not necessarily a bad thing. As we have discussed, it is important to recognize, increase, and utilize the various power bases at work. It is when one expects reciprocity that politics at work gets dangerous. **Reciprocity** means creating debts and obligations for doing something. Suppose you are on a time crunch and must get a report out in two hours but you need help. You ask a coworker to help you. She stops what she is doing and assists you with an hour to spare. You have just created a reciprocal relationship with the coworker. When she is in a crunch, she will not only ask you but expect you to help her out. The workplace is comprised of reciprocal relationships. Unfortunately, sometimes the phrase "you owe me" encroaches on our ability to behave ethically.

Cory has a coworker who helps Cory out with special projects when time is short. When the coworker tells Cory she needs help with something, Cory immediately responds, "Sure, no problem." Unfortunately, there is a problem. The coworker wants Cory to attend a meeting for her and tell people at the meeting that she is home sick when Cory knows she would actually be taking a miniholiday with friends. Cory tells the coworker that it would be unethical to cover for her. "But you owe me!" says the coworker. Cory is unsure what to do. After some thought, Cory tells the coworker that Cory wants to repay the favor and appreciates all the help the coworker provides but Cory's ethics cannot be compromised. Cory should expect some tension between the two, but, in the long run, the worker will respect Cory.

► CORPORATE VALUES/CULTURE

Each company has a corporate culture. A corporate culture is the way a company's employees behave. It is based upon the behavior of its leaders. This culture can be viewed from a corporate level and also from a departmental level. For example, if all the executives within the company are very laid-back and informal, most employees throughout the company will also be laid-back and informal. If a department supervisor is always stressed out and unprepared, the department members will most likely be stressed out and unprepared as well. This behavior also reflects an organization's ethical behavior. Companies that want to be proactive and decrease any type of unethical temptation will have and enforce an **ethics statement.** This is a formal corporate policy that addresses the issues of ethical behavior and punishment should someone behave inappropriately. As Corporate America recovers from its recent scandals, more and more companies are placing great importance on ethics statements. Included in a corporate ethics policy will be a statement regarding **conflict of interest.** A conflict of interest occurs when you are in a position to influence a decision from which you could benefit directly or indirectly.

Cory's company is looking for a flower vendor for an upcoming company event. Cory's uncle owns a local flower shop, and getting this contract would be a big financial boost to his store. Cory wonders if it would be unethical to tell his uncle about the opportunity. After some thought, Cory decides to ask the boss about the dilemma. Cory's boss explains that there is no conflict of interest if Cory does not financially benefit from the contract and encourages Cory to contact the uncle.

If there is ever any possibility that someone could accuse you of a conflict of interest, excuse yourself from the decision-making process. If you are uncertain that there is a conflict, check with your boss or the respective committee. Explain the situation and ask for your boss's or committee's opinion. To avoid a conflict of interest, many companies have strict policies on gift giving. Check with your employer to see if you are able to accept gifts from customers and/or vendors. Most companies do not allow the acceptance of gifts or have a dollar limit on the value of the gift.

◄ **EXERCISE 5–3: Receiving a Gift at Work:** *Your company has a strict policy on not accepting gifts valued over $15. One of the key vendors for your company sends you flowers on your birthday. The arrangement is quite large, so you know it clearly exceeds the $15 limit. What do you do?*

_____

_____

_____

_____

► MAKING ETHICAL CHOICES

As you attempt to make ethical choices at work, it is easiest to do so by remembering the three **levels of ethical decisions.** *The first level of ethics is the law.* When confronted with an ethical issue, you must first ask if the action is legal. If the action is illegal, it is unethical.

Sometimes, a behavior is legal but may be considered unethical (i.e., just because it is legal does not mean it is right). Take the case of an individual who has a romantic relationship with someone who is married to someone else. There is no law that says having an extramarital affair is illegal. However, many consider this behavior unethical. This scenario takes us to *the second level of ethics—fairness.* Your actions/behavior should be fair to all parties involved. If, when making a decision, someone is clearly going to be harmed or is unable to defend himself or herself, the decision is probably not ethical. Note that the concept of "fairness" does not mean that everyone is happy with the outcome. It only means that the decision has been made in an impartial and unbiased manner.

It is understandable that not everyone agrees on what is right and fair. This is where *the third level of ethics—one's conscience*—must be considered. This is also when an ethical decision gets personal. In the classic Disney movie, *Pinocchio,* there was a character named Jiminy Cricket. He was Pinocchio's conscience. He made Pinocchio feel bad when Pinocchio behaved inappropriately. Just like Pinocchio, each individual has a conscience. When one knowingly behaves inappropriately, he will ultimately feel bad about his poor behavior. Some people take a bit longer to feel bad than others, but most everyone at some point feels bad when they have wronged another. Sometimes a behavior may be legal and it may be fair to others, but it still may make us feel guilty or bad. If it does, the behavior is probably unethical.

◄ **EXERCISE 5–4: Honesty, Part I:** *It is 9:00 p.m., it is raining, and you are hungry. You are on your way home from a long workday. You only have $5 in your wallet, so you decide to go to a fast-food drive-through restaurant to get dinner. You carefully order so as not to exceed your $5 limit. You hand the drive-through employee your $5, and he gives you change and your meal. You place it all in the passenger's seat and go home. When you get home, you discover that the fast-food employee gave you change for $20. What do you do?*

_____

_____

_____

_____

Review the scenario; apply the three levels of ethical decision making to the following questions. Is the behavior legal? Is it fair? How do you feel about keeping the money?

Is it legal to keep the money?

Yes ☐   No ☐

Is it fair to keep the money?

Yes ☐   No ☐

How do you feel about keeping the money?

_____

_____

_____

◄ **EXERCISE 5–5: Honesty, Part II:** *Typically, in the fast-food business, employees whose cash boxes are short or over more than once are at risk of being fired. If you initially were going to keep the money, but now you know the employee who gave you too much cash could get fired because you decided to keep the money, would you still keep the money?*

_____

_____

_____

▶ WHEN OTHERS ARE NOT ETHICAL

This chapter discusses how you should behave ethically at work. But what should you do when others are not behaving ethically? Let us go back to the three levels of ethical decision making. Everyone must abide by the law. If someone at work is breaking the law, you have an obligation to inform your employer immediately. This can be done confidentially to either your supervisor or the human resource department. If the accused are executives within the company, you are protected by the **whistle-blower law.** You cannot be fired for informing authorities of a coworker's or an employer's illegal conduct. Whenever you accuse anyone of wrongdoing, make sure you have documented facts and solid evidence. Keep track of important dates, events, and copies of evidence. Your credibility is at stake. Remember, depending on the enormity of the situation, you, as an employee, have three choices: (1) alert outside officials if the offense is illegal and extreme; (2) if the offense is not extreme and is accepted by management, accept management's decision; or (3) if the inappropriate behavior is accepted by management and you are still bothered, you must decide whether you want to continue working for the company.

Cory finds out that a certain coworker received a laptop computer from a vendor for personal use. No other employees received a laptop. The coworker said the laptop was an incentive for the company's good standing with the vendor and, because he was the employee who made the purchases, it was his right to keep the laptop. Cory thinks this is not fair and is unethical. Cory politely checks with the human resource department, and they tell Cory that the coworker can keep the laptop. Cory must accept the company's policy. Although construed as being unethical in Cory's mind, the company found no conflict with its policies. Cory decides the offense is not extreme; and, because it was accepted by management, Cory accepts management's decision.

Another common ethical issue at work occurs in the area of company theft. Company theft is not always large items such as computers or equipment. More often, it is smaller items such as office supplies. Time can also be stolen from the company. If you use company time to surf the Net, make personal calls, or take extra long breaks, you are stealing from the company. You may not realize that taking a pen or pencil home is stealing from your company. Office supplies should only be used for business purposes. Although it is heavily influenced by the company and how others view right behavior from wrong, ethical behavior starts with the individual.

◀ SUMMARY OF KEY CONCEPTS

- ▶ Your ethical behavior is a reflection of the influences of friends, family, religion, and society
- ▶ Ethical behavior starts with the individual
- ▶ You have an obligation to not share confidential information with individuals with whom the business is of no concern
- ▶ Power and power bases are effective tools to use in the workplace
- ▶ Be cautious to not use power and reciprocity in an unethical manner
- ▶ A conflict of interest occurs when you are in a position to influence a decision from which you could benefit directly or indirectly
- ▶ There are three levels to consider when making ethical choices: the law, fairness, and your conscience
- ▶ Reporting unethical behavior that is occurring within your company is called whistle blowing. Whistle blowers are protected by the law

◀ KEY TERMS

charismatic power	ethics statement	networking
coercive power	expert power	politics
confidential	implied confidentiality	power
conflict of interest	information power	reciprocity
connection power	legitimate power	reward power
ethics	levels of ethical decisions	whistle-blower law

◀ REFERENCES

Etzioni, Amitai *A. Comparative Analysis of Complex Organizations*, 4–6. (New York: The Free Press), 1961, 4–6.

French, John R. P., and Bertram Raven. "The Bases of Social Power." In *Studies in Social Power*, (Ann Arbor: University of Michigan Press, 1959), 150–67.

Kotter, John P. "Power, Dependence and Effective Management." *Harvard Business Review* (July–August 1977); 131–36.

Peale, Norman V., and Kenneth Blanchard. *The Power of Ethical Management*, (New York: William Morrow, 1988).

◀ IF YOU WERE THE BOSS

1. You have just been promoted to boss. What are the first five things you should do?

2. What is the best method of dealing with an ethical decision regarding the performance of an employee?

◀ WEB LINKS

http://www.discriminationattorney.com/eeocdfeh.shtml

http://www.whistleblowerlaws.com/protection.htm

http://www.mapnp.org/library/ethics/ethxgde.htm

◀ WORKPLACE DO'S AND DON'TS

Do always behave in an ethical manner	*Don't* behave one way at work and another around your friends
Do keep information confidential	*Don't* break the company's trust
Do recognize and increase your workplace power bases	*Don't* use your workplace power in a harmful or unethical manner
Do remember the three levels of ethical decision making	*Don't* forget the impact your conscience can have on making the right decision
Do report your company's unlawful behavior to authorities	*Don't* constantly complain and point out others' errors

► ACTIVITIES

ACTIVITY 5–1

Is it ever ethical to take paper clips, copy paper, and pens home from work?

Yes ☐   No ☐   Sometimes ☐

Support your answer.

_____

_____

_____

_____

ACTIVITY 5–2

List three examples you have observed in which an individual has conducted personal business in the workplace or at school that could be considered unethical. Why do you believe this behavior is unethical? What type of power was used?

BEHAVIOR	WHY IS IT UNETHICAL?	WHAT TYPE OF POWER WAS USED?
1.	1.	1.
2.	2.	2.
3.	3.	3.

ACTIVITY 5–3

Research a company's conflict of interest policy.

Name of company: _____

Policy: _____

_____

What would you add to the policy to make it better?

_____

_____

(Continued)

ACTIVITY 5–3 (*Continued*)

What would you eliminate?

_____

_____

What should you do if you work for a company that does not have a policy?

_____

_____

ACTIVITY 5–4

List a time when you overheard confidential information that should not have been shared—for example, sitting in a physician's office or overhearing a private conversation while shopping.

_____

_____

How should this situation have been better handled?

_____

_____

_____

ACTIVITY 5–5

Identify at least four potential areas for employee theft on a small scale.

1. _____

2. _____

3. _____

4. _____

Identify at least two potential areas for employee theft on a large scale.

1. _____

2. _____

1. _____ is a moral standard of right and wrong.

2. _____ is your obligation to not share information with individuals with whom the business is of no concern.

3. Everyone at work has some _____. The difference is that some people understand this ability to _____ and use it appropriately.

4. A/An _____ is a formal corporate policy that addresses the issue of ethical workplace behavior.

5. _____ means creating debts and obligations for doing something.

6. A/An _____ occurs when you are in a position to influence a decision from which you could benefit directly or indirectly.

7. The first question for ethical decision making is: Is it _____?

8. The second question for ethical decision making is: Is it _____?

9. The third question for ethical decision making is: How does it _____ _____?

CHAPTER 6

ETIQUETTE/DRESS

OBJECTIVES

▶ Describe and discuss the importance of professional behavior in your career

▶ State the impact dress can have on others' perception of you

▶ Demonstrate a professional and correct introduction and handshake

▶ Demonstrate appropriate professional behavior in business dining situations

▶ Recognize and apply the appropriate use of technology in business/social situations

▶ Utilize professional *etiquette* in appropriate business situations

*Winning is
accomplished
in the preparation
phase, not the
execution phase.*

Anonymous

► EXECUTIVE PRESENCE

The way you look and behave is a reflection of the organization for which you work. You should have the attitude of an executive; this is referred to as an **executive presence**. Projecting an executive presence is important because one of the biggest concerns employers have when hiring is the employee's lack of knowledge regarding basic workplace behavior.

The purpose of this chapter is to provide basics on expected professional behavior on topics including attire, social etiquette, dining, and the appropriate use of technology. There is a reminder of what our parents taught us early in life that some have forgotten, such as smiling and saying please and thank-you. You will encounter many of these social situations daily at work, while other situations may not be as common. All are important.

Some of this information may be new to you, and you may feel awkward when you first implement these positive behaviors. The purpose of this chapter is to prepare you for many of the social experiences you will face in the workplace. Remember, practice makes perfect.

► INFLUENCES OF DRESS IN A PROFESSIONAL ENVIRONMENT

Both your maturity and the importance you place on your job are reflected in the way you behave and dress at work. Because impressions are often made in the first few minutes of meeting someone, individuals rarely have time to even speak before an impression is made. The majority of first impressions are made through your visual **appearance**. This means that your coworkers, bosses, and customers form attitudes based on how you look. Appearance has an impact on how you perform at work. If you dress professionally, you are more apt to act in a professional manner. The more casual you dress, the more casual you tend to behave. Think of your appearance as a frame. A frame is used to highlight a picture. You do not want the frame to be too fancy, because it will take away from the picture. You just want a frame to complement the picture. This appearance frame highlights not only your physical features, including your face, but also your attitude and potential.

◄ **EXERCISE 6–1: Define Your "Frame":** *What does your frame look like? Be honest with these answers.*

Is it trendy, outdated, professional, or inconsistent?

_____

Does it complement your desired appearance as a professional?

_____

If your current frame is not yet professional, what changes need to occur?

_____

_____

_____

For many students, one of the toughest transitions to make when entering the workplace is appropriate dress. Dressing professionally does not have to conflict with current fashion trends. The trick is to know what is acceptable. A basic rule of thumb is to make it a habit to dress one position higher than your current position (i.e., dress like your boss). Doing so communicates that you are serious about your career and how you represent the company. Dressing professionally may not always put you on the cover of a fashion magazine, but it will certainly assist you in projecting a favorable image at work and position you for advancement.

Know the workplace policies. One of the first steps to determining appropriate attire for work is to identify your company's **dress code**. Many organizations have policies regarding appropriate workplace attire. These policies address issues such as required attire, uniforms, hairstyle, undergarments, jewelry, and shoes. Frequently, these policies are included in the employee handbook. If there is no policy, ask your boss if there is a formal dress code and secure a copy. Another important cue to workplace attire is how managers dress. Suits are not always the preferred attire. In some situations, pants are acceptable for women, while in other situations they are not. Please note that sweats (shirts and/or pants) are not appropriate for work.

Once you have identified what your organization considers proper attire, you must begin to create a **work wardrobe**. These are clothes that you primarily wear only to work and work-related functions. You need not invest a lot of money when building a work wardrobe. Start with basic pieces and think conservative. For women, this means a simple, solid skirt in a dark color and a blazer. Skirts should not be above the knee. No one at work asks to see the tags of clothes; therefore, purchase items that fit properly. Men should select dark slacks, a matching jacket, and a tie. Frequently, these items can be found inexpensively at thrift and discount stores. If these items are purchased at a thrift store, take them to the dry cleaners for cleaning and pressing. You will be surprised how professional these items will look. Select items that are made of quality fabrics that will not wear out quickly. Also, make your selections based on fit and comfort. As you begin to earn money, continue building your wardrobe and develop a style that conforms to both company policy and your taste.

▶ TIPS FROM HEAD TO TOE

A woman's outfit should be a reflection of her style and personality—within reason. When dressing for work, your goal is to appropriately frame yourself in a manner that draws attention to your face (i.e., your brains and inner beauty). Regardless of your company's dress code, it is important that women heed several unspoken rules regarding professional dress at work:

▶ *Shower daily.* If needed, use deodorant. If you wear perfume or lotion, use it sparingly. Scent should not be overpowering.
▶ *Clothes should be clean and ironed, and they should fit properly.*
▶ *Hair should be clean, well kept, and a natural color.* Your hairstyle should reflect your profession. Fad hairstyles and unnatural color are inappropriate in many workplaces.
▶ *Makeup should be for day wear.* Makeup is appropriate for work. Makeup that makes people think you are going to a bar after work is not. Do not wear heavy eyeliner, eye shadow in colors that draw attention, or lipstick in bold colors.
▶ *It is not acceptable to wear suggestive clothing.* This means no cleavage and bare midriffs. No matter the current fashion trends, undergarments (bras, panties, and thongs) should not be visible. Remember, skirts should not be above the knee.
▶ *Hands and nails should be well groomed.* Should you use polish, it should be neat and color/artwork conservative. Nails that are too long are inappropriate.
▶ *Jewelry should be kept to a minimum.* Your jewelry should complement your outfit. Do not wear anything that is distracting or that makes noise.
▶ *Shoes should be in good condition.* Keep your shoes polished and free of scuffs. Heels should be in good condition; if not, get them repaired or replaced. Heels should not be too high. Heels that are too high are not appropriate for the workplace, nor are flip-flops. Nylons should be free of runs and snags.

Just like a woman's outfit, a man's outfit should be a reflection of his style and personality. For some positions, a suit may not be appropriate. The biggest wardrobe blunder men make is wearing clothing that is not clean and/or pressed. After checking with your company's dress code, heed these unspoken rules regarding professional dress at work for men:

▶ *Shower daily.* If needed, use deodorant. If you wear aftershave or cologne, the scent should not be overpowering.
▶ *Hair should be clean, neatly trimmed, and a natural color.*

- *Shave and/or trim facial hair.*
- *Clothes should be clean, ironed, of proper fit, and not torn or tattered.*
- *In an office environment, dress pants are the only pants that are professional.* With the exception of casual workdays, jeans are inappropriate. Baggy pants that reveal underwear are also inappropriate. Whenever possible, wear a neutral, plain belt that does not draw attention.
- *Shirts should be tucked in.* A polo shirt or a dress shirt with a tie is best. Shirts should not display excessive wear (check around the collar line). Shirts with inappropriate logos or offensive phrases should not be worn at work.
- *Shoes should be clean and in good condition.* Flip-flops are not appropriate for the workplace. Sock color should match shoe or pant color.
- *Hands should be clean and well groomed* (i.e., clean, trim nails).
- *Hats should not be worn inside buildings.*

◀ EXERCISE 6–2: **Professional Dress List:** *What do you have?*

Take inventory of your current wardrobe.

_____

_____

_____

List clothing you own that you can use for your professional wardrobe.

_____

_____

_____

List the necessities that you are missing.

_____

_____

_____

▶ JEWELRY, BODY PIERCING, AND TATTOOS

Although body piercing and body rings/jewelry appear to be current fads, they are offensive to some individuals. For this reason, it is important that you check with your company regarding its policies. However, in general:

- Nose rings, lip rings, and/or tongue rings are not professional and should not be worn in a professional setting.
- Any other body piercing/body jewelry should not be visible at work.
- More than two earrings worn on each ear is considered unprofessional.
- Earrings and other jewelry should not draw attention. This includes symbols or words that could be considered offensive to others.

Hiding a tattoo is difficult. If you are thinking about getting a tattoo, consider the long-term consequences. They are painful and expensive to remove and are designed to last a lifetime.

► CASUAL WORKDAYS AND SPECIAL EVENTS

Many companies offer something called **casual workdays**. These are days when companies relax their dress code. Unfortunately, too many employees attempt to stretch the term *casual*. If your company has a casual Friday, remember that you are still at work and should dress appropriately. Of course, you can wear jeans if jeans are the preferred attire; just adhere to the *head-to-toe tips* recently presented. Do not wear clothing that is tattered, stained, or torn (even if it is considered stylish).

Your company may also play host or invite you to attend a special function. Holiday parties and receptions are such examples. In these situations, instead of daily work attire, more formal attire may be required. Just as with casual Fridays, stick with the basics provided in the *head-to-toe tips*. Women, if appropriate, wear something in a more formal fabric. Although you have more freedom and flexibility regarding style and length, this is still a work-related function, so remember to dress conservative and not suggestive. Men, check ahead of time and see if tuxedos are preferred. Although seldom required these days, if one is required, you may need to rent one. For most occasions, a suit will suffice.

As a reward for winning Employee of the Month, Cory was invited to attend a one-day conference/luncheon with several managers from Cory's company. Cory had not attended a function like this before and was a little nervous about how to dress and behave in this new business situation. Cory did some preparation and found that dress and behavior are as important in public situations as they are at work. Cory decided dressing more formal would be most appropriate. Cory made sure to shower, clean and trim fingernails, wear polished shoes, and not wear inappropriate jewelry.

► BUSINESS ETIQUETTE

Because we live in a modern society, human interaction is unavoidable. Our society has a standard of social behavior that is called **etiquette**. Typically, when individuals think of etiquette, they think it only applies to the wealthy, high society. This is not true. Socially acceptable behavior should penetrate all demographic and economic groups. Individuals wanting to succeed in the workplace need to heed this protocol and consistently utilize it not only at work but in all areas of their life.

Before we study common areas of business etiquette, we need to define a few terms. Understanding these terms and implementing them into your daily behavior will make it much easier to carry out the desired and appropriate workplace behavior. The first word is **courtesy**. When you display courtesy, you are exercising manners, respect, and consideration toward others. The second word is **respect**. Respect is defined as holding someone in high regard. This means putting others' needs before your own needs. Both courtesy and respect are the keys in becoming ladies and gentlemen at work.

Some of the first words parents teach young children are *please* and *thank-you*. Although they are not used as frequently as they should be, they are extremely powerful words that can actually create power for you at work. Think about it; when someone says "please" and "thank-you" to you, you are more likely to repeat a favor or gesture because your deed was acknowledged. When someone does something nice, verbally say "thanks." Not doing so makes you appear selfish and unappreciative. When you express thanks, individuals will be more likely to continue performing kind acts for you.

Make it a habit to write a thank-you note when someone does something for you that takes more than five minutes or when someone gives you a gift. Do not wait more than three days to write the thank-you note. Write the note as soon as possible. Always send a thank-you note within twenty-four hours of completing a job interview, and remember to send thank-you notes to individuals who agree to be job references for you.

In addition to saying "please" and "thank-you," do not underestimate the value of a simple smile and eye contact. If you have a positive attitude, it will be reflected in your demeanor. When encountering people in the hallways, elevators, and/or meeting rooms, make eye contact and smile.

At times, you will be with individuals who do not know each other. When you are with two people who do not know each other and you know both people, it is your responsibility to introduce the two individuals to each other. This is called an introduction. Politely introduce the least important person to the most important person. For example, "Roger, this is Tim Wilson, the president of our company." "Tim, this is Roger Hue, my next-door neighbor." This rule should be applied in all social situations including dining, meetings, receptions, and parties.

A daily element of business is making and keeping appointments. Always be kind to the receptionist and/or administrative assistant. These individuals are not only the gatekeepers to their bosses; they also control schedules and often wield great power in decisions. When scheduling an appointment, always state your name, the purpose of the meeting, and the desired date/time. If possible, avoid scheduling appointments on Monday mornings. Others are attempting to schedule their own week and are less likely to accommodate you. When keeping an appointment, arrive five minutes early. When you enter the office, greet the receptionist and politely introduce yourself. Then state whom you have an appointment with and the time of the meeting. When entering an office for a meeting, wait to be invited to sit down. After the meeting, extend a handshake and thank the individual for his or her time. If you will be arriving late to an appointment, call and let the other party know you are running late. If you must cancel an appointment, do so immediately and apologize for any inconvenience. Do not just ignore an appointment.

▶ HANDSHAKES

A good handshake conveys confidence. Approach the individual you are greeting and extend your right hand as you verbalize a greeting. For example, "Hello Ms. Jones, my name is Danielle. We met at last week's meeting. It's nice to see you again." Ms. Jones will extend her right hand. Your two hands should meet at the web (see Figure 6–1). Grip the other person's hand and gently squeeze and shake hands.

▶ Do not squeeze the other hand too firmly.
▶ Make certain you shake the entire hand and not just the other person's fingers. Doing so is insulting and implies that you feel you are better than the other person.

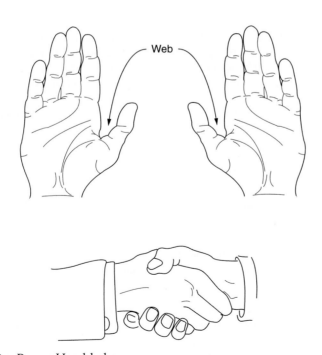

◀ **FIGURE 6–1**   Proper Handshake

- Do not place your hand on top of the other person's hand or pat the hand. Once again, doing so is insulting.
- If your palms are sweaty, discretely wipe your palm on the side of your hip prior to shaking.

Remember to always make eye contact and smile while extending your hand. A good handshake takes practice. Get into the habit of being the first to greet and introduce yourself to others. Practice makes perfect. The more frequently you initiate a good handshake, the more comfortable and confident you will become. See Figure 6–1.

◀ **EXERCISE 6–3: Shake Hands:** *Pair up with a classmate and practice initiating an introduction making sure to include a professional handshake. Rate the quality of the introduction and handshake on a scale of 1 to 5 with 5 being the best. Discuss what improvements should be made.*

▶ DINING

Apart from fast food, few college students are generally comfortable eating in a formal dining situation. Here are a several rules of thumb regarding dining etiquette:

- As soon are you are seated, place your napkin on your lap. If you need to leave the table, place your napkin to the side of your plate. Do not place your napkin on your chair.
- Utensils are set to be used in order of necessity. As your courses are served, start with the outside utensil and work in, toward the plate. The utensils set at the top of the plate are for your dessert.
- When serving coffee, water, tea, or any other beverage available at the table, first offer and serve others at your table.
- Do not order alcohol unless others at your table first order an alcoholic beverage. Abstaining from alcohol is the most desired behavior. If you choose to drink, limit consumption to one drink.
- When bread is available, first offer bread to others at your table before taking a piece.
- Place your bread on the bread plate (located at the top left corner of your dinner plate). Place your serving of butter on the bread plate. Do not butter the entire piece of bread at one time. Tear a piece of bread, and butter only that piece of bread before eating.
- Do not take the last piece of bread or appetizer unless it is first offered to others at your table.
- When your meal arrives, do not begin eating until everyone at your table has been served. If everyone receives their meals except you (you are the last to be served), give others at your table permission to begin eating without you so that their food does not get cold.
- Do not eat your meal with your fingers unless your main course can be eaten without utensils.
- Burping and slurping are inappropriate while dining. If you accidentally burp or slurp, make sure you immediately apologize and say "excuse me."
- When you are finished eating, place your knife and fork together, with the blade facing in and the tines up. When you are only resting and you do not want the server to take your plate away, cross your utensils with the tines facing down.
- It is inappropriate to use a cell phone while dining. If you must take a call, excuse yourself from the table.

In business, you will encounter a variety of dining situations. Some dining experiences will be less formal than others. You will most likely encounter some form of the table setting illustrated in Figure 6–2. Take time to study and review a common place setting to help you understand proper use for utensils, plates, and cups. As you eat, you should use the utensils from outside toward the plate.

1 napkin
2 plate
3 salad fork
4 dinner fork
5 dinner knife
6 teaspoon
7 soup spoon
8 salad plate
9 bread plate
10 butter knife
11 dessert spoon
12 dessert fork
13 water glass
14 beverage/wine glass
15 coffee cup and saucer

◀ **FIGURE 6–2** Table Setting

When Cory arrived at the conference, Cory was glad to be dressed professionally. Everyone there was dressed as a business professional. Cory was introduced to many business professionals. Cory was sure to make eye contact, smile, and properly shake hands when meeting new people. Cory was also careful to follow dining etiquette during lunch. At work the next day, Cory immediately wrote a thank-you note to the managers for being included in the event. At the end of the day, Cory's manager invited Cory into the office and let Cory know what a great impression Cory made at the conference. Several colleagues had mentioned to Cory's manager how impressed they were with Cory's professionalism. Cory realized that doing a little research and being professional were well worth the effort.

A major area of business involves attending social functions. Many invitations request an RSVP, which is French for "répondez s'il vous plaît" (i.e., please respond). As soon as you receive an invitation, send a reply—whether it is an acceptance to attend or regrets. Not acknowledging the invitation and failing to respond are rude.

When you attend a social function, remember that you are attending the function to meet with other professionals, not to receive your last meal.

▶ Refrain from or limit the consumption of alcohol.
▶ Only serve yourself a small plate of hors d'oeuvres and move away from the food table.
▶ Hold your hors d'oeuvres in your left hand, leaving your right hand free to shake hands and greet others.
▶ Do not talk with food in your mouth.

▶ TECHNOLOGY AT WORK

Cell phone usage, messages, voice mail, e-mails—it all gets so confusing! This section provides some basic rules for the appropriate use of communications.

CELL PHONES AND OTHER PORTABLE DEVICES

▶ Turn off cell phones when you are attending a meeting (business, education, religious, or others).

▶ If you are anticipating an emergency call, turn off the ringer of your phone.

▶ Do not use your phone while dining or while attending meetings and performances (including movies).

▶ Do not take or make a call in front of others. Excuse yourself and step away for privacy. Taking or making a call in front of others implies that they are not important.

▶ It is inappropriate to use or display portable music devices when with others.

TELEPHONE MESSAGES

Voice-mail messages are a routine part of conducting business. It is important to remember that a voice-mail impression is equally as important as how you answer the telephone. The following are tips regarding telephone messages:

▶ Keep telephone messages brief.

▶ State your name, purpose of the call, and return telephone number.

▶ Speak slowly and clearly.

▶ Repeat your name and return number at the end of your message.

▶ Promptly return telephone messages.

▶ Keep your voice-mail greetings professional. Cute voice-mail greetings are not professional. Musical introductions or bad jokes do not form favorable impressions when employers or customers are attempting to contact you.

E-MAIL AND COMPUTER USAGE

In addition to all other workplace tools and equipment, your computer at work is the property of the company. Therefore, only use it for company business. This includes Internet use and electronic messaging.

▶ Emoticons (faces made and embedded in e-mail messages) are inappropriate at work.

▶ Do not forward messages that do not involve work-related issues.

▶ Check all messages for spelling and grammar before responding.

▶ Do not send e-mail with large and colorful letters or all capital letters. This is interpreted as yelling and is considered rude.

▶ If you receive a work-related message that requests a reply, respond to the message. Ignoring the message is not only rude, it communicates to the sender that you do not care. You also run the risk that you will be excluded from future messages.

▶ Always include the business subject in the subject line to let the receiver know it is not junk e-mail or a virus. The subject "hello" or "hi" is not appropriate.

▶ Carefully proofread and think about a message before you press Reply to ensure that it cannot be interpreted improperly.

▶ OTHER ETIQUETTE BASICS

▶ *Knock before entering an office.* Do not enter an office until you are invited. If the individual you want to see is with someone else, wait your turn. If the matter is urgent, apologize for interrupting.

▶ *Put others first.* When you are with colleagues and you are taking turns (in line, to order, etc.), allow your colleagues go to first.

▶ *Interruptions.* In today's society, we have so many inputs trying to attract our attention. As a result, we often get anxious to share our point of view in a conversation and fail to allow others in the conversation to complete their sentence. Interrupting is a bad habit and is considered rude behavior. If you accidentally interrupt someone, immediately apologize and ask him or her to continue his or her statement.

▶ *Apologies.* Everyone is human. Therefore, everyone makes mistakes. When you realize that you may have said or done something hurtful to someone, apologize immediately. Apologizing is not a sign of weakness; it is a sign of strength and maturity. Even if you are not sure whether you have offended someone, apologize to avoid any potential misunderstandings. However, do not unnecessarily and continually apologize. Doing so gives you the appearance of being needy and insecure.

▶ *Dominating a conversation.* There is a key to carrying on a successful conversation. The key is listening. Listening means that you value the information the other individual is providing. Too frequently, individuals dominate the conversation with their own personal accounts. In general, this is not appropriate. This behavior becomes annoying when you begin to turn the conversation to yourself. Next time you are in a conversation, listen to how many times you state the words *me, I,* and *my.* Try to minimize the use of these words in your conversation.

◀ SUMMARY OF KEY CONCEPTS

▶ Projecting an executive presence is important in demonstrating knowledge of basic workplace behavior
▶ The majority of first impressions are made through your visual appearance
▶ Both your maturity and the importance you place on your job are reflected in the way you behave and dress at work
▶ You must begin to create a work wardrobe now
▶ Body piercing and body rings/jewelry appear to be current fads; they are offensive to some individuals. Consider the long-term consequences of getting a tattoo
▶ To succeed in the workplace, you need to follow etiquette protocol and consistently utilize it in all areas of your life
▶ Make a habit of thanking individuals either verbally or in writing
▶ Appropriate etiquette at social functions and while dining is as important as professional behavior at work

◀ KEY TERMS

appearance	dress code	respect
casual workdays	etiquette	work wardrobe
courtesy	executive presence	

◀ REFERENCE

Post, Peggy, and Peter Post. *The Etiquette Advantage in Business: Personal Skills for Professional Success.* New York: HarperCollins Publishers, Inc., 1999.

◀ IF YOU WERE THE BOSS

1. As the manager of a bank, one of your employees comes in on a Monday morning with a pierced tongue and purple hair. What should you do?
2. You have just hired a new employee who clearly has no concept of business etiquette. What specific steps would you take to teach your new employee how to behave professionally?

◀ **WEB LINKS**

http://www.ravenwerks.com/practices/etiquette.htm
http://www.youngmoney.com/careers/monstertrak/on_the_job/095
http://www.yorktech.com/department/jobplacement/Profdress.htm

◀ **WORKPLACE DO'S AND DON'TS**

Do wear professional clothes to work	*Don't* wear sweats, tennis shoes, or suggestive apparel at work
Do shower and make sure you are always clean	*Don't* overdo the cologne (or any body sprays)
Do make sure you make eye contact and offer a gentle but firm handshake	*Don't* grasp just the fingers when shaking hands
Do follow formal dining etiquette at work-related functions	*Don't* reach, grab, or overload your plate at the hors d'oeuvres table
Do say "please" and "thank-you" when appropriate	*Don't* assume that the other person knows you are thankful for his or her act of kindness

ACTIVITY 6–1

Assume you are starting a new job as an accounting clerk next week and you need some professional clothes. You need to go shopping for your work wardrobe and are limited to a $50 budget. Make a list of what you need and could buy to get you through your first week of work. Include the cost.

WHAT YOU NEED TO BUY	COST
	$
Total Cost	$50

Prior to being faced with this scenario, what items can you purchase today to begin building your professional wardrobe?

ACTIVITY 6–2

Pretend you are at a business reception and you do not know anyone else in the room. Role-play formal introductions with a classmate, then evaluate your partner's performance by identifying strengths and weaknesses.

Student Name	
STRENGTHS	WEAKNESSES

Student Name	
STRENGTHS	WEAKNESSES

ACTIVITY 6–3

Visit a (non fast food) restaurant to practice proper dining etiquette. While you are doing so, identify five acts of inappropriate behavior others are exhibiting.

	INAPPROPRIATE BEHAVIOR	WHY BEHAVIOR IS INAPPROPRIATE
1.		
2.		
3.		
4.		
5.		

1. The majority of first impressions are made by _____.

2. One of the first steps to determining appropriate attire for work is to identify _____.

3. Give five tips for women for dressing professionally from head to toe. _____, _____, _____, _____, _____.

4. Give five tips for men for dressing professionally from head to toe. _____, _____, _____, _____, _____.

5. A standard of social behavior is called _____.

6. When someone does something nice for you, you should _____.

7. A good handshake conveys _____.

8. Give five rules of thumb regarding dining etiquette. _____, _____, _____, _____, _____.

CHAPTER 7

DIVERSITY

OBJECTIVES

▶ Define *diversity* and realize its impact on performance

▶ Name the various forms of *workplace diversity*

▶ State the basic employee rights and legal protection available for workplace diversity issues

▶ Recognize the negative impact *stereotypes* and *prejudice* have in the workplace and on performance

▶ Identify *cultural* differences and the positive and negative impact these differences have on business

The greatest friend of Truth is time; her greatest enemy is Prejudice, and her constant companion Humility.

Charles Caleb Colton (1780–1832)

▶ DIVERSITY BASICS

Imagine dipping your hand into a large bowl of jelly beans. Pull out a handful of these candies and you will see many bright, beautiful colors. Bite into several of these morsels and you will find that, although they are different colors on the outside, they are exactly the same inside. This is how diversity is in the workplace. On the outside, we may be different; but, on the inside, we are all human beings attempting to do our best with our skills and knowledge.

This chapter addresses workplace diversity, cultural differences, and employee rights regarding these differences. Diversity comes in many forms. Although most people think of diversity as a race issue, the topic goes far beyond race. People are different in many aspects, ranging from ethnicity to the way we wear our hair. As we discuss these issues, it is important to note three primary messages regarding workplace diversity:

▶ No matter what our differences, we must treat everyone with respect and professionalism.
▶ Diversity should be used as an asset that utilizes our differences as ways to create, innovate, and compete.
▶ Workplace diversity should only be an issue when the diversity negatively affects performance.

The following is a common example of workplace diversity: One of Cory's new friends at work has a lifestyle that is not as conservative as Cory's. Although Cory's friend has never openly mentioned his lifestyle, he behaves in a feminine fashion, always talks about his wild weekends, and loves decorating and dancing. Cory really enjoys the workplace friendship with this guy. He is older and watches out for and helps Cory; yet, Cory does not know how to behave around this friend. Cory thinks about talking to coworkers about the new friend and his lifestyle but ultimately decides that personal opinions on one's lifestyle should be kept private. Cory decides it best to maintain a good working relationship with the new friend regardless of lifestyle differences.

▶ FORMS OF DIVERSITY

Workplace diversity means there are differences among coworkers. Whenever people address the issue of diversity at work, they primarily address cultural and racial differences. It is important to note that diversity extends well beyond culture and race. We also differ in age, gender, economic status, physical makeup, intelligence, religion, and sexual orientation, among other things.

The Equal Employment Opportunity Commission (EEOC) enforces laws that protect individuals from workplace discrimination in recruiting, hiring, wages, promotions, and unlawful termination. These laws are based upon Dr. Martin Luther King Jr.'s establishment of Title VII of the Civil Rights Act, which prohibits discrimination based on sex, religion, race or color, or national origin. Since that time, additional laws have been made to further protect individuals from discrimination in the area of age (over forty years), physical and mental disabilities, gender, sexual orientation, hate crimes, pregnancy, and military service. If you ever feel you are a victim of discrimination, first contact your human resource department. If you feel you are still experiencing discrimination, you should contact your state's *Department of Fair Employment and Housing* or the *Equal Employment Opportunity Commission*.

◀ EXERCISE 7–1: **What Do You See?** *Look around the room and list at least ten differences between you and your classmates.*

1.	6.
2.	7.
3.	8.
4.	9.
5.	10.

Race is defined as people with certain physical traits. Racial differences include various ethnicities including Hispanics, Asians, African Americans, Native Americans, and Anglo-Saxons. **Culture** is the different behavior patterns of people. Examples of various cultures may include where you live geographically, your age, your economic status, and your religious beliefs. As the workplace becomes more diverse, it is hard to imagine a workplace that does not include various races and cultures.

As we begin to understand how race and culture impact our workplace, we will begin to recognize how these differences influence our values and behavior. In chapter 1, we discussed that not everyone thinks and behaves like you do. Moreover, people look different and have different value systems. Although we may not like one's looks or agree with others' values or religious beliefs, we must respect everyone's differences and treat them professionally.

Digging deeper into the issue of culture, we need to appreciate the various generational differences and their impact on the workplace as well. Individuals entering the workforce (eighteen- to twenty-two-year-olds) have different needs than those preparing to retire (fifty-five and older). Moreover, these needs reflect priorities, values, and attitudes.

▶ STEREOTYPES AND PREJUDICE

In chapter 1, we discussed the differences in people's attitudes and how these attitudes form our personalities. Everyone is a product of past experience. Individuals use these past experiences to form perceptions about people and situations. A **perception** is one's understanding or interpretation of reality. If we had a positive previous experience, we will most likely have a positive perception of a person or circumstance. For example, if your boss calls you into his or her office, you will either have a positive or negative perception of the upcoming situation. If your boss is a good communicator and you frequently visit his or her office, you will have a positive perception of being called into the office. On the other hand, if your boss only calls you into his or her office for bad news, your perception of reality is that the boss's office only represents reprimands and punishment.

To make situations easier to understand or perceive, we often stereotype. **Stereotyping** is making a generalized image of a particular group or situation. We often take our perceptions and mold groups or situations. These images can be positive or negative, but we generally apply them to similar situations and groups. At work, this can include types of meetings (situations) or members of specific departments (groups). Using the preceding example of the boss and his or her office, one could stereotype that all bosses are good communicators.

It is important to not only know the definition of stereotyping but also to avoid applying stereotypes in a negative manner. Let us use the example of females with blonde hair. A common stereotype is that females with blonde hair are not intelligent. We know this is not true. Prior to responding to a situation, conduct an attitude check to ensure that you are not basing your reaction on a perception or stereotype rather than responding to the current facts and situation.

Using the previous example of attitudes toward females with blonde hair, if we assume that all females with blonde hair are unintelligent (stereotype), we have just demonstrated prejudice. **Prejudice** is a favorable or unfavorable judgment or opinion toward an individual or group based on one's perception (or understanding) of a group, individual, or situation. Typically, at work, prejudice is a negative attitude or opinion that results in discrimination. Therefore, if we do not hire females with blonde hair because we believe they are not intelligent, we are guilty of discrimination. **Workplace discrimination** is acting against someone based on race, age, gender, religion, disability, or any of the other areas we have discussed in this chapter.

Most people harbor some type of prejudice. It is important to recognize in what areas you may be harboring prejudice and begin understanding why. Once you recognize what areas need improvement, begin taking action to decrease your prejudice. One way is to learn about the individual, group, or situation that is causing the prejudice.

What areas of prejudice do you see in your community?

Labeling is when we describe an individual or group of individuals based upon past actions. Labels come from stereotypes. We can attach positive or negative labels to these groups or individuals, and we frequently have the group or individuals live up or down to these standards. We will then watch for supporting behaviors to see if they live up to or dispel the labels we have attached. For example, if we label a coworker as being the smartest person we know, that person may live up to this expectation by behaving as the smartest person (regardless of if he really is). However, he may dispel the label by purposely behaving opposite of a smart person.

◀ EXERCISE 7–3: **Label Yourself:** *Create a personal career label for yourself by writing a statement describing how you want others at work to view you.*

We also make assumptions based on people's language differences and accents. These assumptions may include economic status, intelligence, and social customs. In our melting pot society, it is common for individuals to speak a different language (bilingual) when at home. At work, speaking a second language can be a means of attracting and meeting customer needs. Therefore, being bilingual is a great workplace asset.

Never make fun of people with different cultures or lifestyles. Even jokes that we believe are innocent may cause deep wounds. Moreover, they may not only be offensive but violate one's civil rights. They may be construed as both workplace discrimination and harassment.

For example, Cory is invited to lunch with some new coworkers. During the meal, one of the coworkers tells a joke against a certain ethnicity. Cory politely chuckles at the punch line but is actually offended. Cory wonders how to best handle the situation. Should Cory tell the joke teller that the joke was offensive? Should Cory tell the department supervisor? Cory clearly believes that this type of behavior is inappropriate and could qualify as harassment. Cory decides to informally tell the joke teller that the joke was offensive. If Cory continues to see inappropriate or offensive behavior, Cory has decided to mention the behavior to the department supervisor.

Companies are attempting to better address workplace diversity through several actions. First, they are developing **diversity statements**. These statements remind employees that diversity in the workplace should be an asset and not a form of prejudice and stereotyping. Secondly, they are providing **diversity training** to teach employees how to eliminate workplace discrimination and harassment. Thirdly, they are eliminating the **glass ceiling** and **glass walls**. These are invisible barriers that frequently make executive positions (glass ceiling) and certain work areas such as a golf course (glass wall) off limits to females and minorities. A glass ceiling stops females and minorities from advancing up the corporate ladder through promotions. Glass walls are barriers that prevent females and minorities from certain situations. Finally, proactive companies offer formal mentoring programs to assist in identifying and training women and minorities for promotion opportunities. Remember, people should never receive special treatment because they are female or a minority, but they should be given an equal opportunity. Every employer is responsible for hiring the most qualified candidate.

▶ CULTURAL DIFFERENCES

Our society is a mix of individuals from all over the world. For this reason, it is important to address cultural differences and their impact on the workplace. Cultural differences include, among other things, religious influences and the treatment of individuals based on age and gender, special differences, and family influences.

There are many different religions in the world. Although major U.S. holidays are based around Christian holidays, not everyone who works in the United States is a Christian. Individuals who do not share your religious values are afforded the same rights as you. As mentioned earlier in this chapter, the Civil Rights Act protects individuals from discrimination based on religion. Everyone is entitled to observe his or her respective religious holidays and traditions. Once again, we must be respectful of everyone's individual religious beliefs and not condemn someone for his or her religious difference. Although an individual's religious beliefs should permeate every element of his or her life, it should not be brought into the workplace. As with other issues of diversity, if your religion or someone else's religion impacts performance, the issue must be addressed.

Some countries are very self-centered, while other countries put what is best for society as a priority over personal needs. In some cultures, woman and children are often not treated as equals to men. Although we may not agree with this treatment, we have to respect cultural differences. It is important to understand these differences so you do not offend others. For example, some hand gestures that are commonly used in the United States may be offensive to someone who has come from another country. If you feel you may have offended someone based upon a cultural difference, find out what behavior offended the other person, apologize if appropriate, and make sure you do not repeat the offensive behavior.

Cultural differences have both a positive and negative impact on business. Learning about other cultures can provide insights into new markets and stimulate creativity. With so much diversity among employees and customers, knowing other cultures will result in improved relationships. Outcomes can be negative when companies don not properly train and address cultural differences; this is when opportunities for prejudice and discrimination may emerge.

◀ SUMMARY OF KEY CONCEPTS

- ▶ Workplace diversity means the differences among coworkers. These differences go beyond the color of one's skin
- ▶ No matter what our differences, we must treat everyone with respect and professionalism
- ▶ Title VII of the Civil Rights Act prohibits discrimination based on sex, religion, race or color, or national origin
- ▶ It is important to recognize our stereotypes and prejudice
- ▶ Diversity should be used as an asset that utilizes our differences as ways to create, innovate, and compete
- ▶ Workplace diversity should only be an issue when the diversity negatively affects performance

◀ KEY TERMS

culture

diversity statements

diversity training

glass ceiling

glass wall

labeling

perception

prejudice

race

stereotyping

workplace discrimination

workplace diversity

◀ IF YOU WERE THE BOSS

1. What would you do if you noticed an employee treating another employee in a discriminatory manner?
2. What can you do to minimize workplace discrimination and harassment?

◀ WEB LINKS

http://www.dol.gov

http://www.dol.gov/dol/topic/discrimination/index.htm

http://www.executiveplanet.com

http://www.serve.com/shea/stereodf.htm

◀ WORKPLACE DO'S AND DON'TS

Do know your rights regarding workplace diversity	*Don't* accept defeat in discriminatory situations
Do learn to respect differences in others	*Don't* use your minority status to take advantage of situations
Do be proud of your culture and heritage	*Don't* show prejudice toward others
Do take responsibility for increasing awareness about workplace diversity issues	*Don't* label people

ACTIVITY 7–1

Using the Internet or library, look up three countries. What are the countries' differences in color perception, gender, and religion?

COUNTRY	COLOR PERCEPTION	GENDER	RELIGION
1.			
2.			
3.			

ACTIVITY 7–2

In the United States, the thumbs-up symbol communicates a job well done. Research and identify what the thumbs-up symbol communicates in at least two other countries. What did this activity teach you about various cultures and hand gestures?

COUNTRY	MEANING

Conclusion: What did you learn?

_____

_____

ACTIVITY 7–3

Identify a recent experience or observed act of prejudice. How would you have handled the situation differently?

ACT OF PREJUDICE	HOW YOU WOULD HANDLE THE SITUATION

ACTIVITY 7–4

With a partner, dialogue what you would say if someone offended you with a joke. Was this dialogue easy? Why or why not? Share your findings with your class.

_____

_____

_____

_____

1. Differences among coworkers are referred to as _____.

2. _____ is a group of individuals with certain physical traits, while _____ are different behavior patterns of various groups.

3. The understanding or interpretation of reality is called _____.

4. Making a generalized image of a particular group or situation is called _____.

5. Creating a favorable or unfavorable judgment or opinion toward an individual is displaying _____.

6. Companies provide _____ to teach employees how to eliminate workplace discrimination and harassment.

CHAPTER 8

CUSTOMER SERVICE/QUALITY

OBJECTIVES

▶ Define *productivity* and its impact on organizational success

▶ Identify and define *directional statements*

▶ Know the various types of plans used in an organization

▶ Define the primary business functions and their purpose in an organization

▶ Define *quality* and its importance in business

▶ State the difference between a *product* and a *service*

▶ Identify and describe the importance of *customers* and *customer service*

▶ Describe how to handle a difficult customer

There are only two qualities in the world: efficiency and inefficiency, and only two sorts of people: the efficient and the inefficient.

George Bernard Shaw (1856–1950)

► PRODUCTIVITY IN THE WORKPLACE

Part of your workplace success will be based upon your understanding of the business, the way it is organized, and its overall purpose. Without an understanding of the business as a whole, it is difficult for you to be a good employee. This chapter addresses these issues.

The purpose of a business is to make a profit. Moreover, the business has hired you to be productive. Workplace **productivity** means to perform a function that adds value to the company. Whatever you produce (called *output*) should always assist the company in achieving its mission. It is your responsibility to help the company be successful. There are several ways of doing this. First and foremost, you must behave ethically. You should always make ethical choices that serve the best interest of the company. It is your responsibility to take care of company resources that have been entrusted to you. This includes eliminating waste and producing quality products. As discussed in chapter 1, your attitude assists the company with becoming successful. Maintain a positive attitude. Be an active team member and work to create positive workplace relationships. You should be open to learning new skills.

A company's **mission statement** is its statement of purpose. It identifies why everyone comes to work. An example of a college's mission statement is to make students successful. This means not only providing a solid education but also preparing students to succeed on the job or with their continuing education. If all college employees know their ultimate purpose is to make students successful, every activity they perform on the job should contribute to student success. Either prior to starting your job or within your first week at work, secure a copy of your company's mission statement. If possible, memorize it. A copy should be included in your employee handbook and/or provided to you during the employee orientation. If this information is not provided, ask your supervisor or the human resource department for a copy.

A company will not survive without being profitable; even nonprofit organizations need to make a profit to accomplish their mission. However, a company is not successful just because it turns a profit. There are several important elements that contribute to a company's success. These include satisfied customers who have purchased a quality product produced by motivated employees. Moreover, successful companies are accountable to various stakeholders including their investors, the community at large, the environment, and their employees. Factors within the business environment are always changing, so it is important that companies constantly monitor changes and be proactive in meeting the needs of various stakeholders.

Once a company has identified why it exists, it must identify where it wants to be in the future. This is called a **vision statement**. A company's vision statement is its viable view of the future. For example, a college may want to be the top-ranked college in the nation. It will take work, but it is achievable. In addition to the company's mission and vision statements, every company should have a values statement. The **values statement** defines what is important to (or what the priorities are) for the company. This could include providing a healthy return to investors, taking care of the environment, taking care of its employees, or keeping customers satisfied. Included in the company values statement will typically be the company's code of conduct or ethics statement. As discussed in chapter 7, these statements discuss the importance of behaving ethically in all areas of business.

Together, the company's mission, vision, and values statements comprise the organization's **directional statements**. These statements create the foundation of why the company exists and how it will operate.

For example, Cory's company was updating its strategic plan and was asking for volunteers to sit on various committees. Cory questioned if new employees were qualified to sit on these committees. Cory decided to ask a coworker. The coworker encouraged Cory to participate and said it would be a great way for Cory to learn more about the company, get to know people throughout the organization, and help make positive changes for the company's overall success. Cory's coworker then showed Cory the back side of Cory's name badge. On it was printed the company's mission statement. "This," Cory's coworker proudly said, "is why we come to work everyday." Cory signed up for a committee that afternoon.

Each company should have a strategy. The company's **strategy** is its road map for success. Typically, a **strategic plan** is a formal document that is developed by senior management. The strategic plan identifies how the company will secure, organize, utilize, and monitor its resources. **Company resources** include financial (fiscal), human (employees), and capital (long-term investments).

The formal strategic plan is generally not available to all employees. However, many companies provide brief summaries or overviews to all employees to keep everyone focused on priorities and goals. Just as you created a personal plan earlier in this text, all areas of the company will have smaller plans with stated **goals** and **objectives** that identify how their respective areas will assist in achieving the company's strategy. As defined in chapter 2, a goal is a broad statement or aim while an objective supports the goal. When creating personal goals in chapter 2, objectives were also referred to as *short-term goals*. Remember that an objective must be short-term and measurable. Each area of the company will utilize its respective resources and have its performance monitored based upon the company strategy and goals.

◄ **EXERCISE 8–1: Create Job Goals:** *Assume you started your new job today as a receptionist for a law firm. Write one goal and two objectives for your new job.*

Goal	
Objective 1	
Objective 2	

► LINES OF AUTHORITY

Company functions and resources within the business are organized according to the company's mission and strategy. The way a company is organized is called its **organizational structure**. The graphic visual display of this structure is called the company **organizational chart**. This chart not only identifies key functions within the company but also shows the formal lines of authority for employees. These formal lines of authority are also referred to as the *chain of command*. The formal lines of authority will identify who reports to whom within the company. It is important to remember that you must respect and follow the formal lines of authority within your company. For example, using the organizational chart in Figure 8–1, it is inappropriate for the accounts

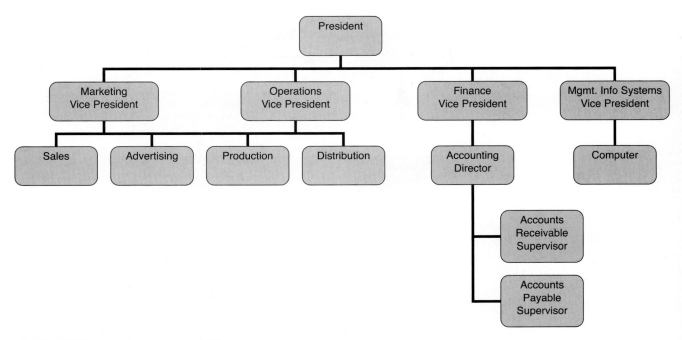

◄ **FIGURE 8–1** Organizational Chart

payable supervisor to directly approach the marketing vice president for a request without prior approval from the accounting director.

This story is a good example of why you should know your organizational structure and identify your superiors. One day Cory was left alone in the department while everyone was away at an important meeting. A tall man walked through the doors and asked to see Cory's boss. Cory explained that the boss was currently out. The gentleman began asking about how Cory felt about the company, including how long Cory had worked for the company and if Cory were able to change one thing in the company what it would be. Cory found the questions strange but interesting. Cory was honest in the answers provided, always keeping the conversation polite and positive but constructive. The gentleman thanked Cory for the input and left. Two weeks later, Cory's boss returned from a meeting and told Cory that the CEO of the company had shared Cory's comments with key executives in identifying ways to improve employee morale. It was then that Cory realized that the earlier conversation was with the CEO of the company. Cory was relieved to have been polite and positive in the CEO conversation but regretted not recognizing the CEO when he first walked into the office.

Each company has a leader (see Figure 8–2). The leader is typically called the **president or chief executive officer (CEO)**. The president or CEO reports to the company **board of directors**. This group of individuals is responsible for developing the company's overall strategy and major policies. The people who become the company's board of directors are elected by shareholders or investors. Smaller companies may not have such a formal structure and/or titles, but every business has investors (owners) and a leader (president). It is important to become familiar with your leaders' names and titles and the formal lines of authority. This will allow you to determine whom you can go to if there is a question or problem. If possible, try to view updated photos of these individuals so that, if the appropriate opportunity arises, as with Cory's experience, you can introduce yourself to them.

Within a typical company structure are three different levels of management (see Figure 8–3). These levels include senior management, middle management, and operations management. **Senior managers or executives** typically have the title of *vice president*. These individuals work with the president in identifying and implementing the company strategy. The time line for **strategic issues** typically ranges from three to five years or more. **Middle managers** typically have the title of *director* or *manager*. These individuals work on tactical issues. **Tactical issues** identify how to link the strategy into the reality of day-to-day operations. The time line for tactical issues is one to three years. **Operations managers**, typically *supervisors* and *assistant managers*, work on **operational issues**. These are issues within the company that occur on a daily

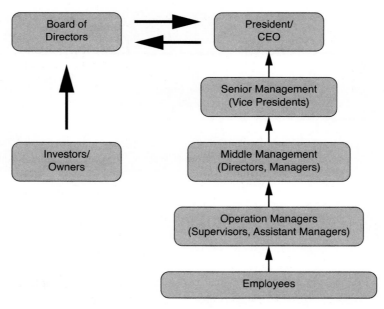

◀ **FIGURE 8–2** Formal Structure

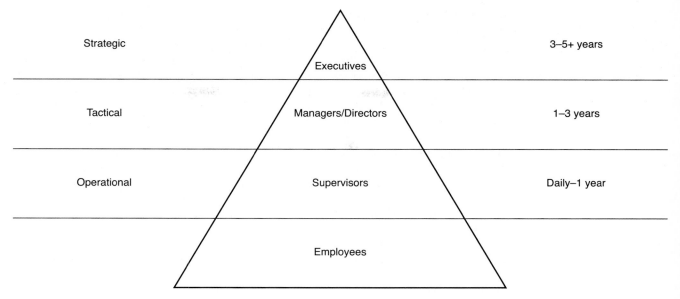

Strategic		3–5+ years
Executives	
Tactical	Managers/Directors	1–3 years
Operational	Supervisors	Daily–1 year
	Employees	

◄ **FIGURE 8–3** Management Levels

basis and/or no longer than one year. As you begin to develop your career, you will have the opportunity to advance into a position of leadership. Your first step into a management position will be that of a **supervisor**. And, although supervisors only concern themselves with operational issues, successful employees and supervisors understand the bigger picture of the company's overall tactics and strategy.

As displayed in a typical organizational chart, companies are typically arranged by major functions. These major functions are frequently referred to as **divisions**. Within these divisions are **departments**. The departments carry out specific functions respective of their division. A number of major functions (divisions) are necessary in business. These include finance and accounting, human resource management, operations, information systems, marketing, and legal counsel.

The **finance and accounting** department is responsible for the securing, distribution, and growth of the company's financial assets. These individuals handle everything within the company that has to do with money. Any invoices (company bills) or incoming cash or checks must be recorded through the accounting department. The accounting department will work with the human resource department on payroll issues regarding your paycheck. Because the primary purpose of every company is to make a profit, you, as an employee, are accountable for how you utilize the company's financial resources. Just as you have a personal budget (refer to chapter 2), every company utilizes **budgets**. A budget is a plan used to allocate money. There are several types of budgets including a **capital budget** and an **operational budget**. The capital budget is used for long-term investments including land and large pieces of equipment. An operational budget is used for short-term items including payroll and the day-to-day costs associated with running a business.

Here is an example that shows the importance of budgeting. One of Cory's coworkers went on vacation. Before leaving, Cory's coworker showed Cory how to order office supplies online and asked Cory to order more supplies if the department fell short. Cory noticed that the department was running low on a few items and decided to place an order. As Cory clicked through the online catalog, Cory saw a lot of items that would be nice to have around the office, including a new hole punch, a label maker, and multicolored vinyl file folders. Cory also thought it would be nice to have a pair of new scissors, a tape dispenser, and other personal desk items. As Cory was about to place the order, Cory was shocked to see that the total was over $1,000. Cory realized that the coworker never gave Cory a budget. Cory decided to order only the necessities and wait to ask the coworker about the other items.

As illustrated in the Cory example, too frequently, nonmanagement employees do not think before they spend the company's money. Before you spend the company's money, ask yourself a simple question: "If I owned this company, would I spend my money on this item?" Answering that simple question makes you more accountable for your actions and makes you think like a business owner. You most likely will not spend your money on frivolous, unnecessary items and will pay more attention to not only adhering to a budget but also identifying ways to save money.

The **human resource management** department deals with recruiting, hiring, training, evaluating, compensating, promoting, and terminating employees. This function deals with the employee (people) side of business. Your first contact with this function will be when you apply and interview for a job. You will also interact with the human resource department for any issue regarding company policy, complaints and grievances, and your terms of employment. The human resource management function is discussed in greater detail in chapter 13.

The **operations** function deals with the production and distribution of the company's product or service. It is the core of the business. Even if your position does not directly contribute to the primary purpose of the company, it is your job to support individuals whose job it is to produce and distribute the product or service.

The **information systems** department deals with the management of information within the organization. This division is responsible for ensuring that the company appropriately utilizes its computer/technology resources. As an employee, you assist and support the information systems department by only utilizing company technology for work-related business. You should report any computer virus and system problems immediately.

Marketing is responsible for creating, pricing, selling, distributing, and promoting the company's product or service. As is discussed later in this chapter, there are internal and external customers and it is every employee's responsibility to assist in satisfying the customer's needs. Therefore, regardless of your position, it is your job to contribute to producing a high-quality, high-value product. You are a walking billboard for your company. Remember that your behavior both at and away from work represents the company. Never speak poorly of your company, coworkers, or the company's product or service.

Finally, the company's **legal counsel** handles all legal matters relating to the business. You should always check with the company's legal department prior to engaging in a contract on behalf of the company.

Large companies may have separate divisions for each of these functions, while smaller companies combine several functions into a single division, department, or position. Note that not all companies have all the formal departments, titles, or organizational charts described in this chapter. Most small businesses will not have such formal structures. However, to be successful, they will have someone who performs these important functions for the business.

▶ QUALITY AND THE COMPANY

If someone asked you to describe a company, you would most likely describe a building, its employees, and the product produced. In some respects, you are right. These are major elements that define a company, but a company needs customers to succeed. Excellent service, quality, and innovation are what will persuade customers to purchase a company's product or service. More important, a successful company's employees and products must make customers want to make a repeat purchase.

As an employee, you are an important part of the company. Every job in the company has a purpose; therefore, every employee is important to a company. Although administration may lead what is being done in the company, your job is necessary to help run the company. This is what makes you an important part of the company. Therefore, you must do your best at all times. **Quality** is a predetermined standard that defines how a product is to be produced or a service is to be provided. Customers demand quality not just in the product they purchase but also from the company employees. If customers do not perceive that they have received a quality product or service, they will not make a repeat purchase.

Customer loyalty is another important element that contributes to the success of a company. If a customer perceives she has received value and a quality product, she will display loyalty to your company by making a repeat purchase. Companies want to build brand loyalty with customers. This means that the customer will not substitute your product for that of a competing product. Customers will be loyal to a company and its products when quality products and service are consistently provided.

Employee loyalty is an employee's obligation to consistently support a company and its mission. Displaying loyalty contributes to a company's success. Employees can show their loyalty in several ways. The most obvious is for you to do your job and do it well. Another way to show loyalty to the company is to show respect for company policies, your coworkers, and the company's customers. Also, you should make every effort to promote the company and its products. To do this, you must understand the company and know the mission, strategy, and business structure of the company you work for.

The success of a company depends on profit. **Profit** is revenue (money coming in from sales) minus expenses (the costs involved in running the business). You can help create profit for your company by monitoring and decreasing expenses and identifying ways to increase sales. You should be aware of expenses you incur at work and make every effort to eliminate waste. You should also find ways to be involved with and take responsibility toward better knowing your customers and the community. As profits increase, the company can grow. This means a company can expand into a larger space, add more sites, offer more services and/or products, increase your pay and benefits, and/or hire additional employees. For you, as an employee, this could result in raises or promotions.

Some companies sell only products, some sell only services, and some sell both. A **product** is a tangible item, that is, something that you can physically see or touch. Appliances, toys, or equipment are examples of tangible products. A **service** is an intangible product. In other words, you cannot always touch or see the product. Examples of services include haircuts, banking, golf courses, and medical services. You need to differentiate between a company's service and customer service. This is explained in more detail later in this chapter.

◄ **EXERCISE 8–2: Compare Product Businesses to Service Businesses:** *Identify the following items as either products or services.*

Item	Product	Service
Movies		
Gasoline		
Photography		
Restaurant		
College class		

▶ WHO IS THE CUSTOMER?

All functions of a company are important. However, what you must remember is that a company cannot survive without customers. This makes it extremely important to know who your customers are and how to treat them. A **customer** is one who buys a service or product. It can be anyone with a want or need who is willing to pay for a product or service that fills that want or need.

A company has internal and external customers. Internal customers are fellow employees and departments that exist within a company. External customers are individuals whom the company serves outside. These include customers, vendors, and investors. You may have a job that never allows you to interact with the company's external customers, but you must serve and treat your internal customers as well as the company expects employees to treat its external customers. Doing so makes it easier for employees who interact with external customers to do so successfully.

_____

_____

How do you want your coworkers to treat you?

_____

_____

A satisfied customer will make a repeat purchase. More important, maintaining satisfied customers is one of the best ways to sell your product or service because they will encourage others to buy your product. In contrast, unsatisfied customers will spread the word about their dissatisfaction even faster than satisfied customers spread the word about their satisfaction. Think about how many times you have been satisfied or unsatisfied about a product or service. When others ask you if you know about a particular product, you will tell them whether your experience was good or bad. The reason satisfaction is important is that most people will tell about the problems and bad experiences without prompting, or without anyone asking. You do not want people bad-mouthing your company or product.

To create a satisfied customer, you need a high-quality product or service and excellent customer service. This can only occur with quality employees producing their product with quality materials (inputs). This concept is best expressed in the equation found in figure 8-4.

▶ QUALITY

When it comes to quality, the expectation of customers is high. With increased technology and competition, customers demand high-quality products and services. Customers expect that a product will last. Customers also expect **value**, which means customers believe they are getting a good deal for the price they have paid. Companies that cannot compete on this issue cannot experience long-term success.

If your job is to help create a product, keep in mind that if you do your job well and the product is of high quality, customers will be happy and keep buying the product. Good-quality products can only be achieved if you, as an employee, are doing your job well.

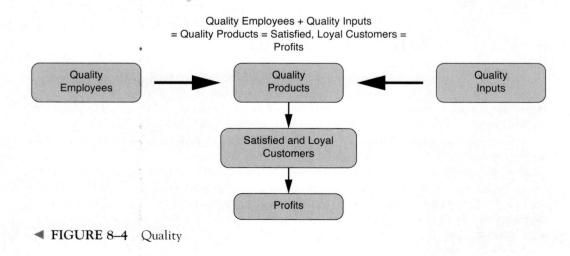

◀ **FIGURE 8–4** Quality

◀ **EXERCISE 8–4: Taking Responsibility for Quality:** *As an employee, list five ways you can take personal responsibility for quality at work.*

1. _____

2. _____

3. _____

4. _____

5. _____

Customers measure product quality by comparing your product to similar products. They also measure quality by how satisfied they are after consuming or using a product. Successful companies include performance monitors in their strategies. Performance monitors identify how success will be measured. An example would be employee evaluations. The evaluation can identify how an employee's performance contributes to customer quality. Monitors, or standards, may include defect rates, expenses, or sales quotas. This evaluation can include areas of quality and service that are done well and those that need improvement. Evaluation criteria can also include areas such as response time, attitude toward customers, and the right use of resources.

As mentioned earlier in this chapter, the marketing department is responsible for the pricing, development, distribution, and promotion of a product. Although these functions are the primary responsibility of the marketing department, projecting a positive image and selling the company's product are the jobs of every employee within the organization. The premise that marketing is everyone's job is commonly referred to as the *marketing concept*.

▶ EXCELLENT CUSTOMER SERVICE DEFINED

An important concept you must remember in regard to workplace quality is the definition of customer service. **Customer service** is the treatment an employee provides the customer, whether the customer is purchasing a service or a product.

Customers expect excellent customer service. They want to be treated with respect and kindness. They not only want but expect employees to be competent, dependable, and responsive. They also expect the business environment to be clean, safe, and organized.

As a **competent** employee, you should know the product(s) your company offers. You should be able to answer questions when the customer asks. Customers expect you to be able to help them decide on a purchase by giving them correct information about the product. If you cannot answer a question, you should be able to direct the customer to another employee who can.

Dependable means that you are capable and honest when assisting a customer. Always speak the truth. Do not pretend to know something when you do not know the answer to a customer's question. Customers expect you to help them solve their problems. There is no shame in admitting that you do not know an answer. You will gain respect in admitting that you do not know all the answers but are willing to find someone who can assist the customer. If there is ever a situation in which you seek assistance from another employee when helping a customer, do not just hand the customer over to the other employee. Whenever possible, stay with the customer and learn from your coworker so that, in the future, you will know the answer the next time someone asks.

A **responsive** employee will provide a customer personal attention. This means that you need to be aware of the customer's need, often before the customer even realizes that need. Some customers like to be left alone to shop for a product but want you near if questions arise. Some customers would like you to guide them step by step when purchasing a product. When a customer approaches your area, make every effort to acknowledge the customer as soon as possible.

Greet him or her and ask the customer if he or she needs assistance. Watch the customer's body language. The customer will let you know if he or she wants to be left alone or wants you to stay nearby. Use the customer's name if you know it. Using the customer's name creates a more personal and friendly atmosphere. Remember, all customers are different and need to be treated differently according to their needs. You need to learn how to satisfy these needs.

A customer also expects a welcoming, convenient, and safe environment. This includes the appearance of the building, as well as the appearance of the employees. As soon as a customer comes in contact with a business, an opinion is formed about that business. There is only one first impression, so it must be good. The appearance of the building and/or employees can be the reason a customer comes to your company in the first place. Keep your workplace clean, and immediately address any potential safety hazards. If there is trash on the floor or a spill of water, clean it up. Take responsibility for keeping your workplace clean and safe. Although addressed in greater detail in chapter 6, make every effort to maintain a professional appearance from head to toe. Your attitude, language, and attire are a total package that creates an image for your customers.

► THE IMPACT OF CUSTOMER SERVICE

Get to know your customers. Good customers will keep coming back to purchase your product. These customers will tell others about your product. Excellent customer service is the biggest reason customers return. With so much competition, the same product can be purchased at many different places. With so many choices and increased competition, often times, the only thing that keeps customers coming back to your business may be the personal service that you have provided them. Your goal is to build a relationship with customers that will make them loyal to you and your business. This is why so many businesses now keep records of their customers. The more information businesses maintain on their customers, the more they are able to provide personal service. With the increased use of technology, many companies maintain databases with such information as past purchases, birthdays, special interests, and return/exchange practices. This helps the company to establish a more personal relationship with the customer and to follow up on sales. It is common to notify customers of upcoming sales of frequently purchased products, send notification of upcoming events, or mail discounts and coupons.

For example, when Cory moved to a new neighborhood and wanted to order pizza, Cory found there were many different pizza parlors. The only way to determine which one to try was to ask others for a recommendation or to just randomly try each one. Because Cory was new to the area and did not know many people, Cory called one of the pizza shops. When Cory called, the employee was friendly and sounded happy to assist with the order. Cory automatically formed a good impression about the pizza shop. When Cory went to pick up the pizza, the inside of the shop was clean, as were the employees. The pizza also tasted good. So the next time Cory wanted a pizza, Cory called the same place. Cory was really impressed when an employee at the pizza shop remembered what was previously ordered and called Cory by name. Cory experienced excellent service.

The success and profitability of a company depends on how you treat your customers. The happier the customers are, the more likely they are to come back. A business needs satisfied customers to not only make repeat purchases but also tell others about their favorable experience. Unhappy customers will tell others to avoid your business. It is important to note that all customer information and records should be kept confidential and should only be used for business purposes.

► THE DIFFICULT CUSTOMER

Customers can sometimes be difficult to deal with. Historically, companies have had the motto "The customer is always right." But, in many instances, the customer may not be right. Although the customer may be wrong, you need to adopt the attitude that the customer is unhappy and do all you can to help the customer solve his or her problem. Have patience, and sympathize with the customer.

Many times, a difficult customer will be unfriendly and may even begin yelling at you. You need to stay calm and not take the customer's inappropriate behavior personally. By remaining calm, you are better able to get the customer to identify the real problem and logically get the problem solved as quickly as possible in a manner that is fair to both the customer and your company.

In order to successfully resolve a difficult customer's complaint, you need to do the following:

1. *Stay calm, let the customer talk, and listen for facts.* This may mean letting the customer vent for a few minutes. This is not easy when someone is yelling at you. However, do not interrupt or say "please calm down." This will only fuel the fire. Pay attention, nod your head, and take notes if it helps you keep focused. Remember, even though the person may be yelling at you, you should not take harsh words personally.

2. *Watch body language.* This may include the tone of voice, eye contact, and arm movement. If a customer avoids eye contact, he or she may be lying to you or not fully conveying his or her side of the story. You should never allow a customer to touch you, especially in a threatening manner. If you feel a difficult customer has the potential to become violent or physically abusive, immediately seek assistance.

3. *Acknowledge the customer's frustration.* Say, "I can understand why you are upset." Let the person know you have been listening to his or her concern by paraphrasing what you have understood the problem to be. Do not repeat everything, just a summary of the concern.

4. *Make sure the problem gets solved.* Whenever possible, take care of the problem yourself; do not just send the customer to someone else. While it is tempting to just call your supervisor or someone else, whenever possible, take care of the customer by staying with him or her until you know the problem is resolved.

5. *Know company policy.* Some difficult customers are dishonest customers and attempt to frazzle employees by intimidation and rude behavior. Know the company policies and do not be ashamed to enforce them consistently. If a customer challenges a policy, calmly and politely explain the purpose of the policy.

6. *Expect conflict, but do not accept abuse.* Difficult customers are a fact of life. Although customers may occasionally yell, you do not have to take the abuse. If a customer shows aggressiveness or is cursing, politely tell him or her that you cannot help him or her until he or she is able to treat you in a respectable manner. If the customer continues the inappropriate behavior, immediately call a supervisor.

◀ SUMMARY OF KEY CONCEPTS

▶ Directional statements include the company's mission, vision, and values statements

▶ The company's strategic plan identifies how a company will secure, utilize, and monitor resources for success

▶ A company's organizational chart is a graphic display of the major functions and formal lines of authority within an organization

▶ Major functions (divisions) that are necessary within a business include finance and accounting, human resource management, operations, information systems, marketing, and legal counsel

▶ Excellent service, quality, and innovation are what will persuade customers to purchase a company's product or service

▶ Customers can be internal customers (other employees) or external customers (individuals outside of your company). A successful company has concern for both internal and external customers

▶ Employees that provide excellent customer service are competent, dependable, and responsive

▶ The customer is not always right, but you need to adopt the attitude that the customer is unhappy and do all you can to help the customer solve his or her problem

◀ KEY TERMS

board of directors
budget
capital budget
company resources
competent
customer
customer service
departments
dependable
directional statements
divisions
employee loyalty
finance and accounting
goals
human resource
   management

information systems
legal counsel
marketing
middle managers
mission statement
objectives
operational budget
operational issues
operations
operations managers
organizational chart
organizational structure
president or chief
   executive officer (CEO)
product
productivity

profit
quality
responsive
senior managers or
   executives
service
strategic issues
strategic plan
strategy
supervisor
tactical issues
value
values statement
vision statement

◀ REFERENCE

Deming, W. E. *Quality, Productivity and Competitive Position,* Cambridge, MA: MIT Press, 1982.

◀ IF YOU WERE THE BOSS

1. How can you get your employees to better relate their workplace productivity to the department's budget?
2. You are the supervisor for a team of employees who have a high number of product defects. They also waste materials. You recognize that product defects and wasted materials impact your department's budget. You have told your team to decrease the amount of wasted materials, but your employees do not seem to care. How can you get them to increase their quality and decrease waste?
3. One of your best customers verbally abuses two of your employees every time she visits your store. Your employees have complained to you several times about this customer. What should you do?

◀ WEB LINKS

http://www.inc.com/resources/startup/articles/20050201/missionstatement.html

http://www.smartdraw.com/tutorials/orgcharts/tutorial1.htm

http://www.personnelinsights.com/customer_service_profile.htm

http://www.cathcart.com/art_grow_business.html

◀ WORKPLACE DO'S AND DON'TS

Do read the company mission statement so you remember why the company pays you to come to work each day	*Don't* ignore the company's directional statements and their application to your job
Do know your internal and external customers. Also know what role you play in ensuring quality and how you contribute to your company's success	*Don't* assume that your only customer is outside of the company and that you have no influence on the company's overall success
Do take responsibility for producing and/or providing quality. Be a role model for other employees by eliminating waste and showing constant concern for quality	*Don't* ignore quality by allowing wasted materials and productivity, and *don't* allow bad attitudes to affect your performance
Do display competence by knowing your company products and policies	*Don't* lie to customers and make up information you don't know regarding company products and policies
Do make every effort to build a professional relationship with your customers by learning their likes and dislikes	*Don't* become overbearing or intrusive when gathering or recording customer data
Do remain calm when dealing with a difficult customer, and seek assistance immediately if a customer becomes abusive	*Don't* tolerate foul language or violence

► ACTIVITIES

ACTIVITY 8–1

Review the following organizational chart and answer these questions.

1. Whom should Linda go to if there is a question about employee benefits?

_____

2. Who is Joyce's immediate supervisor?

_____

3. If Joyce's immediate supervisor is not available, whom should she seek assistance from?

_____

4. Who is ultimately responsible for creating, pricing, selling, distributing, and promoting the company's product?

_____

5. What is Brandon's title?

_____

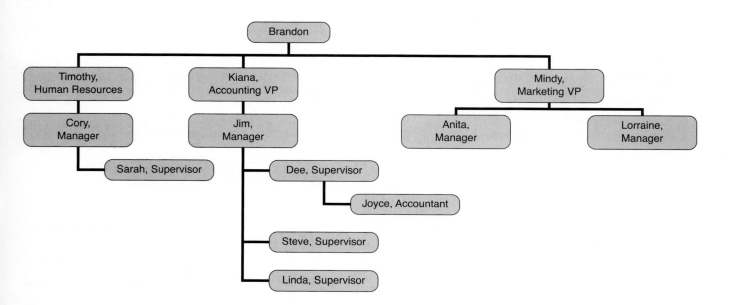

ACTIVITY 8–2

How would you measure performance in the following jobs?

JOB	PERFORMANCE MEASURES
Receptionist	
Customer service clerk	
Forklift driver	
Janitor	
Manager trainee	

ACTIVITY 8–3

What could you specifically do to communicate to your coworkers the importance customer service has on performance and profits?

_____

_____

ACTIVITY 8–4

Thinking about both internal and external customers, identify who the customer would be for the following jobs.

JOB	CUSTOMER
Accounting clerk	
Medical assistant	
Warehouse stockperson	
Mail sorter	
Printing press operator	

ACTIVITY 8–5

When is it appropriate to ask your boss to assist you with a difficult customer?

_____

_____

ACTIVITY 8–6

Describe two different times when you received exemplary customer service. Be specific in identifying how employees behaved toward you.

EXEMPLARY SERVICE ACT	BEHAVIOR TOWARD YOU
1.	
2.	

1. A company's _____ is its statement of purpose and identifies why everyone comes to work.

2. The _____ identifies how the company will secure, organize, utilize, and monitor its resources.

3. The _____ department is responsible for the securing, distribution, and growth of the company's financial assets.

4. _____ is a predetermined standard that defines how a product is to be produced or a service is to be provided. Customers demand _____ not just in the product they purchase but also from company employees.

5. Profit is _____ (money coming in from sales) minus _____ (the costs involved in running the business).

6. A/An _____ is one who buys a service or product.

7. Quality employees + quality inputs = _____ = satisfied, loyal _____ = _____.

8. _____ is when customers believe they received a good deal for the price they paid.

9. _____ is the treatment an employee provides the customer.

10. When dealing with a difficult customer, the first step is to _____, let the _____, and _____ for facts.

CHAPTER 9

ACCOUNTABILITY AND WORKPLACE RELATIONSHIPS

OBJECTIVES

▶ Define and link the relationship among *empowerment*, *responsibility*, and *accountability*

▶ Describe how best to deal with your boss

▶ Describe how to respond when a workplace relationship turns negative

▶ Identify appropriate and inappropriate relationships with your boss, colleagues, executives, and customers

▶ Identify basic workplace expectations regarding social functions and gift giving

You cannot escape the responsibility of tomorrow by evading it today.

Abraham Lincoln (1809–1865)

▶ EMPOWERMENT

In politics, business, and education, everyone should be held accountable for their actions. Unfortunately, too many people do not know what it means to be accountable. This chapter discusses the concepts of accountability and workplace relationships. The concepts of empowerment, responsibility, and accountability are all about choices. These personal choices not only impact how successful you will be at work but have a tremendous impact on workplace relationships.

In chapter 5, we discussed power bases and how workplace power affects politics and ethical behavior. Everyone in the workplace has power. Unfortunately, everyone in the workplace does not use their power appropriately or at all. As companies put an increased focus on quality, correct decision making by employees becomes more and more important.

Empowerment is pushing power and decision making to the individuals who are closest to the customer in an effort to increase quality, customer satisfaction, and, ultimately, profits. The foundation of this basic management concept means that if employees feel like they are making a direct contribution to the company's activities, they will perform better. This will then increase quality and customer satisfaction.

Consider the case of a manager of a retail customer service counter telling his employee to make the customer happy. The manager feels he has empowered his employee. However, the next day, the manager walks by the employee's counter and notices that the employee has given every customer refunds for their returns, even when the return did not warrant a refund. The boss immediately disciplines the employee for poor performance. But did the employee not do exactly what the manager asked the employee to do? Did the manager truly empower his employee? The answer is no. Telling someone to do something is different than showing someone the correct behavior. The employee interpreted the phrase "make the customer happy" differently from the manager's intention. The proper way for the manager to have empowered the employee would have been to discuss the company's return policies, role-play various customer scenarios, and then monitor the employee as the employee applied what had been learned. If or when the employee made errors through the training process, the wrong behavior should have been immediately corrected while good performance received positive reinforcement.

When you, as an employee, demonstrate a willingness to learn, you will have accepted responsibility. **Responsibility** means to accept the power that is being given to you. If you are not being responsible, you are not fully utilizing power that has been entrusted to you. Finally, the whole concept of empowerment and responsibility is useless without accountability. **Accountability** means that you accept the responsibility and must report back to whoever gave you the power to carry out that responsibility. Employees at all levels of an organization are accountable to each other, their bosses, their customers, and the company's investors to perform their best. Each employee must take personal responsibility for his or her performance. Each employee must also be accountable for his or her actions and workplace choices.

One of the best ways to gain respect and credibility at work is to begin asking for and assuming new tasks. If you are interested in learning new skills, speak up and ask your boss to teach or provide you opportunities to increase your value to the company. Assume responsibility for these new tasks and report back (become accountable) on your performance. Remember that worthwhile activities support the company's overall mission. Each project for which you assume responsibility must have a measurable goal. If it lacks a goal, it will be difficult to be accountable for your performance.

As you increase your workplace responsibilities, do not ever be afraid to seek assistance. Also, remember that a great amount of learning and success comes from past failure. When you make mistakes, do not blame others. Determine what went wrong and why. Learn from your mistakes, and view them as opportunities to do better in the future.

Cory is rapidly becoming more confident on the job. Cory wanted to be of more value to the company and began studying the concept of personal responsibility and accountability. Cory was excited about the new concepts that were learned and began requesting extra projects at work. Cory gladly kept the boss informed on the status of each project and reported when each project was successfully completed. The boss noticed how Cory took responsibility not only for personal growth but also for the success of the department. As a result, the boss informs Cory that he is impressed with Cory's willingness to improve and is considering Cory for a promotion.

▶ WORKPLACE RELATIONSHIPS

People who are mature and confident behave consistently around others, while those who are not as secure frequently behave differently around the boss or selected colleagues. Some could argue in favor of this behavior, but it is wrong and immature to behave inconsistently around selected audiences. Boss or no boss, you should behave professionally and respectfully at all times, no matter who is around or watching. This section explains the dynamics of workplace relationships and their impact on performance.

Because we spend more time at work than we do with our families, workplace relationships have a profound impact on productivity. The bottom line is that we must treat everyone respectfully and professionally. It is easy to be respectful and professional to those we like; it is much more difficult doing so with those we dislike. Chapter 12, regarding the topic of conflict at work, addresses the sensitive issue of working productively with those whom we do not like. Unfortunately, developing strong friendships at work can be equally as damaging as creating workplace enemies if we fail to keep professional relationships separate from our personal lives. Socializing with our coworkers is both expected and acceptable to a degree, but do not make workplace relationships your only circle of friends. Doing so is dangerous because it becomes difficult to separate personal and work issues. It also has the potential to create distrust among employees who are not included in your circle of workplace friends. Finally, it creates the potential for you to unknowingly or subconsciously show favoritism toward your friends. Even if you are not showing favoritism, those who are not within the circle of friends may perceive favoritism and may become distrustful of you.

As you become more comfortable with your job and company, you will be in various situations that provide opportunities to strengthen workplace relationships with coworkers, executives, investors, vendors, and customers. The following section discusses selected situations and how best to behave in these circumstances.

▶ EXECUTIVES/SENIOR OFFICIALS

It is often difficult to know how to behave in a room full of executives or senior officials such as members of the board of directors. At work, there are several occasions when you may be in the presence of executives and senior officials. These may include meetings, corporate events, and social functions. While it is tempting to pull a senior official aside and tell him stories about your boss or how perfect you would be for an advanced position, this behavior is both inappropriate and unacceptable. It is important to not draw attention to yourself and always project a positive, professional image. Highlight the successes of your department and not personal accomplishments.

If you are in a meeting that you do not normally attend, do not speak up unless addressed or introduced by the chairman of the meeting. If it is convenient, before or after the meeting, it is acceptable to introduce yourself to senior officials. Remember to not interrupt. Be confident, extend a hand, and state, "Hello, Mrs. Jones, my name is Tim Brandon. I work in the accounting department. It's nice to meet you." Keep your comments brief and positive. Your objective is to create a favorable and memorable impression with the executive. Introduce yourself and make eye contact so that the executive can connect a face, name, and department. Do not speak poorly of anyone or a situation. It is also inappropriate to discuss specific work-related issues, such as wanting to change positions, unless you are in a meeting specifically to discuss that issue. Always let the executive guide the conversation and make sure to read the executive's body language. If the executive's body language includes a nodding head and his or her body is facing you, continue talking. If the executive is glancing away or his or her body is turning away from you, that body language is clearly communicating the executive's desire to be elsewhere. Therefore, tell the executive it was nice meeting him or her, excuse yourself, and leave. Use encounters with executives as opportunities to create favorable impressions for you and your department.

► YOUR BOSS

Typically, there is no middle ground when it comes to workers and their feelings for their bosses. We either love them or hate them. There are three common types of bosses: the bad (incompetent) boss, the abusive boss, and the good boss. Before we discuss how to handle each type, it is important to remember that bosses are human. Like us, they too are learning and developing their skills. Although they are not perfect, we should assume they are doing their best.

Let us begin with the bad or **incompetent boss**. An incompetent boss is one who does not know how to do his or her job. As with every work situation, no matter how bad the boss, you must remain professional and respectful. Make it your mission to make your boss look good. That's right; make your bad boss look good! Doing so demonstrates your maturity and diminishes the tension between you and your boss. Do not worry about your boss receiving credit for your hard work. Incompetence rises to the top. If your boss is a poor performer, others in the company will know your boss is not producing the good work being presented. Therefore, if you are doing good work, it will get noticed by others in the company. If your boss really is not incompetent and you and your boss just have a personality conflict, do not allow your personal feelings to affect your performance. Focus on staying positive and being of value to your boss. Even when your coworkers want to bad-mouth the boss, which is a common occurrence at work, do not give in to temptation. You must remain professional and respectful. Moreover, use your bad boss experience as a time to learn what not to do when you become a boss.

Sometime in your career, you may experience an **abusive boss**. The abusive boss is someone who is constantly belittling or intimidating his or her employees. Abusive bosses generally behave that way because they have low self-esteem. Therefore, they utilize their legitimate and coercive power to make themselves feel better by knocking someone else down. There are several ways to deal with an abusive boss. If the abuse is tolerable, do your best to work with the situation. Although common with employees of abusive bosses, do not speak poorly of your boss in public. If the situation becomes intolerable and is beginning to affect your performance, you have several options. The first is to seek confidential advice from someone in the human resource management department. This expert can begin documenting and observing the situation and take corrective action or provide needed management training to your boss. Remember to be factual in reporting inappropriate incidents. Human resource managers only want facts, not emotions. While tempting, do not go to your boss's boss. Doing so implies secrecy and distrust. If your boss's boss does not support you and/or your immediate boss finds out, your plan will backfire. Finally, if it looks as if nothing and no one can improve your boss's behavior, begin quietly looking for another job either in another department within the company or at a new company. Remember that as an employee, you have rights. If your boss ever acts discriminatory or harassing toward you, document and report the behavior immediately. Your boss cannot make you perform functions that do not reasonably support those identified in your job description. Abusive bosses commonly have employees run personal errands. If you are asked to perform unreasonable functions, you should politely decline.

If you have a **good boss**, be thankful but cautious. A good boss is one who is respectful and fair and is grooming you for a promotion. It frequently becomes tempting to develop a personal friendship with a good boss. You must remember to keep the relationship professional. While it is okay to share important activities occurring in your personal life with your boss (e.g., spouse and child issues, vacation plans), you should never divulge too much information. Take advantage of your good boss and use him or her as a professional mentor. Identify what management qualities make your boss valued and begin imitating these qualities in your own workplace behavior. Regardless of what type of boss you have, always give your personal best.

◀ **EXERCISE 9–1: About Your Boss:** *What kind of boss have you worked for—incompetent, abusive, or good? Provide at least two specific examples to support your assessment. If you have never held a job before, ask a friend or family member.*

What kind of boss?	
Examples to support assessment	

▶ COLLEAGUES

Having friends at work is nice. Unfortunately, when workplace friendships go awry, it affects your job. It is for this reason that you should be cautious about friendships developed at work. A friend is someone whom you trust and who knows your strengths and weaknesses. While we should be able to trust all coworkers, they should not know everything about you. It is important to be friendly to everyone at work. There will be some with whom you want to develop a friendship outside of work, but beware. If there is a misunderstanding either at work or away from work, the relationship can go sour and affect both areas. If one of you gets promoted and suddenly becomes the boss of the other, it also creates an awkward situation for both parties. Even if you can both get beyond this issue, others at work may feel like outsiders or feel you are playing favorites with your friend. Finally, if you only socialize with friends developed at work, you risk the danger of getting too absorbed in work issues. The one common thread that binds your friendship is work. Therefore, it is work that you will most likely discuss when you are together. This can be unhealthy and could potentially create a conflict of interest in the decisions you make at work.

▶ OTHERS WITHIN THE ORGANIZATION

The topic of friendships in the workplace should be extended to those throughout the organization. You are, however, encouraged to increase your professional network by meeting others within your company. As discussed in chapter 5, as we build our connection power, we are gaining additional knowledge and contacts to assist us in performing our jobs and perhaps earning future promotions. This is called *networking*. When you interact with others in the organization, remember to keep your conversations positive and respectful of others. Even if the other individual steers the conversation in a negative direction, respond with a positive comment. Do not ever be afraid to defend coworkers when another employee is talking ill about them.

For example, one day, Cory and a friend were sitting in the break room when Vicki, the department's unhappy coworker, walked in. "I just can't stand John!" declared Vicki. "That's too bad. John's a friend of mine," responded Cory's friend. Vicki stood there red-faced, turned around, and left the room. Cory told the friend that Cory never knew he and John were close. "Well," responded the friend, "we're not personal friends, but we work together." The friend went on to explain that it is easy to eliminate negative conversation when you immediately communicate that you will not tolerate bad-mouthing others. Cory thought that was pretty good advice.

Each company should have a **corporate culture** (**organizational culture**). Think of corporate culture as the company's personality being reflected through its employees' behavior. The company's culture is its shared values and beliefs. For example, if the company's management team openly communicates and promotes teamwork, the company will most likely have excellent communication and successful teams. In contrast, executives who are always stressed and reacting to crisis situations will create a workplace atmosphere based on stress and crisis management. A company's corporate culture has an enormous impact on **employee morale**. Employee morale is the attitude employees have toward the company. This attitude is a result of the company's corporate culture.

_____

_____

_____

What workplace behavior contributes to poor employee morale?

_____

_____

_____

► WHEN RELATIONSHIPS TURN NEGATIVE

Unresolved conflict happens to the best of relationships. Due to a conflict or misunderstanding, a relationship may go bad. Unfortunately, at work, this happens. Sometimes you have no idea what you have done wrong. In other cases, you may be the one that wants to end the relationship. As stated earlier in the text, you do not have to like everyone at work, but no one should know the better. You must show everyone respect and you must behave professionally, even to your adversaries.

If you are the victim of a bad relationship, you need to take the following steps in dealing with the situation:

► If you harmed the other person (intentionally or unintentionally), apologize immediately.
► Tell the other person that you value his or her friendship.
► If the other person accepts your apology, demonstrate your regret by changing your behavior.
► If the other person does not accept your apology and your apology was sincere, you must move on. You must still demonstrate your regret by changing your behavior.
► If you lose the relationship, do not hold a grudge. Continue being polite, respectful, and professional to your lost friend.
► If the lost friend acts rude or inappropriate, do not retaliate by returning the poor behavior. Respond in kindness.
► If the rude and inappropriate behavior impacts your performance or is hostile or harassing, document the situation and inform your boss.

Erin had been one of Cory's favorite coworkers since Cory's first day at work. They took breaks together and at least once a week went out for lunch. One day Cory was working on a project with a short deadline. Erin invited Cory out to lunch and Cory politely declined, explaining why. The next day, Cory asked Erin to lunch and Erin just gave Cory a funny look and turned away. "Erin, what's wrong?" Cory asked. Erin just shook her head and left the room. Cory left Erin alone for a few days, hoping whatever the matter was would boil over and things would be better. After a week of Erin ignoring Cory, things only got worse. Cory decided to try one last time to save the relationship. As Cory approached Erin, Cory said, "Erin, I'm sorry for whatever I've done to upset you and I'd like for us to talk about it." Unfortunately, Erin again gave Cory a hollow look and walked away.

The toughest step when addressing a broken relationship is when the other individual does not accept your apology. We have grown up believing that we must like everyone and that everyone must like us. Because of human nature, this simply is not possible. We cannot be friends with everyone at work. Moreover, people get their feelings hurt and some find it hard to forgive. Your focus at work should be, first and foremost, getting the job done. Any behavior that is not respectful and professional interferes with performance. Remember that the company is paying you to perform. Therefore, if a sour relationship begins to impact your performance, you must respond. First ask yourself if your behavior is contributing to the unresolved conflict. If it is, you must change your behavior immediately. If your wronged coworker is upset or hurt, he or she will most likely begin bad-mouthing you. Do not fuel the fire by retaliating by speaking ill of your coworker. This only makes both of you look petty and immature. Document the facts of the incident and remain a mature adult. If the bad behavior continues for a reasonable period of time and it affects your performance, it is time to seek assistance. This is why documentation is important.

At this point, you must contact your immediate supervisor for an intervention. When you meet with your supervisor, explain the situation in a factual and unemotional manner. Provide specific examples of the offensive behavior and document any witnesses. Do not approach your supervisor to get the other individual in trouble. Your objective is to secure your boss's assistance in creating a mutually respectful and professional working relationship with your coworker. The boss may call you and the coworker into the boss's office to discuss the situation. Do not become emotional during this meeting. Your objective is to come to an agreement on behaving respectfully and professionally at work.

▶ DATING AT WORK

A sticky but common workplace relationship issue is that of dating other employees, vendors, or customers of your place of employment. Because we spend so much time at work, it is natural for coworkers to look for companionship in the workplace. While a company cannot prevent you from dating coworkers who are in your immediate work area, many companies discourage the practice. Some companies go as far as having employees who are romantically involved sign statements releasing the company from any liability should the relationship turn sour. It is highly inappropriate for you to date your boss or if you are a supervisor for you to date your employees. Doing so exposes you, your romantic interest, and your company to potential sexual harassment charges. Your actions will impact your entire department and will most likely make everyone uncomfortable.

If you date customers and vendors/suppliers of your company, use caution. In dating either customers or vendors, you must ask yourself how the changed relationship can potentially impact your job. Remember that you are representing your company 24/7. Therefore, you should never share confidential information or speak poorly of your colleagues or employer. You should be careful to not put yourself in a situation in which you could be accused of a conflict of interest. In short, it is always best to keep your romantic life separate from that of the workplace.

▶ SOCIALIZING

Work-related social activities such as company picnics, potlucks, and birthday celebrations are extremely common. While some individuals enjoy attending these social functions, others clearly do not. You do not have to attend any work-related social function outside of your normal work hours. However, it is often considered rude if you do not attend social functions that occur at the workplace during work hours. If you are working on an important deadline and simply cannot attend, briefly stop by the function and apologize to whoever is hosting the event. If you attend a work-related social function, check to see if guests are being requested to bring items to the party. If you plan on attending, you should bring an item if one is requested. It is considered impolite to show up to a potluck empty-handed. It is also considered rude to take home a plate of leftovers unless offered. Alcohol should not be served on work premises.

Attendance at work-related social events occurring outside the work site is considered optional. As discussed in chapter 6, if the invitation requires an RSVP, be sure to send your reservation or regrets in a timely manner. If you choose not to attend an off-site activity, be sure to thank whoever invited you. This maintains a positive work relationship. If you do attend, do not show up empty-handed and always thank the host for the invitation when arriving and when leaving. If alcohol is being served at a work-related function off of the work site, use caution when consuming alcohol. It is best to not consume at all; but, if you must consume, limit yourself to one drink.

BREAKS AND THE BREAK ROOM

It is a common practice for offices to have a community coffeepot. This means that coffee is available to everyone in the office. Unfortunately, in most cases, the company does not pay for this benefit. The coffee, snacks, and other supplies are typically provided by the boss or someone else in the office. It is common for people to informally contribute to the coffee fund. If you routinely drink coffee or eat the office snacks, you should contribute funds to help pay for this luxury. The same goes for office treats such as doughnuts, cookies, or birthday cakes. If you partake, offer to defer the cost or take your turn bringing treats one day. Many offices have a refrigerator available for employees to store their meals. It is considered stealing to eat someone else's food. Do not help yourself to food being stored in the community refrigerator. If you store your food in this area, remember to throw out any unused or spoiled food at the end of each workweek. Finally, remember to always clean up after yourself. If you use a coffee cup, wash it and put it away when you are finished. Throw away your trash, and leave the break room clean for the next person.

MISCELLANEOUS WORKPLACE ISSUES

While it is tempting to sell fund-raising items at work, the practice is questionable. Some companies have policies prohibiting this practice. If the practice is acceptable, do not pester people nor make them feel guilty if they decline to make a purchase.

It is common and acceptable to give a gift to a friend commemorating special days such as birthdays and holidays. However, you do not have to give gifts to anyone at work. If you are a gift giver, do so discreetly so as to not offend others who do not receive gifts from you. If you advance into a management position, do not give a gift to just one employee. If you choose to give gifts, you must give gifts to all employees and treat everyone equally.

It is also common for employees to pitch in and purchase a group gift for special days such as Boss's Day and Administrative Assistant's Day. While it is not mandatory to contribute to these gifts, it is generally expected that you contribute. If you strongly object or cannot afford to participate, politely decline without attaching a negative comment. If price is the issue, contribute whatever amount you deem reasonable and explain that you are on a budget. If you are the receiver of a gift, verbally thank the gift giver immediately and follow up with a handwritten thank-you note.

SUMMARY OF KEY CONCEPTS

▶ It is important to take responsibility for the job you perform by being accountable for your actions
▶ Keep workplace friendships positive, but be cautious that these relationships not be your only friendships away from the workplace
▶ If a workplace relationship turns negative, remember to remain professional and respectful
▶ It is best to refrain from dating anyone at work
▶ Practice good etiquette at social functions that occur within the office

KEY TERMS

abusive boss	employee morale	incompetent boss
accountability	empowerment	responsibility
corporate culture (organizational culture)	good boss	

◀ REFERENCE

Deming, W. E. *Quality, Productivity and Competitive Position,* Cambridge, MA: MIT Press, 1982.

◀ IF YOU WERE THE BOSS

1. How can you get employees excited about assuming additional responsibilities?
2. If you noticed employee morale dropping in your department, how would you respond?
3. How would you handle two employees whose friendship had turned negative?
4. You never give your employees gifts, but one of your employees always gives you gifts for holidays, birthdays, and boss's day. Is it wrong for you to accept these gifts?

◀ WEB LINKS

http://www.librarysupportstaff.com/coworkers.html#principles

http://www.iaap-hq.org/careercenter/Workplace_Relationships.htm

http://www.relationships.com.au/relations_in/landing.asp

◀ WORKPLACE DO'S AND DON'TS

Do take responsibility for your performance and success at work	*Don't* wait for someone to tell you what to do
Do display consistent, professional behavior	*Don't* behave appropriately only when the boss is around
Do always make your boss look good	*Don't* speak poorly of your boss
Do create positive relationships with coworkers	*Don't* make your workplace friendships your primary friendships away from work
Do practice business etiquette at work-related social functions	*Don't* ignore the importance of behaving professionally at work-related social functions

ACTIVITY 9–1

You are supposed to attend a meeting the next day. Overnight, you have a family emergency. What should you do? Explain your answer.

_____

_____

_____

_____

ACTIVITY 9–2

Your boss is always bad-mouthing or belittling your coworkers. You do not like it and you wonder what he says about you when you are not around. What should you do?

_____

_____

_____

_____

ACTIVITY 9–3

The company that services your office equipment has hired a new salesperson. This person does not wear a wedding ring and flirts with you. If you go out on a date with this person, what are at least three potential problems that could occur (work related)?

1. _____

2. _____

3. _____

ACTIVITY 9–4

Is it appropriate to discuss the following company information with individuals outside of the company? Why or why not?

INFORMATION	YES OR NO	WHY OR WHY NOT?
1. Key clients/customers		
2. Financial information		
3. Boss's work style		
4. Company mission statement		
5. Names of members of the company board of directors		

1. _____ is the attitude employees have toward the company.

2. If you ever harm another, immediately _____.

3. Any behavior that is not _____ or professional interferes with _____.

4. Be cautious in engaging in _____ with coworkers, customers, vendors, or your boss.

5. You _____ have to attend any work-related social function outside of your normal work hours.

6. If _____ is being served at a work-related function off of the work site, use caution when consuming, or better yet, do not _____.

7. If you partake of office treats, it is good manners to _____.

8. Just like at home, you must always _____ in the break room.

9. It is best to not sell _____ items at work.

CHAPTER 10

COMMUNICATION

OBJECTIVES

▶ Define the impact effective *communication* has in the workplace

▶ Name the key elements of the communication process

▶ Name the three types of communication media

▶ Describe the dangers of becoming emotional at work

▶ Demonstrate proper formatting for *business letters* and *memos*

▶ Demonstrate basic telecommunication etiquette

The most important thing in communication is to hear what isn't being said.

Peter Drucker (1909–2005)

► WORKPLACE COMMUNICATION AND ITS CHANNELS

Imagine going to work; sitting at your desk; and, for one day, sending and receiving no communication. If there were no face-to-face contact, no telephone or cell calls, no meetings, and no memos to receive or write, business would come to a complete standstill. No matter how talented you are at your job, if you cannot communicate with others, you will not succeed, much less have a job. This chapter discusses the process and importance of effective communication in the workplace and provides information on how to improve your workplace communication skills.

At work, you have an obligation to share appropriate, timely, and accurate information with your boss, your coworkers, and your customers. As we jump into the topic of workplace communication, you must remember that improving your communication skills is an ongoing process. As explained in chapter 5, information is power. In regard to workplace communication, your goal is to be known as an overcommunicator.

While eating lunch with employees from other departments, Cory listened to employees complain about how their bosses did such a poor job communicating with them. The employees complained that they never knew what was going on within the company. Cory had no reason to complain because Cory has a manager that makes every effort to share whatever information the manager knows with Cory's department. After each managers' meeting, Cory receives an e-mail outlining major topics that were discussed at the managers' meeting. During Cory's department meeting, Cory's manager reviews the information a second time and asks his employees if there are any additional questions. Cory appreciates the fact that Cory's manager enjoys and values communicating important information with his employees.

In the workplace, there are two primary communication channels. These include formal and informal communication. Whether it is formal or informal communication, you have a professional obligation to share timely and relevant information with the appropriate people. **Formal communication** occurs through the formal lines of authority. This can include communication within your immediate department, your division, or throughout your company. Formal communication can occur either vertically or horizontally. Formal vertical communication can occur coming down the organization chart (via written correspondence, policies and procedures, and directives and announcements from management), or going up the organization chart (reports, budgets, and requests). Formal horizontal communication occurs among individuals or departments at the same or close organizational levels.

The second type of communication channel is that of the informal organization. **Informal communication** occurs among individuals without regard to the formal lines of authority. For example, while eating lunch with friends, you may learn of a new policy. A major form of the informal communication network is called the *grapevine*. This informal communication network frequently highlights matters of importance to employees. Although the grapevine is an informal source of communication, it usually is not 100 percent accurate. While it is important to know about current events of the workplace, it is important that you not contribute negative information to the grapevine. If inaccurate information is being shared and you are aware of the facts, clarify the information. If someone shares information that is harmful to the company or is particularly disturbing to you, you have a responsibility to approach your boss and ask him or her to clarify the rumor.

When the grapevine is targeting individuals and their personal lives, it is called *gossip*. Gossip is hurtful and inappropriate. Do not be part of personal attacks on individuals. Any time you contribute to negative conversation, you lose credibility with others. By your actions, you communicate both immaturity and unprofessional behavior. Your job is to clarify misinformation when necessary and assist in defending the rights of others. Should someone begin sharing gossip with you, politely interrupt and tell the individual that you really do not want to hear the information and transition the conversation to a more positive subject. You have a right to defend your coworkers from slander (individuals bad-mouthing others), just as you would expect your coworkers to defend you. After a while, your colleagues will learn that you do not tolerate gossip at work and they will reconsider approaching you with gossip.

In that same manner, refrain from speaking poorly of your coworkers and boss. As a result of human nature, you may not enjoy working with all of your colleagues and bosses. You do not have to like everyone at work, but you must treat everyone with respect. Gossip is a form of disrespect. No matter how much someone annoys you at work, do not speak poorly of him or her. It only displays immaturity on your part and communicates distrust to your colleagues. Even if someone speaks poorly of you, do not reciprocate the bad behavior.

▶ THE COMMUNICATION PROCESS

Communication is the process of a sender sending a message to an individual (receiver) with the purpose of creating mutual understanding. As simple as this definition is, a lot of barriers hinder the process of creating mutual understanding and successful communication. Communication is important for maintaining good human relations. Without basic communication skills, processes break down and an organization may collapse. This is why you need to know and understand the communication process (see figure 10–1).

Communication starts with a **sender** wanting to convey a message. The sender must identify what message needs to be sent and how best to send this message. The sender has several options for sending the message. The message can be sent verbally, written, or nonverbally. Identifying the message and how it will be sent is called **encoding.**

Once the sender encodes the message, the message is sent to a receiver. **Decoding** is when the receiver interprets the message. The receiver then sends **feedback** on the sender's message based upon the receiver's interpretation of the original message.

Due to barriers, the communication process can break down. First, the sender must clearly identify the real message that needs to be sent. Once the message is identified, the sender needs to figure out how best to send (encode) the message in a manner that will be properly interpreted (decoded) by the receiver. If the sender is not a strong communicator, his or her verbal, written, or body language may be misinterpreted by the receiver and the message may be doomed before it is even sent. The receiver can assist with the communication breakdown if he or she incorrectly interprets the message.

Another barrier to effective communication is **noise.** Noise is anything that interrupts or interferes with the communication process. The noise can be audible (you can actually hear it with your ears), or the noise can occur in your mind (thoughts).

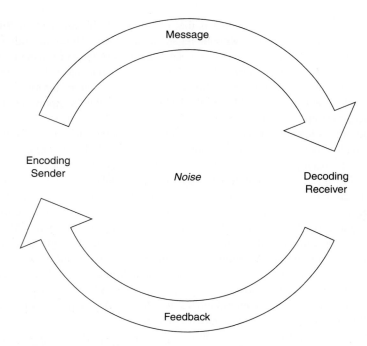

◀ **FIGURE 10–1** Communication Process

◀ **EXERCISE 10–1: Identify Noises:** *Identify at least four noises you experience during class.*

1. _____

2. _____

3. _____

4. _____

A supervisor in another department really irritates Cory. Cory has never shared this irritation with anyone. One day, Cory was asked to attend a meeting led by the irritating supervisor. As Cory sat in the meeting, Cory had a hard time focusing on the message. Cory's mind was wandering with both audible and mental noise. At the end of the meeting, Cory was embarrassed that there were no notes to share. Cory's dislike for the irritating supervisor affected Cory's ability to listen and be a good receiver. Cory learned a hard lesson that day and made a commitment to be open to every communication, regardless of Cory's like or dislike of the sender.

Communication can only be complete and effective if all of the components of the communication process work together to effectively send the message as it is meant to be sent. In order for this to happen, the sender must choose the right medium and overcome noise. The receiver must then be willing to accept the message and provide feedback to acknowledge that the message has been received correctly.

As previously stated, a key element to effective communication is the communication medium (how the message will be sent). Communication media include verbal, nonverbal, and written communication. Let us further explore these three types of communication media.

▶ VERBAL COMMUNICATION

Verbal communication is the process of using words to send your message. The words you select are extremely important. If you only use basic words in your communications, you may appear uneducated or inexperienced. In contrast, if you use a highly developed vocabulary, you may appear intimidating or arrogant. If others do not know the definitions of the words you are using, they will most likely not ask for clarification for fear of appearing ignorant. Therefore, your intended message will fail. When selecting words for your message, identify whether these words can be misinterpreted in any way. Many times, we assume our receiver is thinking our same thoughts. This is highly unlikely.

Finally, you must learn to stop and listen. Too frequently, a person will have so much to say that he or she does not stop to give the receiver time to respond. The receiver's response is the only way you, as a sender, can verify that your message has been properly received. Therefore, when improving your verbal communication, you must learn when it is appropriate to not speak. Keys to effective listening include making eye contact with the sender and taking notes.

▶ NONVERBAL COMMUNICATION

Nonverbal communication is what you communicate through your body language. You do not have to utter a word and you can still send a very strong message. Body language includes eye contact, facial expressions, tone of voice, and the positioning of your body. Nonverbal communication also includes the use of silence and space.

When people are nervous or excited, they frequently speak fast. When you increase the speed of your speech, you increase the probability that your message will be misinterpreted. Your tone of voice also conveys or creates images. It adds to others' perception of you, which either enforces your message or detracts from the message.

The most obvious form of body language is eye contact. When you look someone in the eye, you are generally communicating honesty and sincerity. At other times, looking someone in the eye and coupling that look with a harsh tone of voice and an unfriendly facial expression may imply intimidation. Those who fail to look someone in the eye risk conveying to their receiver that they are not confident or, worse, are being dishonest. It is important to make eye contact with your audience (individual or group). However, when making eye contact, do not stare. Doing so is considered rude and intimidating. Actively work at making appropriate eye contact with your receiver. If your direct eye contact is making the receiver uncomfortable, he or she will look away. Be aware of his or her response and adapt your behavior appropriately.

Eye contact is part of the larger communication package of your facial expression. A receiver will find it difficult to interpret your eye contact as sincere and friendly when your message is accompanied by a frown. A smile has immense power and value. A nod implies that you are listening or agreeing with a sender's message. Even the positioning of your head can convey disagreement, confusion, or attentiveness.

◄ **EXERCISE 10–2: Body Language:** *With a partner, take turns communicating the following emotions through body language. Note how the sender signals to communicate the emotion.*

Emotion	Signal
1. Concern	
2. Distrust	
3. Eagerness	
4. Boredom	
5. Self-importance	
6. Interest	

Another important element in body language is the use and positioning of your body. Having your arms crossed in front of your body can be interpreted in several ways: as being cold, angry, or uninterested. When you are not cold, having your arms crossed implies that you are creating a barrier between yourself and the other person. To eliminate any miscommunication, it is best to have your arms at your side. Do not hide your hands in your pockets. In speaking with others, be aware of the positioning of your arms and those of your audience. Also, be aware of the positioning of your entire body. Turn your body toward those to whom you are speaking. It is considered rude to turn your back to or ignore someone when he or she is speaking. In this case, you are using your entire body to create a barrier. Avoid this kind of rude behavior. This only communicates immaturity on your part.

The use of your hands is extremely important in effective communication. Through varied positioning, you can use your hands to nonverbally ask someone to stop a behavior or be quiet or to reprimand another. Your hands will also expose any nervous gestures you may have. Once again, when around others, be aware of the positioning of your hands. If you have any nervous gestures such as popping your knuckles, biting your nails, or continually tapping your fingers, take steps to eliminate these habits.

Apart from a handshake, touching another person at work is not acceptable. People in our society frequently place a hand on another's shoulder as a show of support. However, others could interpret that hand on the shoulder as a threat or sexual advance. Therefore, keep your hands to yourself.

You must also be aware of the space you allow between you and your receiver. Standing too close may be interpreted as intimidation or may imply intimacy. Neither is appropriate for the workplace. Distancing yourself too far from someone may imply your unwillingness to communicate.

Another element that affects nonverbal communication is emotion. You must make every attempt to not become emotional at work. However, reality may cause you to express emotions that oftentimes cannot be controlled. You must make every effort to control your emotions in public. If you feel you are beginning to cry or have an outburst of anger, excuse yourself. Go somewhere private and deal with your emotion. If you are crying or distraught, splash water on your face and regain control of your emotions. If you are getting angry, assess why you are angry, control your anger, and then create a strategy to regain control of how best to handle the situation. Any overt display of anger in the workplace is inappropriate and could potentially jeopardize your job. When you become emotional at work, you lose your ability to logically deal with situations. Practice effective stress management and think before you respond.

Finally, it is important to understand the appropriate use of silence. Silence is perhaps one of the most important communication tools you have. Silence communicates to your audience that you are listening and are allowing the other party consideration. Not immediately responding to a message gives the sender time to clarify or rephrase a message.

◄ **EXERCISE 10–3: Silence:** *You are trying to negotiate a pay raise with your boss. As you role-play this scenario, practice the effective use of silence. How did the use of silence affect the outcome?*

_____

_____

_____

_____

As you can see, there are a lot of variables involved in effective nonverbal communication. It is important to interpret body language within its entire context. For example, if you are communicating with a colleague with whom you have a positive working relationship and your coworker crosses his or her arms, your coworker is most likely cold. Consider the entire package: environment, relationship, and situation.

▶ WRITTEN COMMUNICATION

Writing is an important element of effective workplace communication. Your written communication conveys your aptitude and attitude. Because the receiver of your message will not have verbal and nonverbal assistance in interpreting your message, it is vital to take great care to ensure that the correct message is being communicated. Because you are not present when the message is received, you must remember that the receiver will be drawing additional conclusions about you based upon the grammar, vocabulary, and presentation/formatting you use in your written communication.

As you advance in responsibility within an organization, you will be required to conduct an increasing amount of written business communications including writing memos, e-mail messages, and business letters. Written business correspondence represents not only your professionalism and intelligence but also that of your organization. It is for this reason that you should consistently present your written correspondence in a professional manner. Make sure all written communication is error free by proofreading the message prior to sending. The key to written communication is to choose words that clearly and concisely communicate your message. You must make sure your message is clear. The three most common forms of written communication in the workplace are letters, memos, and electronic messages. Written communication should be typed (word processed). The only exception to this rule is when you are sending a handwritten thank-you note.

The first step in any professional correspondence is to state an objective. Determine exactly what it is that you want to communicate. Write a draft message and make sure it is free of anger or negative emotions. If the purpose of your correspondence is to address a negative situation (e.g., complaint), make sure your message addresses the situation and not a person. With all written forms of communication, do not send or write any message conveying anger. A good rule of thumb is to always put good news in writing and be cautious when sending negative information in writing. Put bad news in writing only when necessary.

After you have drafted your message and eliminated negative emotions, again review your correspondence and delete unnecessary words. Keep your correspondence short and simple. Do not be too wordy, and try to minimize personalization words (*I, my*) as much as possible. Make sure your correspondence not only communicates your core message but also clearly communicates how you want the reader to respond to your communication. Include contact telephone numbers and a deadline if relevant.

Although it is important to keep your correspondence simple, you want to project a professional image, not that of an elementary student. Get a thesaurus and identify and substitute words to project a more mature image. Make sure you know the definitions of the words you are using and that you are using words appropriately. Utilizing a thesaurus is an excellent way to expand your vocabulary. Remember to not overdo it, and use words in the correct context.

After you have completed writing your message, identify who should receive the message. Share your correspondence only with individuals who need to know the information. However, make sure you have shared the information with individuals whom the correspondence affects. When writing business correspondence, you have several options. These include a business letter, business memo, an e-mail message, and a thank-you note.

▶ THE BUSINESS LETTER

A **letter** is used when your message is being sent to an individual outside of your organization. External audiences may include customers, vendors, suppliers, or members of the community. Letters should be written in proper business format and sent on company letterhead. Every letter sent should be error free. Proofread, sign, and date the letter before mailing. Make sure your message and expected follow-up activity to the letter are clear. Remember, the message needs to be conveyed to the receiver in a professional and concise manner.

Business letters should be written on company letterhead. Company **letterhead** is paper that has the company logo, mailing address, and telephone numbers imprinted on quality paper. Figures 10–2 and 10–3 provide an example of the correct letter format.

An important element of a business letter is the mailing envelope. Remember that the envelope helps create a first impression. Make sure you address the envelope with the same information that is in the inside address. The letter should be folded properly. This is done by folding in thirds; start with the bottom and fold it up one-third of the way. Then fold the top over the bottom and put it in the envelope with the opening on the top. Number 10 envelopes are normally used for business letters.

▶ THE BUSINESS MEMO

Business memos (sometimes called *interoffice memorandums*) are used internally, that is, when the written communication is being sent to a receiver within an organization. A memo should include the receiver's name, sender's name, date, and subject. Again, as with a business letter, it is important to include all facts needed to get the message across, but be brief and to the point. In general, memos should be no longer than one page. Figures 10–4 and 10–5 illustrate the proper way to format a business memo.

▶ THE BUSINESS E-MAIL

Electronic mail (e-mail) is becoming a more popular form of internal and external communications. With internal e-mail messages, you can directly type a message or attach a formal memo to your e-mail. E-mail creates more efficient communication within an organization and with individuals outside of the organization.

When sending an e-mail, always include a subject in the subject line. The subject line should clearly state the purpose of the e-mail. You should not use *HI* or *HELLO* as the subject line. Because of the spread of common computer viruses, it is also inappropriate to use the words *URGENT* or *IMPORTANT* as a subject line.

As with the use of all workplace equipment, e-mail should only be used for business purposes. Remember that e-mail messages are an important element of professional workplace communication. Therefore, do not use emoticons (happy faces, winks) in your messages. Doing so at work takes away from your professionalism. It is also important to refrain from forwarding messages that are not work related. Maintain an organized and updated electronic address book. Make every attempt to preserve the confidentiality of your address book.

<table>
<tr>
<td>

(Students do not type QS and DS, these are shown for correct spacing).

Since most business letters will be on letterhead (preprinted business address), you need about a two-inch top margin. Then enter the current *date*.

The *inside address* should have the title, first and last name of receiver.

The *salutation* should have title and last name only.

For the *body,* all lines begin at the left margin. Use a colon after the salutation and a comma after the complementary closing.

Keep the *closing* simple.

The writer's first and last name should be four enters or returns after the closing to give the *writer* room to sign (remember to have the writer sign).

Typist's initials
Enclosure is used only if you add something in the envelope with the letter.

</td>
<td>

August 1, 2007

QS (4 enters or returns)

Ms. Suzie Student
Word Processing Fun
42 Learn Avenue
Fresno, CA 93225

DS (2 enters or returns)
Dear Ms. Student:

DS
The first paragraph of a letter should state the reason for the letter. If you had any previous contact with the receiver, mention it in this paragraph.

DS
The second (and possibly a third) paragraph should contain details. All information needed to be communicated should be here.

DS
The last paragraph is used to close the letter. Add information that is needed to clarify anything you said in the letter. Also, add any follow-up or contact information.

DS
Sincerely,

QS
Sarah S. Quirrel

Sarah S. Quirrel
Instructor

DS
sbb
Enclosure

</td>
</tr>
</table>

◀ **FIGURE 10–2**   Letter Format

▶ THE THANK-YOU NOTE

As mentioned in the etiquette chapter, a thank-you note is a powerful tool for building relationships. When you express thanks, individuals are more likely to continue performing kind acts for you. A thank-you note should be handwritten, in pen, and on a notecard. Thank-you notes do not need to be lengthy; generally, just a few sentences are sufficient. Make it a habit to write a thank-you note when someone does something for you that takes more than five minutes or when someone gives you a gift. Write and deliver the note as soon as possible. Figure 10–6 shows the correct format and key elements of a thank-you note.

▶ DOCUMENTATION

One final element of effective communication is documentation. Documentation is an important paper trail that assists us in remembering important events that have occurred. Frequently, this is used for personal reasons or as supporting evidence. Documentation may be necessary for an instance in which a policy is not enforced or an abnormal event has occurred that has the potential to evolve into conflict at a later date. These events may support performance issues, business

August 1, 2007

Ms. Suzie Student
Word Processing Fun
42 Learn Avenue
Fresno, CA 93225

Dear Ms. Student:

It was a pleasure speaking with you over the telephone earlier today. I am delighted that you have agreed to serve as a guest speaker in my Communications class. The purpose of this letter is to confirm the details of the upcoming speaking engagement.

As I mentioned in our conversation, the date for your scheduled lecture is Thursday, October 14, 2007. The class meets from 6:00 p.m.–8:30 p.m. You may take as much time as you need, but if possible please allow a student question and answer period. There are approximately sixty students, and the classroom contains state-of-the-art technology. If you have specific technology requests, please do not hesitate to contact me. Enclosed is a parking permit and map of the campus directing you to the appropriate classroom.

Once again, thank you for continued support of our students. I and my students are looking forward to you sharing your communications insight and expertise with us on October 14. If you have any additional information, please do not hesitate to contact me via e-mail at S.Quirrel@teaching.com or call me at 123-456-7890.

Sincerely,

Sarah S. Quirrel

Sarah S. Quirrel
Instructor

sbb
Enclosure

◀ **FIGURE 10–3**   Letter Example

relationships, and business operations. Every employee should have some method of recording relevant business situations if needed for future reference to protect yourself and/or your employer. Although there are numerous methods of documenting and retaining important information and events, the basic elements to be recorded remain the same.

Effective documentation records the *who, what, when, where,* and *why* of a situation. Basic elements in effective documentation include the date, time, and location the event occurred. It is also important to note the event itself (e.g., who said what or did what). Also, note who was present when the major event occurred and how witnesses to the event behaved or responded to the event. Your documentation is for your personal reference. Therefore, your documentation can be kept electronically, in a journal, or through minimal notations on a calendar. Whatever system you choose, remember to keep your documentation in a secure, private location. It is not necessary to—nor should you—record every event that occurs at work. If there are any supporting memos, be sure to keep copies in a private file, preferably in a secure location. If you are ever called upon to defend your actions, you will have the ability to easily gather pertinent information.

Start the memo about two inches from the top of the page.

Double-space after each *heading*. Bold and capitalize just the headings, not the information.

Use initial caps in the *subject line*.

Body—single-space, no tabs, left align. Double-space between paragraphs.

MEMO TO: Loretta Howerton, Office Manager
       (DS)
FROM: Lawrence Schmidt, OA/CIS Trainer
       (DS)
DATE: January 6, 2007
       (DS)
SUBJECT: Memo Format for Internal Correspondence
       (DS)
A memorandum is an internal communication that is sent within the organization. It is often the means by which managers correspond with employees, and vice versa. Memos provide written records of announcements, requests for action, and policies and procedures.You should use first and last names and include the job title.
       (DS)
Templates, or preformatted forms, often are used for creating memos. Templates provide a uniform look for company correspondence and save the employee the time of having to design a memo. Word processing software has memo templates that can be customized.You should customize the template so it has the company name and your department name atthe top.Make sure you change the date format. It should be as it is seen at the beginning of this memo.
       (DS)

Reference initials (typist's initials)
Attachment notation, only if needed (if you attach something)

sbb
Attachment

◀ **FIGURE 10–4** Memo Format

MEMO TO: Loretta Howerton, Office Manager

FROM: Lawrence Schmidt, OA/CIS Trainer

DATE: January 6, 2007

SUBJECT: Accounting Department Computer Training

This memo is to confirm that the computer training for the accounting department will occur on February 1, 2007 in the large conference room. Although the training is scheduled from 9:00 a.m.–11:30 a.m., I have reserved the room for the entire morning, beginning at 7:00 a.m.

As we discussed last week, this may be a good opportunity to offer breakfast to the department prior to the training. If this is something you would like to pursue, please let me know by next Tuesday, and I will make the proper arrangements. Thank you again for the opportunity to provide computer training to your team.

sbb

◀ **FIGURE 10–5** Memo Example

▶ TELECOMMUNICATION

With the increased use of technology in the workplace, the proper use of cell phones, voice mail, answering machines, and facsimile machines becomes increasingly important. When using a *cell phone,* keep in mind that there are proper times and places to use it and there are times and places

Include the date.	*June 3, 2007*
Start your note with a salutation and the receiver's name.	*Dear Mrs. McCombs,*
Be brief but specific about why you are thanking the person. Include how you benefited from the person's kindness. Do not begin every sentence with *I*.	*Thank-you for loaning me your book on business etiquette. I especially liked the chapter on social events and dining. Your constant encouragement and mentoring mean so much to me.* *Sincerely,*
Use a complementary closing, and do not forget to sign your name.	*Mason Yang*

◄ **FIGURE 10–6**   Thank-You Note

where a cell phone should not be used. Just as it is impolite to interrupt someone who is talking, it is also impolite to interrupt a conversation with a cell phone ringing and/or answering a cell phone. There are two basic guidelines for using your cell phone. First, it is OK to have a cell phone ring and/or answer your phone if you are alone at your desk or office. Secondly, when at a luncheon or meeting, turn your cell phone off or on vibrate. If it vibrates, do not answer it. Politely excuse yourself from the table or room and take the call in private. Although these guidelines are for business purposes, they should pertain to personal use as well.

If you are not with another individual, make every attempt to answer the *telephone* after the first ring. Smile when you are talking. Although the caller may not be able to visually see you, your smile will be communicated through your attitude and tone of voice. Speak clearly and slowly. Most voices get higher when the rate of speech increases. Be cautious to not speak too softly or too loudly. If you receive a message, remember to promptly return the call. It is rude to not return a message.

If you are with someone else when the phone rings, ignore the call and let the call go into your voice mail. If you must take the call, explain to the individual in your presence that you are expecting a call (or must take the call) and apologize for the interruption. When taking the call, if possible, be brief, take a message, and return the telephone call after you are finished with your face-to-face meeting.

Do not have a voice-mail message that contains music or humor. Your message should be brief and professional. Provide a friendly greeting, and include your name in the message. Remember to check your message mailbox at least once a day. If you are leaving a message on someone else's voice mail, remember to speak clearly and slowly. Always state your name, when you are calling, the purpose of your call, and a return telephone number.

► FOUL LANGUAGE

Your words reflect what is going on in your heart and mind. There is never an appropriate time to use profane and offensive language at work. Even in times of stress or at social functions, you are representing your company and must always do so in a professional manner. Practice self-control. Attempt to eliminate foul or offensive language from your personal and professional vocabulary. Doing so will rid your heart and mind of negativity. If you happen to slip by utilizing inappropriate language at work, immediately apologize. Make a mental note of what situation caused you to behave poorly and learn from the experience. Ask yourself how you could have better handled the situation and mentally rehearse a proper, more acceptable method of verbally handling a challenging situation.

► POTENTIAL OFFENSIVE NAMES

Names that could be considered sexist and offensive are inappropriate in a business setting. In fact, using inappropriate names toward coworkers will expose you and your company to a potential sexual harassment lawsuit. These include names such as *honey, sweetie,* and *sexy.* Even if the individual acts as if he or she is not offended by the names, the person may actually be offended or insulted but afraid to tell you. Eliminate potentially offensive names from your workplace vocabulary. In addition, do not use gender-specific titles when referring to certain job titles. For example:

INSTEAD OF:	USE:
Postman	Postal carrier
Policeman	Police officer
Waitress	Server
Stewardess	Flight attendant
Maid	Housekeeper

► NOT ALWAYS ABOUT YOU

Closing our discussion on communication, we address one word that often dominates our vocabulary. This word frequently turns listeners off; unfortunately, too often, the sender is unaware of its overuse. The word is *I.* Be cautious with the use of this word. Self-centered people use it to draw attention, while others who may not be confident may use the word to protect themselves. They may not know how to turn the conversation to others, so they choose to stay in a safety zone. When you are using verbal communication, think before you speak. If your initial sentence includes *I,* try to rephrase your message.

◄ **EXERCISE 10–4: Checking for I:** *Take five minutes and interview a classmate about college and his or her career choice. While you are getting to know each other, keep track of how many times your new friend says the word I.*

◄ SUMMARY OF KEY CONCEPTS

- ► Effective communication is necessary for workplace success
- ► The goal of communication is to create a mutual understanding between the sender and the receiver
- ► There are appropriate times to utilize both the formal and informal communication channels
- ► The communication process involves a sender, a receiver, noise, and feedback
- ► It is important to thoughtfully consider the right words to increase the chance of successful verbal communication
- ► Because the receiver of your message will not have verbal and nonverbal assistance in interpreting your message, it is vital to take great care with all written messages
- ► Listening and silence are effective tools for effective communication

◀ KEY TERMS

business memos	feedback	letterhead
communication	formal communication	noise
decoding	informal communication	sender
encoding	letter	

◀ REFERENCE

Parsons, G. *Basics of Communication.* 1982.
http://www.cedresources.ca/docs/modules/comm.doc

◀ IF YOU WERE THE BOSS

1. One of your employees uses bad grammar that is reflecting poorly on your department's performance. How can you get a handle on this problem?
2. Employees keep saying they never know what is going on at work. What steps would you take to increase workplace communication?

◀ WEB LINKS

http://www.career.fsu.edu/ccis/guides/write_eff.html

http://owl.english.purdue.edu/handouts/pw/p_memo.html

http://members.aol.com/nonverbal2/entries.htm#Entries

http://www.casaa-resources.net/mainpages/resources/sourcebook/listening-skills.html

◀ WORKPLACE DO'S AND DON'TS

Do recognize the importance effective and professional communication has in the workplace	*Don't* ignore opportunities to improve your communication skills on a daily basis
Do carefully think through your message and the appropriate medium	*Don't* be in such a hurry to send your message that an incorrect message is sent
Do always demonstrate professionalism in the formatting, word choice, and grammar in your written communications	*Don't* write and send messages when you are angry
Do express kindness to others with both your words and body language	*Don't* utilize foul language at work or at home
Do leave professional voice-mail messages that include your name, a return number, and the purpose of your call	*Don't* have a cute or annoying message on your voice mail

► ACTIVITIES

ACTIVITY 10–1

Without infringing on someone's privacy, discreetly observe a stranger's body language for approximately five minutes. Make sure you are far enough away to not hear him or her speak. Name at least two assumptions you can make by simply watching the person's gestures, movements, and expressions.

GESTURE, MOVEMENT, OR EXPRESSION	ASSUMPTION
1.	
2.	
3.	

ACTIVITY 10–2

Watch a television news show for a half hour. Document at least two facial expressions of an individual being interviewed. Do the individual's facial expressions match his or her statements?

FACIAL EXPRESSION	MATCH STATEMENTS: YES OR NO
1.	
2.	

ACTIVITY 10–3

Review the following letter and identify five errors. How should they be corrected?

April 21, 2007

Sandra Wong, Vice President
Human Resource Department
Robinson Enterprises
55123 W. Robinson Lane
Prosperity, CA 99923

Dear Ms. Wong,

It was a pleasure speaking with you this afternoon regarding the average salary you pay your receptionists. This data will be useful as our company begins creating a new receptionist position for our California site.

I am most appreciative of your offer to mail me a copy of your most recent salary guide for all production positions. I look forward to receiving that guide in the mail. As a thank-you for your kindness, I am enclosing coupons for our company product.

If there is any information I can provide to assist you, please let me know. Thank-you again for your cooperation.

Sincerely,

Cory Kringle

WHAT ARE THE ERRORS?	HOW TO CORRECT
1.	
2.	
3.	
4.	
5.	

ACTIVITY 10–4

Review the following memo and identify five errors. How should they be corrected?

MEMORANDUM

Re: Budget Meeting

To: Mason Jared

From: Cory Kringle

Date: May 1

Hey Mason. I wanted to remind you that we have a meeting next week to talk about next year's budget. Bring some numbers and we'll work through them. Bye.

-Cory

WHAT ARE THE ERRORS?	HOW TO CORRECT
1.	
2.	
3.	
4.	
5.	

ACTIVITY 10–5

Role-play what to say to someone who is inappropriately talking on his or her cell phone, such as someone interrupting your meeting.

---

1. The two types of workplace communication include _____ and _____ communication.

2. A major form of the informal communication network is called _____.

3. When the _____ is targeting individuals and their personal lives, it is called _____.

4. When _____ are displayed at work, it becomes difficult to think and behave in a logical manner.

5. Nonverbal communication is what we communicate through our _____.

6. _____ communicates to your audience that you are listening and are allowing the other party consideration.

7. Make sure all _____ is error free by proofreading prior to sending.

TEAMWORK, MOTIVATION, AND LEADERSHIP

OBJECTIVES

▶ Define a *team* and its function

▶ Identify the characteristics of a team player

▶ Describe what motivates team players

▶ Identify the characteristics of effective *leadership*

▶ Name a leader's responsibilities

▶ Describe ways to develop leadership skills

The price of greatness is responsibility.

Sir Winston Churchill (1874–1965)

► TEAMS AND PERFORMANCE

Good human relations are all about attitude and getting along with others. Most individuals have experienced being part of a successful team. Perhaps it was a sports team, or maybe it was in school when a group of students successfully completed a big project. Whatever the task, no doubt you were part of a team that was comprised of individuals who shared a goal and respected each other. These important factors resulted in success. Learning to get along with others is a skill that is necessary in the workplace. You will most likely be working with others in a group or as part of a team. Each team should strive toward creating synergy. **Synergy** is that extra excitement that occurs when people are truly working together as a team. This chapter discusses teamwork, factors vital for team success, and the impact teams have on an organization's overall performance.

In the workplace, working in a **group** means you and one or more people share a common goal. Every group has a leader that defines what happens in order to reach a goal. The most common group in a workplace is a department. As a department, your boss will be the one assigned to lead your group in accomplishing the department's goal.

Most companies use **teams** to accomplish goals. You and one or more other people will make up a team. The team will be assigned the task of reaching a goal. In a team setting, it is the responsibility of everyone in the group to decide how and when to reach the goal. Each team member needs to have a sense of ownership for the team's performance. This occurs when team members are active participants and are accountable to fellow team members.

Several types of teams exist at work. Teams that occur within the organizational structure are formal teams. **Formal teams** are developed within the formal organizational structure and may include functional teams (e.g., individuals from the same department) or cross-functional teams (individuals from different departments). **Informal teams** are comprised of individuals who get together outside of the formal organizational structure to accomplish a goal. Examples of informal teams include a company softball team and a group of coworkers collecting food for a local charity. In each team situation you are involved with, it is important that you get along with your team members and act professionally. Your performance for getting the job done depends on this team effort. A team comprised of individuals who behave professionally performs better.

Every team goes through five stages of team development: forming, storming, norming, performing, and adjournment. In the **forming stage,** you are getting to know and forming initial opinions about your team members. You are making assumptions based on first impressions. Sometimes these impressions are right; other times, they are wrong. In stage two, the **storming stage,** some team members begin to have conflict with each other. When team members accept other members for who they are (i.e., overcome the conflict), the team has moved into the **norming stage.** It is only then that the team is able to go into the **performing stage** and begin working on its task. Once the team has completed its task, it is in the **adjourning stage** to bring closure to the project. Note that it is normal for a team to go through these phases. Some teams successfully and rapidly move through the forming, storming, and norming phases and get right to work (performing), while other teams cannot get beyond the initial phases of forming or storming. Make every effort to move your team along to the performing stage, and recognize that minor conflicts are a part of any team development. Successful teams move beyond the conflict and accept each member for his or her unique talents and skills.

You may work with people you know and see every day in the workplace. However, you may have to work with a team of people you have never met before. Some team members may be from your immediate department (functional teams), some may be outside of your department (cross-functional teams), and some may be from outside of the company. Good people skills and a willingness to lead are what make employees valuable to a team.

In a team situation, you will usually have your own job to do but you are also accountable to your fellow team members. The success of others within the company depends on how you do your job. Although you may be working independently from your team members, it is still important that you get your job done on time and correctly. An effective team member is able to work with everyone on the team. You may have to work with a person with whom you do not care to work. No matter what disagreements you may have, you need to get along with this person and be professional at all times. This is a skill needed for any job.

► CHARACTERISTICS OF A TEAM MEMBER

A good team member is one who does his or her job in a manner that is productive toward the end project. This means being trustworthy, being efficient, and communicating at all times. Common team projects include improving product quality, providing excellent customer service, and creating and/or maintaining company records.

As a team member, you should know the objectives and goal of the team. Every activity you perform for your team should support the team's objectives and goal. In chapter 2, you learned how to create personal goals. Organizations do the same thing. When you have a team working on a specific project, there is a goal; so the first step is to set objectives to reach your goal. Do not just jump into the project. You do not want to reinvent the wheel or waste time and money. The best way to avoid these common mistakes is to solicit ideas and input from all team members.

Once the team has identified its goal and objectives, the team can identify various alternatives or solutions on how best to successfully achieve the goal. One popular way of doing this is through brainstorming. Brainstorming is a way of identifying alternatives to a problem while withholding comments on the alternatives. The reason brainstorming is so successful is that it is fast and provides members the opportunity to contribute different ideas. Brainstorming starts with the presentation of a problem, for example, how can we improve office communication. Members then have a set time to make any suggestion for improving office communication. The suggestions can be obvious (e.g., a newsletter) or fun and creative (have a weekly office party off site). No matter the suggestion, everyone is to withhold comment and judgment on the idea until the brainstorming session is over. Recommendations are recorded on a board for everyone to view. In effective brainstorming sessions, even an off-the-wall comment such as the suggestion to have a weekly office party off site may spark an idea that contributes to solving the problem (e.g., have a companywide gathering).

◄ **EXERCISE 11–1: Brainstorm for Saving:** *Working in a small group, brainstorm for as many ideas as possible to help you and/or your classmates save money while going to college. List the top three ideas.*

1. _____

2. _____

3. _____

Although conflict is a natural part of team development, occasionally, there are teams that are filled with conflict. As you will learn in chapter 12, there are various ways to overcome conflict. First and foremost, do not let one member ruin the synergy of the team. If possible, confidentially pull the member aside and ask that person what it is about the team or project that he or she finds objectionable. Also, ask that team member how he or she feels the issue can best be resolved. Calmly and logically help the individual work through the issues. Accept the fact that he or she may not (1) recognize there is a problem, (2) share, or (3) want to come to a solution. If you or others on the team attempt to solve the problem with the difficult team member and he or she rejects the effort, your team needs to move forward without that person. Do not give one member so much power that he or she negatively affects the efforts of the entire team. Although team conflict is a natural stage of team development, it should never cripple a team. When the problem team member is not around, do not allow other team members to talk negatively about the individual. Your job is to be a productive, positive team member who assists in successfully accomplishing the team's goal.

In addition to knowing the goals of the project and what your roles and responsibilities are in the team effort, you also need to know the responsibilities of all the other team members. Whenever possible, identify ways to support other team members and assist them in accomplishing the team's objectives. Take responsibility to attend all team meetings and be on time. Participation, sharing, support, understanding, and concern are all part of being on a team. During the meetings, make every effort to be involved in discussions and determine what work is needed for accomplishing the goal. Do not be afraid to speak up during team meetings. The key is to successfully complete the team goal. Some of your ideas may not be considered, but that does not mean they are not important. Speak up; you may have the winning idea. Also, remember to be responsible and finish your assignment in a timely manner. As a group, you should review all aspects of the project together before completing the project. To make the project successful, team members must be accountable to each other.

Cory's department was having problems meeting its production goal. The manager asked the department to form a team and create a plan for increasing production. Cory volunteered to be on this team. It was the first team project Cory had been involved in, and Cory did not know what to expect. Fortunately, Cory had a good team leader. The team leader sat down with the team and helped the team identify its goal and objectives so that team members knew exactly what needed to be done. At the next meeting, the team leader led a brainstorming session. Some good ideas were mentioned. Cory had an idea but was not sure it should be mentioned. However, the team leader noticed Cory was not participating and asked Cory for ideas. Cory decided to share the idea. It turned out the team liked the idea, and it became an important part of the project plan.

Communication is a key element of effective teamwork. You should not make assumptions. If you have questions regarding an aspect of the project, respectfully speak up. As mentioned earlier in this chapter, it is normal for teams to experience conflict. If others do not agree with your ideas, keep a positive attitude. If your team takes a wrong turn, do not waste time on blame; take corrective action and learn from any mistakes that are made. Each team member should be able to state his or her position and ideas; it should then be a team effort to decide which ideas to use. Do not assume that any team member's idea will not be worth hearing. The whole point of a team project is to get as many ideas as possible in order to come up with the best solution for reaching the goal. If the team makes a decision with which you did not agree and you have expressed and explained your objection and the team still decides to continue, you should support the team's decision and continue assisting the team in achieving its goal. Conflict is a normal part of teamwork, but you must learn to work through conflict. This is where open, honest, and timely communication with all team members is important.

Your team members need to trust you to do your part in getting the work done. Make sure you do not let your team members do your work because you know they will do it. Many times, in a team situation, one member contributes nothing because that member knows he or she can. If you have a lazy team member, you should still do your best and try to work around that person. Eventually, that person will lose respect from other team members and they will not work with that person on projects. Try talking to that team member and find out why he or she is not doing his or her share. If the team member provides a good reason, suggest that he or she excuse himself or herself from the team. If the team member just simply refuses to perform, you may need to talk to your supervisor and get him or her replaced.

◀ EXERCISE 11–2: **Good Team Member Characteristics:** *Name the two most important characteristics you would want to see in your team members. Be specific and explain why these characteristics aid in a team's success.*

Characteristic	How Does this Help the Team Achieve Success?
1.	
2.	
3.	

▶ MOTIVATION

Motivation is an internal drive that causes people to behave a certain way to meet a need. What they do is a result of trying to fill that need. If your needs are not met, you change your behavior. Team members need to be motivated to achieve success. Several factors can contribute to motivating team members. The most obvious motivation factor is money. However, when working in teams, monetary payment often may not be the motivating factor.

Motivation comes from within. A team member's motivation may be a sense of accomplishment that could result in a future promotion. Perhaps the motivation is the sense of responsibility and the achievement of a goal, which is self-satisfaction. Or perhaps the motivation factor is the social acceptance you receive from others for being part of a successful team. For others, the motivation factor may just be a matter of keeping their job. Perhaps the team project will be the key to keeping the company in business or increasing customer satisfaction.

Abraham Maslow created a hierarchy of needs (see figure 11–1). This hierarchy of needs essentially states that throughout one's lifetime, as individuals' needs are met, they move up a pyramid (hierarchy) until they self-actualize and assist others with their needs. Organizational behaviorists have adapted Maslow's hierarchy to a typical workplace. Maslow's lowest level, **physiological needs,** translates to basic wages. Everyone works to receive a paycheck, which is used for food and shelter. The next step up the pyramid is **safety needs**. Individuals desire not only a safe working environment but also job security. It is only after individuals, receive basic wages and security at work that they invest in workplace relationships, thus reaching the **social needs** level. Employees who encounter workplace bullies or a poor supervisor cannot progress to the next level until positive workplace relationships are made. The next level on the pyramid is **self-esteem needs.** This is when employees flaunt workplace titles, degrees, and awards. Their need is to inform others of their accomplishments. The final stage of the hierarchy is that of **self-actualization.** In a workplace, this is when employees have successfully had their needs met and now desire to assist others in meeting their needs. They do so by becoming mentors or coaches or by finding other means of helping others achieve their goals. Because each level has a different goal, you need to find what motivates you in that level.

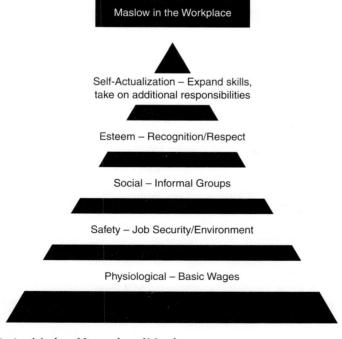

◀ **FIGURE 11–1**   Maslow Hierarchy of Needs

◀ **EXERCISE 11–3: Self-Motivation:** *What level of Maslow's hierarchy are you on? What motivates you when doing your work or class assignments? Why? What do you think your boss or instructor thinks motivates you? Why?*

What level (Maslow) are you on?	What motivates you?	Why?	What does your boss think?

Maslow's theory is still used today to explain what motivates employees and how humans respond to motivational factors. Each level of the pyramid addresses different ways people need to be motivated. As a team member, you need to recognize that not everyone is motivated; nor do others always have the same needs as you. Observe other members' behaviors and words, then try to determine where they are on the pyramid. Once you figure out what others' needs are, you assist in creating an environment that helps fill those particular needs. Remember, motivation is an internal drive. You must motivate yourself. Others can only help provide a motivating environment.

◀ **EXERCISE 11–4: Identify the Need:** *Evaluating the following comments, determine what need on Maslow's hierarchy is being expressed. Refer to figure 11–1.*

Comment	Need Expressed
I have done a similar project in the past; can I help you?	
I need a raise this year.	
Anyone want to join me for lunch?	
I received a sales award; would you like to see it?	

If you are in level 1 (physiological needs), you may be motivated by having any job in which you get paid enough money to pay for your living quarters, food, and clothing. After feeling comfortable, you will move into level 2 (safety needs). Here, you may want to get a job with better pay so you can move to a neighborhood where you feel safe. In addition to job security and workplace safety, you need security for your home and family. Once you have reached that level of security, you move to level 3 (belonging and love). At this level, you will have motivation in the area of human relationships. Once again, in addition to workplace relationships with coworkers and your boss, you will have relationships with others in family, clubs, religious groups, or even work groups. The next level (esteem) is where you desire recognition for what you do; you want to do the best you can do. After reaching all these levels, you move to the top level of the pyramid (self-actualization). This is where you have become what you want to be and spend your time assisting others in achieving their goals. Maslow believed very few people ever make it to the self-actualization level.

One final point regarding Maslow's theory is that individuals can quickly move from one level to another. It is common to have an off day in which you are not motivated to perform. If you find yourself having an off day, take time out and ask yourself what situation put you in a nonproductive frame of mind. Use positive self-talk to get back on track and be productive. In some situations, you may not be able to control the situation that affected your performance. An example may be work layoffs or a workplace safety issue. In one of these instances, try to identify what element of the situation you can control and work from there. Remember that you are the only one who can control your attitude.

If you find yourself in a situation in which you no longer have a desire to work and this lack of motivation lasts more than a week, you may be experiencing burnout. **Burnout** is the desire to no longer work. It is most commonly caused by stress, which, when applied to Maslow's theory, translates into a low motivating work environment. Signs of burnout include:

- ► Being frequently tardy or absent
- ► Continual complaining
- ► Lack of concern for quality
- ► Clock watching and being easily distracted
- ► Gossiping
- ► Desire to cause harm to the company (theft or damage property)

If you have seriously tried to improve your current work situation and still find yourself at a dead end, you may need to consider a job change. Continuing in a job in which you are not motivated for a long period of time is destructive not only to you but also to your company and coworkers.

► LEADERSHIP

In most companies, when reference is made to *leaders,* people think of managers. But the reality is that every employee should display leadership. **Leadership** is a process of one person guiding one or more individuals toward a specific goal. We all can be leaders. A leader does not need to be a manager or a supervisor. Note that not all bosses are leaders. Leaders motivate others through relationships. At work, these relationships are based on trust, professionalism, and mutual respect. A leader is one who will help guide and motivate others. In other words, a leader will help others want to successfully get the job done. In comparison, a boss who is not a leader will just tell others what job to get done without guiding and motivating.

From the preceding examples, you can see that you do not need a title or degree to be a leader. At work, make an effort to assume a leadership role. In a leadership role, you need to know the project and its purpose. You need to know your team players' (or coworkers') strengths and weaknesses. You need to be someone others can trust. You also need to remember that it is a team process, not just your own process for getting a job done. As a good leader, you must know how to problem solve and make sure you plan for projects. In order to do this, you must know your job. A good leader also knows when to follow.

Effective leaders do not do all the work themselves. They learn to delegate. Delegating means you assign part of a project to someone else. The most important thing to remember is that you cannot do it all yourself. However, as the leader, you are responsible for seeing that the project does get done. Remember, if you are the leader, you must oversee the project. As a leader, you need to empower others, teach them, and mentor them. If you are a team member, work with the leader and do your part in the project. Ultimately, the leader takes responsibility, so make sure you take your responsibility seriously and get the job done.

► BECOMING A LEADER

At work, you may be assigned a leadership position by your boss or your team or simply because no one else wants to lead. No matter how you obtain a leadership position, you need to be prepared to lead at all times. You need to know what it is like to serve on a team and what skills are necessary to be a team leader. Begin preparing today by learning new skills through continual learning or by attending workshops. Observe successful leaders and/or find a mentor to help you develop good leadership skills. Learning new skills will enable you to think and act like a leader. You will also improve your communication skills, which is necessary for effective leadership.

Effective leaders display characteristics that make them stand out from others. These skills include excellent communication skills, the ability to work with and earn the trust of others, consistent ethical behavior, and focus and vision. Although these skills are not developed overnight, remember that you have the ability to become a successful leader not only in your workplace but also in every other area of your life.

◀ **EXERCISE 11–5: Leadership Characteristics:** *List five people whom you consider leaders. Next to their names, list the characteristic that makes them a successful leader.*

Leader	Leadership Characteristic
1.	
2.	
3.	
4.	
5.	

◀ SUMMARY OF KEY CONCEPTS

▶ Most companies use teams to accomplish goals
▶ An effective team is comprised of individuals who share a goal and respect each other
▶ A good team member is one who does his or her job in a manner that is productive toward the end project
▶ Although team conflict is a natural stage of team development, it should never cripple a team
▶ Communication is a key element of effective teamwork
▶ Motivation is an internal drive that causes you to behave a certain way to meet a need
▶ Everyone has the ability to become a successful leader

◀ KEY TERMS

adjourning stage	leadership	self-actualization
burnout	motivation	self-esteem needs
formal teams	norming stage	social needs
forming stage	performing stage	storming stage
group	physiological needs	synergy
informal teams	safety needs	teams

◀ REFERENCES

Maslow, Abraham. *Motivation and Personality*, 2nd ed. New York: Harper & Row, 1970.

Maxwell, J.C. *The 21 Irrefutable Laws of Leadership.* Nashville: Nelson Business, 1998.

Tuckman, B.W., and M.A.C. Jenson. "Stages of Small Group Development Revisited." In *Group and Organizational Studies,* 2nd ed., 419–27. 1977.

Zemke, Ron. "Maslow for the New Millennium." *Training* (December 1998): 54–58.

◀ IF YOU WERE THE BOSS

1. You have assembled a group of employees into a team to reach the goal of improving customer service in your department, but all they do is argue when they meet. What should you do?
2. Your employees have successfully met their production goals this week. Based on Maslow's motivation theory, how can you motivate them to meet next week's goals?

◀ WEB LINKS

http://www.nwlink.com/~donclark/leader/leadhb.html

http://www.affinitymc.com/Five_Facets_of_Leadership.htm

http://www.deepermind.com/20maslow.htm

◀ WORKPLACE DO'S AND DON'TS

Do be an active participant by being accountable to fellow team members	*Don't* ignore team meetings and deadlines
Do be a good team member by being trustworthy and efficient and by communicating at all times	*Don't* allow negative team members to disrupt the team's performance
Do express yourself during team meetings	*Don't* think your ideas are not of value
Do recognize that people are motivated by different factors	*Don't* ignore initial signs of burnout
Do make every effort to increase your leadership skills	*Don't* leave the leadership process up to others

ACTIVITY 11–1

Write about a time when you belonged to a successful team. Identify at least three specific factors that made the team successful.

TEAM SITUATION	
1.	
2.	
3.	

ACTIVITY 11–2

Research President Abraham Lincoln and answer the following questions.

What key leadership qualities made him unique?

_____

_____

What challenges did he face?

_____

_____

How can you apply lessons learned from your President Lincoln research to your leadership development?

_____

_____

ACTIVITY 11–3

If you were teaching this class, what specific topics or activities could you include in the course to help students better meet each level of Maslow's hierarchy?

LEVEL	MOTIVATION FACTOR
Self-actualization	
Esteem	
Social	
Safety	
Physiological	

1. _____ hierarchy of needs is used to explain _____.

2. Every team goes through _____: forming, _____, norming, _____, and _____.

3. _____ is a way for teams to identify various alternatives or solutions on how best to successfully achieve the goal.

4. A/An _____ is one who will work with others to help guide and motivate.

5. Communication with all team members must be _____, _____, and _____.

6. _____ is an internal drive; therefore, no one can motivate you. Others can only provide a _____ environment.

7. _____ is the desire to no longer work. It is most commonly caused by _____.

8. At work, _____ are based on trust, professionalism, and mutual respect.

CHAPTER 12

CONFLICT AND NEGOTIATION

OBJECTIVES

- ▶ Define *conflict* and its impact on performance
- ▶ Name and describe the various conflict management styles and the appropriate time to utilize each one
- ▶ Describe the process and purpose of *negotiation*
- ▶ Define the various forms of workplace *harassment*
- ▶ Identify resources available to employees who are confronted with workplace harassment
- ▶ Describe how to deal with a hostile work environment or *workplace bully*
- ▶ Name warning signs of workplace violence

Whenever you're in conflict with someone, there is one factor that can make the difference between damaging your relationship and deepening it. The factor is attitude.

William James (1842–1910)

► CONFLICT

Unfortunately, a common element of working with individuals is conflict. Although most individuals regard conflict as a negative experience, it does not always have to be negative. Conflict can result in a positive experience if you approach it with the right attitude. This chapter addresses the issue of conflict and its impact on performance. The chapter also presents various methods of dealing with conflict in addition to tips on how to deal with difficult people. Finally, this chapter addresses the issues of harassment, workplace violence, and negotiation.

Conflict occurs when there is a disagreement or tension between two or more parties (individuals or groups). Although conflict at work cannot be avoided, you can control your reaction to the conflict. Conflict means that individuals are looking at a situation from different perspectives, which is not always a bad thing. Different perspectives mean diversity of thought.

If you view conflict as a breakdown in communication, you should work on overcoming the problem instead of finding fault or blame. How an individual deals with conflict reflects his or her attitude, maturity level, and self-confidence. When someone disagrees with you or hurts you, a natural tendency is to become angry. The next common reaction is to retaliate to get even. Unfortunately, this behavior does not reflect that of an individual who is striving to become a logical, mature professional. In general, follow these basic rules when dealing with any conflict:

- ► Remain calm and unemotional
- ► Be silent and listen
- ► Try to see the disagreement from the other person's perspective
- ► Explain your position and offer a solution
- ► Come to a solution

Rarely, if ever, does anyone win when people respond in anger. An individual who becomes emotional cannot manage his or her logic in resolving the issue. It is for this reason that, when confronted with conflict, you should remain calm and unemotional. You should acknowledge your hurt feelings or anger, but do not let it dominate your response. With a clear mind, it is easier to view the disagreement from your opponent's side. Try to identify why your opponent behaved the way he or she did. Before responding, identify what message was being sent. Look for facts and feelings. This will help you identify if the message was misinterpreted because of an emotional response or miscommunication. It could just be a difference of opinion. This includes identifying what message was misinterpreted, along with who sent or interpreted the wrong message.

After seeing the disagreement from "the other side," calmly and rationally explain your position along with a solution. This is the step that could easily lead to an argument if you become emotional. While explaining your position, your opponent may interrupt and state his or her position. Do not argue. Allow your opponent to talk while you remain quiet and listen. This is a tough job because we want to defend our opinions. Remember, you are responding in a mature, professional manner. When the opponent is done speaking, take your turn. If your opponent again interrupts, ask him or her if you can take your turn responding. In your conversation, look for common ground. Identify what it is exactly that you are disagreeing over. Get your opponent to agree on the point of contention. Try to give several alternatives to solving the problem, and then agree on a solution.

The following list offers a few basic concepts to remember when dealing with conflict in the workplace:

- ► No one except you can control how you respond to a situation.
- ► Do not let your feelings dictate your actions. When confronted with conflict, remain calm and unemotional.
- ► Attempt to resolve a conflict immediately and at the lowest level (start with the offender) before talking with a supervisor.
- ► Accept responsibility for your actions and apologize if necessary.
- ► Retaliation (getting even) is not the answer.
- ► Keep your conflict issues confidential.
- ► Document an offensive or inappropriate behavior regarding the conflict.
- ► Seek assistance within the company to resolve the conflict.
- ► If an internal remedy cannot be reached, seek outside assistance.

◀ **EXERCISE 12–1: Handling Interruptions:** *Role-play a conversation with a classmate about the best way to take notes in class. Have the other classmate interrupt you several times. Practice handling the interruption in an adult, mature manner. What did you say to that person?*

_____

_____

_____

_____

_____

▶ CONFLICT MANAGEMENT STYLES

Depending on the offense and workplace situation, there are several methods of dealing with conflict. These include forcing, avoiding, accommodating, compromising, or collaborating.

If the behavior is offensive or unacceptable, you should use the **forcing management style.** This is when you deal with the issue head-on. Remember to remain calm and unemotional. Do not turn the discussion into an argument. Your goal is to communicate that the inappropriate behavior is unacceptable and provide your solution to the problem. Forcing behavior means you get your way. The other party has no say whatsoever.

The **avoiding management style** should be used when you do not want to deal with the conflict. Sometimes we avoid a conflict because the offense is not a big enough deal to upset others. Other times, we avoid the conflict because we are not strong or confident enough to stand up for our rights.

If preserving a relationship is a priority, you may use the **accommodating management style** with the offender and let him or her have his or her way without the offender knowing there was ever a conflict.

A **compromising management style** occurs when both parties give up something of importance to arrive at a mutually agreeable solution to the conflict. This differs from the **collaborating management style** in which both parties work together to arrive at a solution without having to give up something of value.

When faced with conflict, your goal is to create a situation that is fair to all involved parties. This is called **negotiation.** Both sides can come to an agreement if both parties:

▶ Want to resolve the issue
▶ Agree on an objective
▶ Honestly communicate their case/situation
▶ Listen to the other side
▶ Work toward a common solution that is mutually beneficial

In working toward a successful negotiation, remember to practice good communication skills. As stated in the preceding list, listen. Do not interrupt or pass judgment until the other side has stated its case. Watch the other party's body language through hand and arm gestures and body positioning. Attempt to identify whether the other party is willing to resolve the issue. Also evaluate the party's ability to make eye contact. Put aside your personal feelings and focus on coming to a mutually agreeable solution.

If two parties are not able to resolve an issue themselves or if the issue affects workplace performance, it is common for a neutral third party to serve as a **mediator.** The mediator's primary objective is to assist the two feuding parties in coming to a mutually agreeable solution.

If you consistently avoid conflict, evaluate your motives. While it is acceptable to use **passive behavior** at times, there are appropriate times to use **assertive behavior.** It is important to stand up for your rights. In doing so, it is also important that you do not violate the rights of others. Professionals should behave in an *assertive* manner. Individuals who are assertive stand up for their rights without violating the rights of others. You should never be ashamed to stand up for your rights and share your concerns. While individuals exhibiting **aggressive behavior** also stand up for their rights, they do so in a manner that violates others' rights generally in an offensive manner. Others do not have to be harmed or put down for you to be heard or for you to have your way.

◀ EXERCISE 12–2: **How to Handle Poor Quality:** *You are in a restaurant eating lunch with coworkers and are served a poor quality meal. Identify both assertive and aggressive responses to the situation. If you were the waiter, how would you respond to both behaviors?*

Assertive Behavior	Waiter Response to Assertive Behavior	Aggressive Behavior	Waiter Response to Aggressive Behavior

Someone loses when aggressive behavior is exhibited. Remember to treat everyone in a respectful, professional manner. If you are offended or see that someone else's rights are being violated, speak up. You can stand up for your rights (or those of another) without harming others. Do not demean others as a form of retaliation when someone displays aggressive behavior toward you.

▶ HARASSMENT

Discussed in more detail in chapter 13, the human resource department is your advocate for unlawful harassment. The Equal Employment Opportunity Commission (EEOC) defines **sexual harassment** as unwanted advances of a sexual nature. The two types of sexual harassment are quid pro quo and hostile behavior. **Quid pro quo harassment** is behavior that is construed as reciprocity or payback for a sexual favor (e.g., you sleep with your boss and he or she gives you a raise). The EEOC states that quid pro quo harassment can also include "verbal, visual or physical conduct of a sexual nature." **Hostile behavior harassment** includes any behavior of a sexual nature by another employee that you find offensive. The EEOC states this behavior can include "verbal slurs, physical contact, offensive photos, jokes, or any other offensive behavior of a sexual nature." Harassment can occur between a man and a woman, a man and another man, or a woman and another woman. It also does not limit itself to a boss and employee relationship.

Names that could be considered sexist and offensive are inappropriate in a business setting. Using inappropriate names toward coworkers will expose you and your company to a potential sexual harassment lawsuit. These include names such as *honey, sweetie*, and *sexy*. Even if others act as though they are not offended by the names, they may be offended or insulted but afraid to tell you so. Eliminate these words from your workplace vocabulary.

In addition to sexual harassment policies, companies should also have a policy regarding professional behavior. Every employee should be treated in a respectful and professional manner by coworkers. The policy regarding workplace behavior prevents workplace incivility and communicates to all employees that unprofessional behavior will not be tolerated. In the workplace, there will be individuals whom you may not care to befriend. You do not have to be friends with all of your coworkers, but you are required to respect your colleagues and treat everyone in a professional manner. You should not be rude. Choose to be courteous. Rude behavior ignores the individual and is immature behavior. Rude behavior is not professional behavior. Courteous behavior means that you are polite. You do not have to like your coworkers, but they should not be aware of your negative feelings toward them. Mature adults treat every coworker with courtesy and respect.

◄ **EXERCISE 12–3: Identify Harassment:** *What kind of behavior have you exhibited that could be construed as harassing?*

_____

_____

_____

How can you change your behavior or attitude to ensure that no one is offended by or could misinterpret your behavior as inappropriate?

_____

_____

Every company should have an antiharassment policy. Moreover, employers should provide antiharassment training and a protocol for filing and investigating a complaint. If you are a victim of harassment, you should take the following steps:

1. If the behavior is offensive but relatively minor, tell the individual that his or her behavior is offensive and ask him or her to stop. Document the conversation in your personal notes. Make sure your documentation includes the date, time, and any witnesses to the incident.
2. If the behavior continues or if the behavior is extremely inappropriate and/or outrageously offensive, immediately contact your supervisor or human resource department. Tell the person you contact what happened, that you are offended by the harassing behavior, and that you want to file harassment charges. Provide facts and names of anyone who witnessed the offensive behavior.

Once you have filed a complaint to your employer, he or she has a legal obligation to conduct a confidential investigation. Remember that everyone is innocent until proven guilty. On that same note, you must not feed the rumor mill with information regarding your complaint. Remain professional and reserve comments for the investigative interview. Document the dates and times of whom you speak with regarding the complaint, interviews, and comments made. When the investigation is complete, the supervisor or human resource department will render a decision. If you are not satisfied with the outcome, you have the right to file a complaint with the Department of Fair Employment and Housing or the Equal Employment Opportunity Commission. It is unlawful for an employer to retaliate against or punish anyone who files a sexual harassment claim, even if the claim is found to be without merit. No one should be punished for filing a claim.

Harassment policies are extremely important policies. You should behave appropriately and not exhibit behavior that could be offensive to others. This includes off-color jokes, inappropriate touching, inappropriate conversations, and suggestive attire. Many times, individuals think they are joking when in fact their behavior is offensive to others.

Katie, the mailroom clerk who works in Cory's office, returned from a vacation at the beach. When Cory asked Katie about her vacation, she told Cory and Cory's officemates all about her new tattoo. One of Cory's coworkers, John, asked where on her body she got her tattoo. Katie grinned at John and said she would show him later. The next day, when Katie delivered the mail, John again asked Katie when he would get to see her tattoo. Katie smiled and went on her way. For the next few days, John kept asking about the tattoo and Katie kept smiling and walking away. The following week, John was called into the boss's office. Cory later found out that Katie filed sexual harassment charges against John based on John's curiosity regarding Katie's new tattoo.

◀ **EXERCISE 12–4: Identify Violations:** *Whose rights were violated in the previous story regarding Katie, John, and the tattoo? Justify your answer.*

_____

_____

_____

If you were Katie, how should you have handled the situation differently?

_____

_____

_____

If you were John, what should you have done differently?

_____

_____

_____

▶ WORKPLACE BULLIES

Even if you are treating everyone with respect, you may have a coworker who is not reciprocating with the same respectful and professional behavior. Many times in a workplace, there is an employee who is rude and unprofessional. These types of employees are called **workplace bullies.** Workplace bullies always seek ways to intimidate or belittle coworkers. Sometimes bullies publicly harass coworkers. Other times, they are discreet in their harassing tactics. Employees who are consistently rude and who bad-mouth other employees or demonstrate intimidating behavior are displaying workplace incivility. Both bullying and incivility can result in a hostile work environment, which contributes to both an increase in stress-related performance issues and, worse yet, workplace violence. Workplace bullying and incivility are not only immature behavior; they are unacceptable in the workplace. If you experience workplace bullying:

▶ Do not retaliate with the same bad behavior. Remain calm and unemotional. Remember that the bully enjoys seeing that he or she has upset you. While it is tempting to seek sympathy from coworkers, keep the issue confidential.

▶ Document dates, words, and witnesses of inappropriate behavior.

▶ Share your factual and documented information with your boss or human resource department, and file a formal complaint.

▶ If you feel your company has not appropriately resolved the issue in a reasonable time and manner, seek outside assistance. This assistance can come from a union, state or federal agency, or private attorney.

▶ KNOW YOUR RIGHTS

Every employee has a right to work in an environment free from harassment, discrimination, and hostility. Note that your boss and human resource department cannot assist you in resolving the conflict if they are not aware of the issue. Always share your concerns regarding harassment, discrimination, and workplace incivility immediately with your superiors. Prior to seeking outside assistance, you must exhaust all internal remedies (company resources that exist to take care of these issues). If you feel you need outside assistance to preserve your rights, several state and federal resources are available to assist you. These include your state's Department of Fair Employment and Housing, the Federal Equal Employment Opportunity Commission, your State Personnel Board, the Department of Labor/Labor Commission, and the Department of Justice. These resources are available to act on your behalf and ensure you are being treated in a fair and nondiscriminatory manner.

▶ RESOLVING CONFLICT AT WORK

Several steps should be taken when attempting to resolve a conflict at work. They are presented in figure 12–1. Whenever you are faced with a conflict, you must attempt to resolve the issue as quickly as possible. No matter the size of the conflict, deal with the issue immediately. Too often, individuals ignore a problem and hope it will go away. Unfortunately, these unresolved molehills frequently grow into giant, unresolved mountains. If you choose to utilize an accommodating or avoiding conflict resolution style, you need to accept your decision to not bring the conflict to the attention of the offender and move on.

If the conflict is affecting either yours or someone else's performance, inform your immediate supervisor. During this step, you need to think like a boss and ask yourself if the matter is appropriate to be brought to the attention of a superior. You never want to appear as a complainer. Be sure to document relevant information. If the problem continues and you are not satisfied with the way your immediate supervisor is handling the situation, contact the human resource management department. Members of this department will review existing policies and, if the situation warrants, they will conduct an investigation. If you are not fully satisfied with their

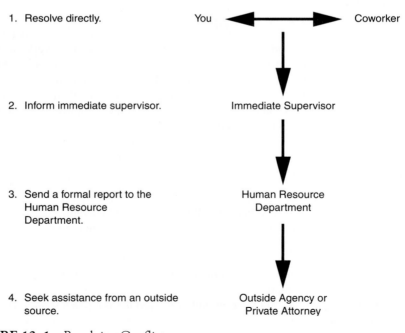

◀ **FIGURE 12–1** Resolving Conflict

decision or handling of the situation, you have the right to seek assistance from a private attorney or an outside government agency identified earlier in this chapter. Prior to seeking assistance from any outside agency, attempt to resolve the problem within your organization's structure. If you have representation from a union, involve the union as early in the process as possible. The legal term for this activity is *exhausting all internal remedies*.

▶ RESOLVING A CONFLICT UNDER A UNION AGREEMENT

If you belong to a union and you have a conflict with your supervisor or any other member of management, you need to refer to your union contract to identify what steps and rights are afforded you by being a union member. Every workplace represented by a union has a shop steward. The **shop steward** is a coworker who is very familiar with the union contract and procedures available to assist you in resolving the conflict. A problem or conflict that occurs in a union setting is called a *grievance*. Go to your shop steward and share your concern, along with any documentation or evidence you may have. The shop steward will meet with you and your supervisor to attempt to resolve the issue. If the issue cannot be resolved at this level, a union representative will meet with the human resource management department. The issue will continue to work up the chain of command until it is resolved. This process is called a **grievance procedure.** If you are represented by a union, it will assist you in protecting your rights through the grievance process. However, its purpose is not to shield you from punishment if you are guilty of wrongdoing.

▶ WORKPLACE VIOLENCE

Unresolved conflict has the potential to escalate into workplace violence. According to the U.S. Department of Labor, workplace violence is the third leading cause of workplace fatal injuries. Workplace violence includes any type of harassing or harming behavior (verbal or physical) that occurs in the workplace. This violence can come from coworkers, a boss, a customer, or a family member. It is vitally important that you recognize the warning signs and take appropriate precautions to decrease the probability that you become a victim.

If you are a victim of harassment, seek assistance and report any unprofessional behavior to your boss or to the human resource department before the behavior escalates to violence. Your personal life can impact workplace performance as well. If you have a personal issue that you feel may impact the workplace, share your concerns and seek confidential assistance from a coworker, your boss, or the human resource department as soon as possible. Most companies offer employee assistance programs (EAPs) that provide free confidential counseling. Even if your company does not offer this benefit, it may be able to help you identify an appropriate community resource to assist you.

Cory shares a cubicle with a woman who is newly married. She appeared to be happily married and had told Cory about the romantic dinners and gifts her new husband provided. One day, the woman showed up to work and kept to herself. Throughout the morning, Cory found it strange that she kept covering her face. Finally, as it neared lunch hour, Cory asked the woman if everything was okay. The woman looked up at Cory with a black eye and a bruised face and told Cory that she was leaving her husband. She went on to tell Cory that the husband had become increasingly jealous of any friendship the woman had with other men and had hit her the night before. Cory asked her if she felt safe. The woman responded, "No." Cory reminded the woman about the confidential and free EAP benefit their company offered. Cory then offered to help the woman arrange an appointment with the EAP.

As exemplified in Cory's experience, stress at home can impact your performance at work. If you feel your conflict (either at work or at home) does not warrant professional assistance, find a friend with whom you can confidentially and neutrally discuss the issue. Many times, victims of domestic violence fail to seek assistance out of embarrassment or fear. Your employer will want to assist you. You should not have to go through a hostile experience alone.

Remember to take responsibility at work to ensure that you have a safe working environment. Keep your work area and access to and from your workplace well lighted and secure. Never be afraid to ask for an escort to and from your car if you are working nontraditional work hours or park your car in a remote location. Keep emergency phone numbers posted in a visible area next to your phone and know where all the emergency exits are located. Finally, remember to always report suspicious behavior or situations that have the potential to become violent. It is much better to be safe than sorry.

▶ AGREE TO DISAGREE

As we learned in this chapter, conflict frequently cannot be avoided. In your efforts to work in harmony with your coworkers, you will find that others will hurt you. As important as it is to apologize when we have harmed others, it is equally as important to forgive. Too often, coworkers have apologized and the harmed individual has failed to forgive. Forgiving does not mean that you have forgotten the hurt. It does mean that you will give the individual another chance to prove his or her apology was sincere by a change in behavior.

A mature coworker is always willing to forgive and not hold grudges. Those who hold grudges never forgave in the first place and are seeking a means of retaliation. Doing so demonstrates immaturity. Remember, you do not have to like all of your colleagues, but you must always demonstrate professionalism and respect. Conflict at work is inevitable. How you allow the conflict to affect your performance is your choice.

◀ **EXERCISE 12–5: Resolving Issues:** *Identify grudges you have held or people you need to forgive. Make a point of resolving one of those issues within the next week.*

_____

_____

_____

_____

◀ SUMMARY OF KEY CONCEPTS

▶ A natural element of working with others is conflict
▶ How you deal with conflict determines your maturity level and professionalism
▶ Depending on the offense and workplace situation, there are several methods of dealing with conflict
▶ Employees have a right to work in an environment free from harassment
▶ Immediately report any harassing behavior
▶ Always attempt to resolve conflict at the lowest level, as soon as possible
▶ Recognize the warning signs and take appropriate precautions to decrease the probability that you become a victim
▶ It is considered immature to hold grudges. If you cannot resolve a conflict, sometimes it may be best to agree to disagree

◀ KEY TERMS

accommodating management style
aggressive behavior
assertive behavior
avoiding management style
collaborating management style

compromising management style
conflict
forcing management style
grievance procedure
hostile behavior harassment
mediator

negotiation
passive behavior
quid pro quo harassment
sexual harassment
shop steward
workplace bullies

◀ REFERENCES

Rahim, M.A., and T.V. Bonoma. "Managing Organizational Conflict: A Model for Diagnosis and Intervention." *Psychological Reports* 44 (1979): 1323–44.

State of California Department of Fair Employment and Housing. *The Facts about Sexual Harassment.* CADFEH-185 (04.04). Sacramento, CA, 2004.

U.S. Department of Labor Office of Labor-Management Standards within the Employment Standards Administration, Washington, DC www.dol.gov.

United States Equal Employment Opportunity Commission. Washington, DC www.eeoc.gov.

United States Occupational Safety and Health Administration. U.S. Department of Labor, Washington, DC www.osha.gov.

◀ IF YOU WERE THE BOSS

1. A fellow supervisor always wants to argue about an issue before arriving at a decision. Knowing this is typical of this person's behavior, how should you handle your next confrontation?
2. One of your employees tells you that another employee has been harassing him. What should you do?

◀ WEB LINKS

http://www.negotiationskills.com/qadeal.html

http://www.cdc.gov/niosh/violcont.html

http://www.afscme.org/health/violtc.htm

http://www.osbar.org/public/legalinfo/1104.htm

◀ WORKPLACE DO'S AND DON'TS

Do resolve a conflict as quickly as possible and at the lowest level	*Don't* allow a small conflict to grow over time
Do utilize the appropriate conflict-management style	*Don't* demonstrate aggressive behavior when standing up for your rights
Do know your rights regarding sexual harassment and discrimination issues	*Don't* utilize offensive language or hostile behavior
Do document any activity that you feel may escalate into potential problems	*Don't* retaliate when a workplace bully behaves inappropriately
Do agree to disagree when a conflict cannot be resolved	*Don't* hold grudges or behave in an immature manner

► ACTIVITIES

ACTIVITY 12–1

Based on what you learned in this chapter, identify the proper way to deal with these poor boss behaviors.

POOR MANAGEMENT QUALITY	HOW TO DEAL WITH
1. Uses foul language	
2. Steals company property	
3. Tells you to lie	
4. Allows employees to harass other employees	
5. Takes all the credit for everyone else's work	

ACTIVITY 12–2

Name at least three specific steps you can take to decrease the probability that workplace violence will occur in your office.

1. _____

2. _____

3. _____

ACTIVITY 12–3

You need a new printer and have decided to approach your boss and negotiate for the new piece of equipment. Research various options and prices for the printer that you are requesting.

What key information should you prepare before *your meeting?*

_____

_____

What key points should you share during *the meeting?*

_____

_____

ACTIVITY 12–4

Identify a time you felt you were harassed or had your rights violated.

Based on the information you learned in this chapter, what should you have done differently?

_____

_____

What outside resource could/should you have contacted?

_____

_____

1. _____ occurs when there is a disagreement or tension between two or more parties (individuals or groups).

2. Your goal when _____ is to create a win-win situation for all involved parties.

3. There are two types of sexual harassment: _____ and _____ environment.

4. _____ harassment is when payback is expected for a sexual favor. It can also be construed as verbal, visual, or physical conduct of a sexual nature.

5. A/An _____ includes any behavior of a sexual nature by another employee that you find offensive. This could include verbal slurs, offensive photos, jokes, or any other offensive behavior of a sexual nature.

6. _____ always seek ways to intimidate or belittle coworkers.

7. If you belong to a/an _____ and you have a conflict with _____, you need to refer to your _____ to identify what steps and rights are afforded you by being a union member.

8. It is important to _____ when you have harmed others.

HUMAN RESOURCE MANAGEMENT

OBJECTIVES

▶ Identify the primary functions performed by the *human resource department*

▶ State the primary components of an *employee orientation* program

▶ Describe the purpose and use of an *employee handbook*

▶ Explain the concept of *employment-at-will* and *right-to-revise* clauses

▶ Identify the various types of employment status

▶ Name the primary types and appropriate use of employee benefits

▶ Explain the importance and appropriate use of an *open-door policy*

*Eighty percent of success
is showing up.*
Woody Allen
(1935–)

► HUMAN RESOURCE DEPARTMENT

One of the first departments you will interact with at your new job is the **human resource department.** This department is responsible for hiring, training, compensation, benefits, performance evaluations, complaints, promotions, and changes in your work status. This very important department can assist you with work-related matters.

► EMPLOYEE ORIENTATION

Typically, on your first day of work or within the first few days of employment, you will experience an **employee orientation.** This is the time when the company's purpose, structure, major policies, procedures, benefits, and other important matters will be explained. You may also be issued company property at this time, including a name badge and keys if necessary. This is the time to begin meeting people and identifying potential mentors. Mentors are individuals who will work with you in developing your skills and abilities.

It is important to understand your new company. This includes knowing the major products or services the company provides as well as the key people in charge. These questions are explained in the company's mission and the company's organization chart. The mission statement states why the company exists. The organization chart identifies the lines of authority, key departments, and individuals in charge. Pay attention to the names of key executives and their titles such as the company president, CEO, and/or vice presidents. If possible, view current photos of these individuals; if you ever have the opportunity to meet them in person, you will know who they are.

► EMPLOYEE HANDBOOK

After a general overview of the company, you will be given a copy of the **employee handbook.** The employee handbook is an important document that outlines an employee's agreement with the employer regarding work conditions, policies, and benefits. Some of these policies are legally required, while others are rules of conduct and/or benefits from the company. Keep this handbook and use it as a reference for major workplace issues. Important sections of the handbook will be reviewed with you. Be sure to ask questions on topics that you do not fully understand. After the handbook is reviewed with you, you will be asked to sign a statement affirming that you have received the handbook, have read the handbook, and agree to its contents. This is a legal agreement. Therefore, do not sign the statement until you have completely read the handbook and fully understand its contents. Most employers will give the employee a day or two to return the agreement.

For example, during Cory's employee orientation, Cory received an employee handbook. With all new employees present, a man from the human resource department went through the handbook. Unfortunately, Cory was so overwhelmed with new terms, policies, and signing forms that Cory was not confident that any information was truly understood. Cory kept the handbook along with all the other employment paperwork on the dining room table and thought about throwing it away. Cory figured the human resource department had copies of everything that was important but decided to keep all the information just in case it was needed. About three weeks later, Cory's friends wanted to take a minivacation on an upcoming holiday and invited Cory. Cory was not sure the company gave that day as a holiday but remembered that something about holidays was mentioned in the orientation meeting. Unsure of whom to ask without appearing foolish, Cory suddenly remembered the employee handbook. Using the handbook, Cory immediately identified company holidays and was thankful not to have thrown the policy book away.

▶ DRESS CODE

Every employee should be aware of the company **dress code.** Dress codes vary by company depending on the product or service, the specific work area, and health/safety concerns. If your company has a mandatory uniform, the company dress code is typically spelled out in detail. If a uniform is not required, you should identify what is and is not acceptable attire. Some codes include vague terms such as *professional attire*, while other companies may use the terms *appropriate undergarments and shoes*. Even if your company does not provide specific information regarding suitable workplace attire, you should always dress appropriately. First and foremost, your attire should pose no safety hazards. Unstable shoes and footwear that do not provide protection are not appropriate. Dangling jewelry that could be caught in equipment is also inappropriate for work. Your undergarments, including bras, boxers, underwear, or thongs, should never be visible. You are expected to come to work clean (shower and brush your teeth). Cleanliness includes neatly maintained head and facial hair and hands, as well as control of body odor. Be conservative in the use of perfume, cologne, hair, and jewelry. Clothes should be clean and well maintained. Finally, your clothing should never carry any offensive words or comments. If you ever have questions regarding the company dress code or appropriate attire, check with your boss or the human resource department.

▶ EMPLOYMENT-AT-WILL AND RIGHT TO REVISE

Legally required in many states, a major policy statement that is usually placed at the very beginning of the employee handbook is called **employment-at-will.** This policy applies to any employee that is not hired as a contract employee for a stated period of time. Contract employees literally have contracts outlining the terms, start dates, and end dates of employment. Employment-at-will employees are not contractually obligated to work for the company for a specified period. You can quit any time you want. On that same token, your employer can terminate your employment at any time.

◀ **EXERCISE 13–1: Your State's Employment-at-Will Law:** *Although legally required in many states, some small employers do not properly inform their employees of their employment-at-will. How can you check to see if your state has an employment-at-will law?*

_____

_____

_____

_____

An employer also has the **right to revise** or change employment policies. You may be asked to sign separate statements affirming that you understand both the employment-at-will and right-to-revise policies if they are applicable.

There should also be statements in the employee handbook regarding equal employment opportunity and discrimination. These policies state that the company does not discriminate nor allow unlawful harassment of any kind (including sexual harassment, hostile workplace, or hate crimes).

▶ EMPLOYMENT STATUS

Another important section of your handbook will include employment status definitions, including introductory employees, part-time employees, full-time employees, and temporary employees. These classifications are typically determined by the number of hours worked per week and/or the length of your employment with your company.

Part-time employees work less than forty hours a week. Depending on your employer, part-time work hours can vary based upon workload. **Full-time employees** work forty or more hours per week. Any employee who works more than forty hours per week is entitled to overtime pay. **Temporary employees** are hired only for a specified period of time, typically to assist with busy work periods or to temporarily replace an employee on leave.

For most companies, new employees who are hired for full-time positions are first considered **introductory employees.** There will be a period (typically one to three months) in which the employer will evaluate your performance and decide if he wants you as a regular employee. On that same note, you have that period to determine if you want to work for the employer. At the end of this period, you will be given a performance evaluation. If the employer is happy with you, you become a regular employee and begin receiving benefits and all other entitlements that are due to full-time employees. If the employer is not happy with your performance, he can terminate you without cause. No excuses need to be given. If your performance is not yet acceptable but the employer thinks you demonstrate potential, the introductory period may be extended for one to three additional months.

As a new employee, it is important that you identify

▶ Whether your company has an orientation/introductory period
▶ The length of your orientation/introductory period
▶ When you become eligible for benefits
▶ Factors that will be used to evaluate your performance

After determining the length of your orientation/introductory period, secure a copy of your job description and performance evaluation. Your **job description** outlines your job duties and responsibilities (i.e., why they are paying you to come to work every day). Your **performance evaluation** identifies how your performance will be measured. Performance evaluations contain various criteria that measure your daily productivity, efficiency, and behavior. Common factors used to evaluate your performance reflect the duties and responsibilities included in your job description. Additionally, your involvement in work-related activities, ongoing education, and ability to assume new responsibilities may be reflected in this document. Both your job description and your performance evaluation will assist you in becoming a better employee and in moving past the introductory period and into that of a full-time, permanent employee.

◀ **EXERCISE 13–2: Evaluating Performance:** *If you were the boss of an accounting firm and you hired a new accountant, what factors would you use to evaluate your new accountant's performance?*

Evaluation Factor	How Measured?
1.	
2.	
3.	

▶ HOW TO BEHAVE AT PERFORMANCE EVALUATIONS

As previously mentioned, most employers typically provide performance evaluations immediately after completing an introductory period and then once a year thereafter. Although the prospect of someone providing feedback on your performance can be a bit intimidating, remember that this is a time for you to obtain information on how you can be a better employee. Performance evaluations provide a time not only for your supervisor to give you feedback on performance but also for you to share your desire for additional training and responsibilities.

Every employee should receive advance notice of an impending evaluation and performance criteria. Based upon the preestablished criteria, you should keep a historical record of your past performance. This may include notes and letters from customers, coworkers, and vendors. It may also include your personal documentation of events detailing when you displayed excellent judgment and/or behavior. On occasion, a supervisor provides the employee a blank copy of the upcoming evaluation form and asks the employee to complete a self-assessment. Use this opportunity to provide an honest review of your performance. Do not be overly favorable nor overly critical in your self-assessment. Be honest. Refer to the evidence and documentation you collected to support your assessment. After you have completed your self-assessment, take a photocopy of your document and return the original to your supervisor.

During your formal evaluation, sit quietly and listen to your supervisor's assessment of your performance. If there is anything negative regarding your performance that is included in the evaluation that you do not agree with, take notes; but do not interrupt your supervisor. Share your concerns only when your supervisor is finished talking or asks for feedback. Support your comments with your documentation. Even if you do not agree with your supervisor's response after you have presented your evidence, do not argue or challenge your supervisor during the assessment. At the end of each appraisal form is an area for the employee's signature. Immediately under the signature area should be a statement that the employee's signature does not constitute agreement with everything contained in the assessment but only that the employee received an evaluation. If you do not agree with any negative statement included in your evaluation and the appraisal form *does not* contain the preceding statement, do not sign the evaluation. If you do not agree with the negative statements included in your evaluation and the appraisal form *does* include the statement, sign the evaluation; but attach a written response regarding what areas you specifically do not agree with and state why. Provide supporting documentation and evidence to your attached statement. Do not write an emotional response. Make sure your statements are factual, and do not attack your supervisor or anyone else. Stick to the issues. Both your original evaluation and your written response will be forwarded to the human resource department and will become a permanent part of your personnel file. You should also receive a photocopy of your evaluation.

Remember to keep photocopies of your evaluations. They serve as legal documentation of your performance. They also serve as excellent reference material for future employers.

► BENEFITS

Most employees relate employee benefits with health care. Fortunately, employee benefits extend well beyond health benefits and vacations. During your orientation, someone will explain what benefits you will receive as a regular employee. These benefits may be **direct benefits** (monetary) and **indirect benefits** (nonmonetary) such as health care and paid vacations. Note that in most states employers do not have to offer health benefits. They do so as an incentive to attract a qualified workforce. Typically, only full-time, permanent employees are entitled to major benefits. During your employee orientation, you will learn when and if you qualify for benefits. Some employers allow their employees to select which benefits best meet their lifestyle needs. Providing employees their choice of which benefits to choose is called a *cafeteria plan*. Most benefits become effective immediately, while others may become effective after you have successfully passed your orientation period. If you are not clear as to when your benefits become effective, check with your human resource department.

If you qualify for benefits, you will be given paperwork to complete. It is important to provide accurate information. Your employer does not expect you to complete all the forms in one day and will most likely have you return them the following day. Keep all your copies of these forms in a secure place for easy reference. Your personal medical information is protected confidentially, so access to your medical information is restricted. Not even your boss should have access to this information. The only people within your company that will know your medical information will be those that are administering your health benefits.

◀ **EXERCISE 13–3: Choosing Benefits:** *Assume you are in a cafeteria plan and only qualify for four benefits from the following list. Which four would you choose and why?*

Salary	Medical	Dental
Vision	Emergency	Company car
Well child care	Day care	Prescriptions
Paid vacation	Life insurance	Retail discounts
Paid holiday	Free parking	Personal days
Paid training	In-house promotions	Free meals
Family medical	Bonuses	Flexible scheduling

Benefit	Why This Benefit Is Important to You
1.	
2.	
3.	
4.	

◀ **EXERCISE 13–4: Identifying Personal Information:** *Workplace organization begins your first day on the job. What personal information/documents should be kept for easy reference?*

1.

2.

3.

4.

5.

6.

Employers offer health benefits as an incentive to attract and keep good employees. Common health-related benefits include medical, vision, and dental insurance. **Medical benefits** include coverage for physicians and hospital visits. Physician coverage sometimes includes psychological (therapy), chiropractic (bone alignment/massage), and physical therapy (rehabilitation) services. If you or someone in your family utilizes these services, make sure you understand the coverage and stipulations. Check for emergency room access and coverage, as well as coverage for pharmaceuticals (prescription drugs). **Vision benefits** include care for your eyes. Some plans pay for eyeglasses only, while others pay for contact lenses and/or corrective surgery. Once again, be familiar with your plan and its coverage. **Dental benefits** provide care for your teeth. Check to see how frequently you are allowed to see your dentist for routine checkups. Typically, this is twice a year. Identify if your plan pays for cosmetic dental care such as teeth whitening or braces.

Most people utilize health benefits only when faced with an obvious health issue. While it is easy to put off routine checkups, it is in your best interest to practice preventive care. As soon as you become eligible for your benefits, schedule an appointment with a physician for a routine physical if you have not been to a doctor in some time. Get your vision checked, and see your dentist. This is important not only for preventive purposes but also to establish relationships with medical professionals. Because both you and your employer are paying for these benefits, it is important that you take advantage of these benefits when you become eligible. Finally, this may be a good time for you to evaluate your health status. If you need to shed a few pounds or eliminate a poor health habit such as smoking or drinking, now is a good time to change your behavior.

◄ **EXERCISE 13–5: Take Some Healthy Action:** *Identify three concerns regarding your health. Then make a commitment to begin improving these concerns by completing the following table.*

Healthy Action	Goal	Deadline
1.		
2.		
3.		

Employers may give you several choices for health policies. While few if any policies pay 100 percent of your health expenses, employees typically need to pay a copayment, or small percentage of the total fee. Many health insurance programs provide a list of medical professionals and health facilities that accept their insurance. Any time you do not use one of these preferred providers, the health insurance will not pay for your care or it will only pay a small percentage. At that point, you are responsible for the rest of your bill. When selecting a health program, carefully review the list of providers and facilities for familiarity and convenience. Do not forget to check emergency access, well child care, preventive care, or any other medical care you may need now or in the future.

Federal law requires that every employee receive **mandatory time off** for jury duty, voting, military leave, domestic violence issues, and crime victim related issues. Depending on the size of your company and the state in which you live, you may or may not get paid for this time off. Federal law also protects employees from pregnancy discrimination.

◄ **EXERCISE 13–6: Health-Care Considerations:** *In selecting health-care providers for you and your dependents, what issues are important considerations?*

Provider	Major Considerations
Physician	
Hospital	
Dentist	
Vision	
Pharmaceuticals	

As your benefits are being explained to you in detail, find out who else is entitled to these benefits. Frequently, these benefits are available to spouses and children. You may have to pay a bit more if you add people to your coverage, but it may be worth the extra cost. As healthcare costs continue to increase, it is important that you and your family have the security and needed access to quality health care.

Ask if your company offers a **retirement plan.** As explained in chapter 3, you are not too young to begin thinking about your retirement. If your company has a retirement plan, join it and start saving now. If you have these retirement funds automatically deducted from your earnings prior to receiving your paycheck, you will most likely not miss the money but you will appreciate the funds as they increase. Many company-sponsored retirement savings plans are tax deferred, which means you do not pay taxes on these funds until you retire. This provides an added incentive to begin planning for your future.

Payroll, paydays, accrued vacation, and sick days or sick leave are terms used to discuss monetary benefits. Your employee handbook identifies when you are paid. Typically, payday is every two weeks or on the fifteenth and thirtieth of each month. Your paycheck is in two parts. One part is the actual check (or a statement if your check is directly deposited into your bank account). The second part of your paycheck is called your pay stub. This stub contains very important information including hours worked, total pay, taxes paid, and any other deductions that were taken from your paycheck. Everyone must pay taxes. Any money taken from your original earnings is documented on your pay stub. Always keep your payroll stubs in a file for tax purposes and later reference. The Internal Revenue Service (IRS) recommends you keep these records on file for three years.

Find out what vacations and holidays your new employer provides and if you get paid overtime for working on a holiday. Identify how many days of vacation you will receive and when it will become available to you. Some companies also provide a personal day. This is one day that an employee can take off without explanation. However, provide your employer ample notice prior to taking this day. All information regarding vacations and holidays should be clearly communicated in your employee handbook. If it is not, be sure to obtain this information from either your supervisor or the human resource department.

If you have a family or are planning a family, it is important to identify company policies on pregnancy and family leave. There are laws to protect you from pregnancy discrimination and provide relief in these situations. Some employers even provide additional benefits beyond those required by law. Regardless of whether you currently have or are planning a family, emergencies happen with parents and other loved ones and you may need to take a leave of absence in the future.

One final benefit your company may offer is called an **employee assistance program (EAP).** This benefit typically provides free and confidential psychological, financial, and legal advice. An EAP benefit is generally extended to everyone who lives in your household. If you are experiencing a stressful situation at work or home, take advantage of this benefit.

Cory's best friend has a family cabin and invited Cory to spend a long weekend at the lake. Unfortunately, Cory had only been on the job for two months and had not accumulated any vacation time. Cory really wanted to go to the cabin. Cory remembered that the company provides sick leave and one personal day a year. Being on the job for such a short period of time, Cory wondered if it would be okay to either call in sick or take a personal day so soon. What would you do? After some thought, Cory realized that it would be unethical to lie by calling in sick. Cory also thought it would not be responsible to take a personal day so early on the job. As a result, Cory called the friend and suggested that perhaps they could meet up at the cabin later in the year. As difficult as Cory's decision was, Cory valued the new job and did not want to do anything to risk losing credibility or responsibility at work.

▶ OPEN-DOOR POLICY/GRIEVANCE PROCEDURES

Every company should have an **open-door policy.** Think of this policy as more of a "we're here to listen and help" policy. The purpose of an open-door policy is to communicate to employees that management and the human resource department are always available to listen should the employee have a concern or complaint. As discussed in chapter 12, the easiest way to deal with conflict is immediately, openly, and honestly. Doing so keeps a small problem from becoming big and keeps big problems from reoccurring. Do not be afraid to speak with your supervisor or the human resource department on any workplace issue that causes you concern.

▶ UNIONS

Depending on the size and nature of your company's business, you may have the opportunity to join a union. A **union** is an organization whose purpose is to protect the rights of employees. This organization is a third party that represents you and your colleagues' interests to your employer. Theoretically, if managers are doing their jobs, there is no need for unions. Unfortunately, this is not always the case. Unions negotiate on behalf of employees and typically negotiate higher salaries, better benefits, and improved working conditions. This comes with a cost. Employees pay a fee to a union for this representation. Moreover, as a union member, you are trusting that the union will always act on your behalf. Employees have the right to unionize (become members of a union), and they also have the right to choose not to join a union. You cannot be a manager and a union member. Union membership is only for nonmanagement employees.

If your company's employees are represented by a union, the union will contact you and invite you to become a member when you begin employment. Additional employment issues, including the handling of grievances, holidays, vacations, and other issues are outlined in your **union contract.** The union contract and the employee handbook are equally important documents. There are three types of membership agreements a union may have with employers: **union shop, agency shop,** and **open shop.** Check with your employer to see which agreement your employer has. Under a union shop, you do not have to be a member of the union to secure employment. However, after a specified time period (generally three months), you are required to join the union. Under an agency shop agreement, you do not have to join the union after a specified time. However, you are required to pay a fee to the union because you are enjoying the benefits of being represented by the union. Finally, under an open shop agreement, employees do not have to join the union, nor are they required to pay a fee for representation.

If you choose to join the union, you will be given a copy of the union contract. This is a very important document. The union contract addresses specific work-related issues that your employer and the union agree upon. These issues include work schedules, benefits, pay, performance measures, and a grievance procedure. You should take time to carefully read the contract and keep it in a place where you can easily use it for later reference. You also should know the names of and how to contact union officials who can assist you with work-related issues.

Your primary union contact will be the *shop steward* or *union representative*. This individual is an employee of your company but has agreed to serve as a primary contact between company employees and the union. The shop steward or union representative knows the union contract in great detail and will make every effort to assist you with a work-related issue. If you have a concern with how your supervisor or another manager of your company is treating you, do not hesitate to contact the shop steward or union representative.

Whenever the union contract comes up for renewal, union officials may ask union members for input on topics to be included in the new contract. These topics are called **bargaining issues.** If the union and your employer cannot come to an agreement regarding issues contained in the new contract, the negotiating has come to an **impasse.** At this point, every employee covered in the contract is working without a contract. The union may choose several tactics to get management (your employer) to support the concerns of the union. These tactics may include going on strike, picketing, or conducting a work slowdown. A **strike** occurs when employees walk off the job. During a strike, all employees who are members of the union must support the strike. They are not allowed to go to work. This means the company will not pay them. Most unions, however, will provide striking employees some funding in an attempt to make up for these lost wages. **Picketing** is when union employees stand outside the workplace and inform others of the current disagreement between the employer and the union. However, as a union employee during a picket, you are still working and receiving a paycheck. Employees only picket during nonwork hours. A **work slowdown** is when employees work but significantly decrease their output until the employer meets the union contract objectives.

During an impasse, a company also has methods to get the union to support management's contract terms. Because the union employees are working without a contract, an employer may choose to lock out union employees until a contract is approved. A **lockout** occurs when union employees cannot work and do not get paid until a contract is approved. Management may also choose to contract with other companies to produce the company product or service; or managers assume extra duties to reduce the amount of work available for regular, unionized employees. The management's strategy is to decrease the amount of work (and pay) available to union employees until a contract that favors the employer is approved.

Once a new contract is presented, every union member has a right to vote on approving the contract. It is imperative that you exercise your right to vote on the new contract. Remember that the union contract dictates work rules, benefits, and other issues important to your work environment. Not voting means that you do not care about these issues. At other times, the union will provide opportunities for employees to become union representatives. If you are interested in becoming more involved in the union, explore these opportunities. Once again, all union members will be given the opportunity to vote for their representatives. Exercise your right to vote on any union-related issue.

Take an active role in knowing what services are available to you through the union, the names of union officials who can assist you, and what value and services the union provides through its representation.

◄ SUMMARY OF KEY CONCEPTS

▶ The human resource department is responsible for all hiring, training, compensation, benefits, performance evaluations, complaints, promotions, and changes in your work status

▶ An employee orientation is the time to learn all about a company, its major policies, and employee services

▶ The employee handbook is an important document that outlines an employee's agreement with his or her employer regarding work conditions, policies, and benefits

▶ Employee benefits may include direct (monetary) benefits and indirect (nonmonetary) benefits such as health care and paid vacations

▶ You should be aware of and take advantage of benefits that are available to you

▶ Be aware of paydays, paid holidays, and sick leave policies

▶ Unions are designed to protect the rights of employees

◄ KEY TERMS

agency shop	human resource department	performance evaluation
bargaining issues	impasse	picketing
dental benefits	indirect benefits	retirement plan
direct benefits	introductory employee	right to revise
dress code	job description	strike
employee assistance	lockout	temporary employee
program (EAP)	mandatory time off	union
employee handbook	medical benefits	union contract
employee orientation	open-door policy	union shop
employment-at-will	open shop	vision benefits
full-time employee	part-time employee	work slowdown

◄ REFERENCE

United States Equal Employment Opportunity Commission. Washington, DC. www.EEOC.gov.

◄ IF YOU WERE THE BOSS

1. How should you handle an employee who keeps coming to you asking for information regarding major policies, vacations, and benefits?
2. How can a boss consistently communicate an open-door policy?

◄ WEB LINKS

http://www.dol.gov/ebsa/publications/10working4you.html
http://www.busreslab.com/policies/goodpol2.htm

◀ WORKPLACE DO'S AND DON'TS

Do read and keep your employee handbook for future reference	*Don't* ask your boss questions if you have not already referred to your employee handbook
Do utilize a calendar to identify upcoming paydays and company holidays	*Don't* demonstrate poor planning and be unaware of important days at work
Do take advantage of your company's employee assistance program	*Don't* wait until an issue dramatically affects your performance to seek help
Do ask for clarification if you have questions regarding appropriate dress in the workplace	*Don't* dress in a manner that brings attention to you or does not professionally represent your company
Do immediately speak with your boss if there is a conflict regarding your work	*Don't* wait until a workplace issue gets out of control to share your concerns with your boss

ACTIVITY 13–1

At the end of your orientation period, you may be given a formal performance evaluation. Identify and discuss with the class three typical areas that employers look at in performance evaluations.

1.	
2.	
3.	

ACTIVITY 13–2

Using the information from Exercise 13–6, Health–Care Considerations, assume you are now eligible for health benefits and must choose specific health-care providers. Identify a local physician, eye doctor, dentist, and hospital that you would visit. Why did you select these providers? How did you go about selecting them?

	NAME	WHY SELECTED	HOW SELECTED
Physician			
Eye doctor			
Dentist			
Hospital			

ACTIVITY 13–3

A coworker does not like you and is constantly demonstrating rude behavior toward you. You have attempted to resolve the disagreement, but the coworker refuses to act civil and professional. You resolve to ignore the behavior until an upset customer approaches you and says that your colleague has bad-mouthed you and the customer was offended. What do you do?

_____

_____

_____

_____

ACTIVITY 13–4

An executive at your new workplace starts making inappropriate comments of a sexual nature to you. What do you do?

---

1. During a/an _____, the company purpose, its structure, major policies, procedures, benefits, and other important matters are explained.

2. A/an _____ is a benefit that provides free and confidential psychological, financial, and legal advice.

3. Many companies offer _____ savings plans that are tax deferred for use at a later date.

4. A paycheck has two parts: the _____ and the _____.

5. What you wear to work should never pose a _____.

6. A/an _____ communicates to employees that management and the human resource department are always available to listen should the employee have a concern or complaint.

7. _____ exist to protect the rights of employees when management is not doing its job.

NETWORKING AND RESUMÉS

OBJECTIVES

▶ Define *networking* and its importance to a professional future

▶ Develop a professional *networking list*

▶ Create and update your *resumé*

▶ Create a *cover letter* and professional reference list

▶ Create a *job search portfolio*

CHAPTER 14

Whenever you are asked if you can do a job, tell 'em, "Certainly I can!" Then get busy and find out how to do it.

**Theodore Roosevelt
(1858–1919)**

► PROFESSIONAL NETWORKING

Throughout this text, you have learned how to survive and be successful in the workplace. The importance of maintaining a positive attitude throughout your career cannot be stressed enough.

There will be a time in your future that you will be looking for a job or a new position. This is why networking now and throughout your career is important. **Networking** is the act of creating professional relationships. Think of networking as a connection device.

A professional network is important when you begin searching for a new job either within or outside your current company. Developing a professional network is easy. You tell a person who tells others, then those people tell others, and soon you have many people who know that you want a job. Look at figure 14–1 to see how a network grows.

Almost every person you know can be included in your network. Include the following people in your network list:

- ► Coworkers
- ► Supervisors
- ► Instructors
- ► Family
- ► Friends

Cory has been working as an account clerk for a year now. Throughout the year, Cory has been learning new skills and has learned several new software packages. In addition, Cory has attended several workshops and conferences. Cory knows that in the next year or two the office manager is planning on retiring. Cory would like this position or a similar one. Now is the time for Cory to begin networking. Cory begins by letting coworkers and supervisors know how much Cory has learned in this job. In addition, Cory mentions the new skills and software packages learned over the last year and shares future goals. Cory then tells family members and friends the same thing. This is the beginning of Cory's professional network. Cory creates a written network list and starts keeping track of the people on the list in order to keep them updated.

In addition to adding people you know, there are many other ways to develop and generate your network. One such way is volunteering for community organizations. This gives you a chance to meet many people in different organizations and in different positions throughout the community. Another way is to join clubs. Again, this is a way to meet different people from different companies and from different industries. When you attend workshops, conferences, and seminars, you get a chance to meet people from different corporations that are in your same career field. Another great method to grow your professional network is for you to conduct

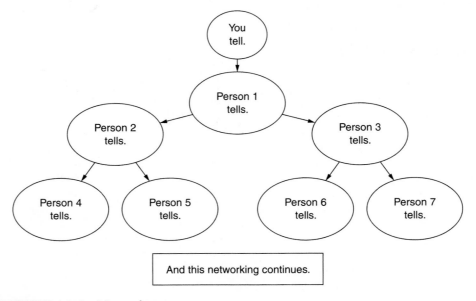

◄ **FIGURE 14–1** Networking

informational interviews. An informational interview is a way to find out about a company or specific career field. You can ask questions about jobs, hiring, and the culture of the company by meeting and talking with others you have added to your professional network.

You are networking when you:

▶ Attend professional or trade association meetings
▶ Talk to other parents when attending a child's sporting or music event
▶ Volunteer for a local park cleanup day
▶ Visit with other members of your social clubs or religious groups
▶ Talk to your neighbors
▶ Strike up a conversation with a stranger waiting at the veterinarian's office
▶ Post messages on mailing lists or in chat rooms
▶ Talk to salespeople who are visiting your office

◀ **EXERCISE 14–1: Identify Your Current Network:** *Name at least three places where you have met people who could be on your professional network list.*

1. _____

2. _____

3. _____

Once you have established a professional network, it is important to maintain that network. This is done by keeping in touch with the people on your list. Keep them updated with your career growth and plans. You can do this by keeping track of who is included in your network and note the last time you updated your information. A **network list** should include the network contact's name, address, telephone number, and e-mail address so you can easily get in touch with each person. You should provide each contact that is actively assisting with your job search a copy of your most current resumé. Keep the contacts on your network list updated throughout your job search. When keeping in contact with members of your network, be sensitive to their time. Do not annoy or be inconsiderate in your behavior and interactions with individuals in your network.

▶ YOUR RESUMÉ

As you begin your career, you will need to create a resumé. A **resumé** is a formal document that presents a person's knowledge, skill, and abilities to potential employers. Throughout your career, it is important to continue to update your resumé. You may not be planning to find a new job or get promoted now, but a time will come when you need a current resumé. Do not wait until that time to create or update your resumé. It is important that you have all current job-related information on your resumé. You need to continually update and include accomplishments you achieve throughout your career. If you wait until you need a resumé, you may forget the important information. As just discussed in the previous section, you should continually be increasing your skills. Add these new skills and experiences to your resumé.

A career objective is a statement to introduce your skills and interest in the position. If you include a career objective on your resumé, it should be specific to the job for which you are applying. Through research, you will identify company needs; you should then apply this information when writing your objective.

Cyber resumés are designed to be sent through the Internet. Companies often drop these into a database to fill open positions. These resumés are then scanned for key words listed in the job posting. Cyber resumés should be saved in plain text. Do not use tables, text formatting (bold, italics, underline), bullets, or headers.

Once you have completed a resumé, update it at least once a year. After you have reached a significant, new skill level, it will be time to change your resumé format. If you are starting in your career, you should create a resumé using the **functional resumé format.** This format is used to emphasize relevant skills when you lack related work experience. A functional resumé focuses on your skills and education. This is done by listing your career objective, relevant skills, and education before any work experience. Most functional resumés are only one page in length. Refer to figure 14–2 for the functional resumé setup. See figures 14–3 and 14–4 for examples.

As you grow in your career, you can change to the **chronological resumé format.** This format emphasizes your related work experience and skills. You should have your employment history, in reverse time order (most recent job first), listed at the beginning of the resumé. Remember to stress major accomplishments and responsibilities of each position. Highlight important activities you have accomplished in your job. Do not assume the reader will know what you have done. Be specific; if necessary, add a second page to your resumé. If your resumé is two pages, be sure you put your name at the top of the second page. Refer to figure 14–5 for the chronological resumé setup. See figure 14–6 for an example.

Make sure your resumé includes both job specific skills and transferable skills. **Job-specific skills** are those that are directly related to a specific job. If you were to leave that job and change careers, those skills would probably not be useful. For example, if you are a medical billing clerk who knows how to use a specific program such as Medical Manager, you will not need to use these skills if you change jobs and become a teacher.

Transferable skills are skills that are transferred from one job to the next. If you change careers, you will still be able to use these skills in any job. For example, if you are a medical billing clerk, you may have consistent contact with patients and must practice patience and be positive when dealing with your customers. If you become a teacher, that skill is transferable to the children in your classroom. You should list both types of skills on your resumé. Employers want you to have the basic skills needed to perform the job, but they also look for transferable skills. They want to know if you are a team player when needed, reliable, a good communicator, get along with others, and so on. The term **soft skills** refers to the people skills needed to get along with others.

Be specific with the skills you list on your resumé, such as computer skills. The term *computer skills* can be too general and typically includes many different areas: networking, programming, applications, data processing, and/or repair. An employer needs to know what specific computer skills you possess. Be specific in your explanation, for example, by informing the employer of your skill level (e.g., basic, intermediate, or advanced) with specific software.

If you are bilingual (speak or write a second language), include this information in your resumé. Let the employer know if you read, write, or just speak that language.

◀ **EXERCISE 14–2: List Your Skills:** *List as many as possible of your job-specific skills and your transferable skills. If you do not have any job-specific skills, list the job skills you will have after finishing your schooling.*

Job-Specific Skills (Related to Your Career Job)	Transferable Skills (Can Be Used in Any Job)
1.	1.
2.	2.
3.	3.
4.	4.
5.	5.

Organize your skills by listing what is needed for the job first. You need to write with energy. Use action verbs, also referred to as *power words*, and quantify your accomplishments. For example, instead of stating "started a new accounts receivable system," use "developed a new accounts receivable system that reduced turnaround time by 20 percent."

Use power words whenever possible. They describe your accomplishments in a lively and specific way. Use some of the power phrases listed in table 14-1 and table 14-2.

When creating a resumé, see the resumé setup and sample resumés found later in this chapter and follow these important tips:

✓ Make sure your objective is job specific.
✓ If you are starting out in your career, use a functional resumé; education and skills are listed before work experience. Keep your resumé to one page.
✓ If you have work experience in your career, use a chronological resumé; experience and skills are listed before education. If you need two pages, put your name on the second page.
✓ Include job-specific and transferable skills.
✓ List experience and education with most recent first.
✓ Watch for consistency in tense: if you have words ending in *ing* or *ed* under an area, make sure they all end the same.
✓ Do not use bullets throughout your resumé; use them to emphasize your skills.
✓ Do not use different color fonts or highlights on your resumé.
✓ Make sure your resumé is consistent in both setup and formatting (periods at the end of each line, alignment of dates, date format, bold/italics, etc.).
✓ Do not use a word processing program template.
✓ List your high school in the education section only if you are using a functional format and have not graduated from college.
✓ Use *telephone*, not *phone* (this is slang).
✓ Use the postal abbreviation for your state, for example: the state is *CA*, not *Ca.*, not *Ca*, not *C.A.*
✓ Any reference statement does not belong on your resumé. Do not list references on the resumé. References should be on a separate sheet and provided only when requested.

Create a list of professional references that the potential employer can contact. Instead of listing these on your resumé, create a separate page for references. Do not send this list with your resumé unless it is requested by the employer. However, you should have a copy available because employers usually ask for references after they have interviewed you. Make sure you have asked each person on this list if he or she will be a reference. Also, be sure each person on this list will provide a positive reference. Have at least three names to give as references. Include each reference's name, telephone number, address, relationship, and e-mail if available. References can be past or present employers and supervisors, coworkers, instructors, or someone with whom you have volunteered. Do not use relatives, friends, or religious leaders unless you have worked or volunteered with or for them.

You should have at least three letters of recommendation. A letter of recommendation is a written testimony from another person that states that you are credible. The letters should not be more than two years old. These letters can be from past or present employers, coworkers, instructors, or someone you worked for as a volunteer.

In addition to keeping your resumé updated, you should update your reference list. Make sure your references are relevant to your career. Check to see if they are still willing to serve as references. In addition, make sure you have your letters of recommendation updated.

When you believe your resumé is perfect, have someone you trust review it for punctuation, grammar, and other potential mistakes. Make sure you check it several times before sending it to a potential employer. Look at the Functional and Chronological Resumé Setups for formatting tips.

YOUR NAME
Your Address
City, State ZIP
Telephone Number (Include Area Code)
E-Mail Address (Remove Hyperlink)

OBJECTIVE

Headings can be on the left or centered, 12- or 14-point font, and uppercase or initial cap.
Headings should be formatted the same throughout the resumé.
Make sure the spacing is equal between each section.

QUALIFICATIONS (OR SKILLS)

- Related to the job, they can be job-related skills or transferable skills.
- Most relative to the job are listed first.
- Bullet (small round or small square only) these items to stand out.

EDUCATION

You may list before qualifications.
Do not list high school.
Include the years attended.
List schools in chronological order, most recent attended first.

> Skills and education need to be emphasized. List your skills and education before any work experience.

WORK EXPERIENCE

Include: *Name of Company and City, State*—No Addresses
Job title, if part-time, dates employed (month, year)
List the jobs in chronological order with most recent date first.
List the duties, responsibilities, and achievements.
Be consistent in your setup.
Use the same tense throughout (*ed* or *ing*).
Do not use complete sentences or *I, me,* or *my*.

OTHER CAPABILITIES

Optional—Items in this section may not be directly related to the job but may interest the employer.

Notes to Keep in Mind

✓ Watch periods, punctuation.
✓ Watch spelling.
✓ Keep to one page.
✓ Use a regular font, no color, 12-point font (except heading).
✓ Use resumé paper, no dark or bright colors.
✓ Do not use full sentences or *I, me,* or *my*.
✓ References are not necessary; you will have a separate sheet with references.

◄ FIGURE 14–2   Functional Resumé Setup

Cory Kringle

4 Tolearn Avenue

Fresno, CA 93705

559-442-4333

ckringle05@jasper.com

OBJECTIVE

To obtain a position as an Account Clerk with XYZ Company which will allow me to utilize my skills in a dynamic company.

SKILLS

- Knowledgeable and accurate in general ledger and journal posting
- Basic software knowledge of QuickBooks
- Knowledge of account receivables and account payables
- Experience with Microsoft Office, including Word, Excel, Access, PowerPoint, and Outlook
- Ten-key at 150 cspm
- Type 50 wpm accurately
- Excellent English grammar, spelling, and punctuation skills
- Accurately follow oral and written instructions
- Strong attention to detail
- Positive attitude, motivated, and organized

EDUCATION

California State University, Fresno, CA	8/06–present
Accounting	

Fresno City College, Fresno, CA	5/06
Associate Degree in Business, Certificate of Completion in Account Clerk Program	

WORK EXPERIENCE

S and L Accounting   1/06–5/06
Account Clerk Volunteer (work experience course)
Assisted the accountant by answering telephone, bookkeeping, data entry in Excel and QuickBooks, verifying totals, making copies, faxing, and other clerical duties when needed.

Bret's Hamburger Haven   1/05–12/05
Cashier/Food Service
Worked as a team member to assist customers with food orders, cleaned, handled cash, and trained new employees.

◄ FIGURE 14–3   Functional Resumé Example 1

DENISE S. SHORE

1408 North Ferris, Fresno, CA 93702
559-451-5899   dshore02@yahoo.com

OBJECTIVE

To obtain a position as an Office Assistant with XYZ Company that will enable me to utilize my current skills and education.

QUALIFICATIONS

- Type 50 wpm
- Experience with Microsoft Office, including Word, Excel, Access, PowerPoint, and Outlook
- Accurately proofread and edit documents
- Knowledge of records management
- Positive telephone skills
- Excellent oral and written communications skills
- Positive attitude, motivated, and organized
- Excellent customer services skills

EDUCATION

2004–2006   Fresno City College   Fresno, CA
AA Degree Business & Technology
Clerical Administration Certificate

EXPERIENCE

06/2003–present   Target   Fresno, CA
Cashier
Responsibilities include: providing customer service, cashiering, handling of money, placing merchandise on the floor, helping return gobacks, processing of merchandise being put on the floor, stocking of merchandise in back/stockroom, training new hires.

02/1998–05/2003   Burger King   Fresno, CA
Cashiering/Counter Person
Responsibilities included: assisted guests with their orders, ensured a safe and clean work environment, and assisted other team members as needed.

◄ FIGURE 14–4   Functional Resumé Example 2

YOUR NAME
Your Address
City, State ZIP
Telephone Number (Include Area Code)
E-Mail Address (Remove Hyperlink)

OBJECTIVE

Headings can be on the left or centered, 12- or 14-point font, and uppercase or initial cap.
Headings should be formatted the same throughout the resumé.
Make sure the spacing is equal between each section.

WORK EXPERIENCE

Include: *Name of Company and City, State*—No Addresses
Job title, if part-time, dates employed (month, year)
List the jobs in chronological order with most recent dates first.
List the duties, responsibilities, and achievements.
Be consistent in your setup.
Use the same tense throughout (*ed* or *ing*).
Do not use complete sentences or *I, me,* or *my.*

> Emphasis is on your work experience in your career. List your work experience first.

QUALIFICATIONS (OR SKILLS)

- Related to the job, they can be job-related skills or transferable skills.
- Most relative to the job are listed first.
- Bullet (small round or small square only) these items to stand out.

EDUCATION

You may list before qualifications.
Do not list high school.
Include the years attended.
List schools in chronological order, most recent attended first.

OTHER CAPABILITIES

Optional—Items in this section may not be directly related to the job but may interest the employer.

Notes to Keep in Mind

✓ Watch periods, punctuation.
✓ Watch spelling.
✓ Use a regular font, no color, 12-point font (except heading).
✓ Use resumé paper, no dark or bright colors.
✓ Do not use full sentences or *I, me,* or *my.*
✓ References are not necessary; you will have a separate sheet with references.

◀ **FIGURE 14–5**   Chronological Resumé Setup

Forrest S. Gunther

2833 Follie Land
Pasadena, CA 93705
214-111-4322
F_gunther@yipae.com

EDUCATION

California State University, Fresno, CA   5/05
Bachelor degree in accounting

Fresno City College, Fresno, CA   5/03
Associate degree in accounting, certificate of completion in account clerk program

PROFESSIONAL WORK EXPERIENCE

Anderson, Bolt, and Company CPA   6/05–present
Accountant
AP, AR, general ledger, general journal, quarterly taxes, and payroll. Supervise account clerks.

Randy and Son Construction   6/03–6/05
Account Clerk
Answer telephone, record journal and ledger for bookkeeping, data entry in Excel and QuickBooks, verify totals, make copies, fax, and other clerical duties when needed.

SKILLS

- Experience and accurate in general ledger and journal posting
- Extensive knowledge of QuickBooks and MAS 90
- Experience with account receivables and account payables
- Experience with Microsoft Office, including Word, Excel, Access, PowerPoint, and Outlook
- Supervisor and leadership skill
- Excellent English grammar, spelling, and punctuation skills
- Accurately follow oral and written instructions
- Strong attention to detail
- Positive attitude, motivated, and organized
- Ten-key at 200 cspm
- Type 60 wpm accurately

◄ FIGURE 14–6   Chronological Resumé Example

◄ **TABLE 14–1** Skills Power Phrases

POWER PHRASES FOR SKILLS SECTION

- Ideal oral and written communications skills
- Understanding of office practices and procedures; ability to operate fax machine, copy machine, and ten-key machine; ability to enter data; ability to effectively interpret policies and procedures; work well under the pressure of deadlines; establish and maintain a positive working relationship with others; ability to communicate
- Accurate typing skills at _____ wpm
- Experienced with Microsoft Office, including Word, Excel, Access, PowerPoint, and Outlook
- Excellent English grammar, spelling, and punctuation skills
- Accurately proofread and edit documents
- Strong attention to detail
- Accurately follow oral and written instructions
- Excellent attendance and punctual record
- Maintain confidentiality
- Positive attitude, motivated, and organized

◄ **TABLE 14–2** Experience Power Phrases

PHRASES FOR WORK EXPERIENCE

- Prepared reports and other materials requiring independent achievement
- Enjoy working in a flexible team situation
- Established and maintained positive and effective working relationships
- Planned, scheduled, and performed a variety of clerical work
- Maintained office equipment and supplies
- Proofread forms and materials for completeness and accuracy according to regulations and procedures
- Processed and prepared materials for pamphlets, bulletins, brochures, announcements, handbooks, forms, and curriculum materials
- Provided training of temporary or new employees
- Maintained department files and records
- Demonstrated ability to receive incoming calls and route them efficiently
- Processed purchase requisitions, ordered and distributed supplies, and maintained inventory control
- Responsibly planned and conducted meetings

► COVER LETTERS

A **cover letter** is most often the first impression a potential employer will have of you. It serves as an introduction to your resumé. Employers use cover letters as screening tools.

When writing your cover letter, use a friendly but professional tone. Include information about the company that shows the employer you have done some research on the company. This may include knowing the key product or service, company growth plans, and/or recent community involvement.

In your letter, point out how you can meet the employer's needs. This is accomplished by reflecting the skills and qualifications the employer is asking for in the advertisement and/or job description. Let the employer know what you can offer the company, not what you want from the company. Do not just duplicate the resumé; instead, expand the areas of interest to the employer.

Be careful not to begin most of your sentences with the word *I*. Instead, focus the attention toward the employer. This puts the company first and makes its needs more important. Do this by beginning the sentence with what the company will receive with your skills. For example:

Instead of writing, "*I* am proficient in Word 2003 and WordPerfect,"
Write, "*Your* company will benefit from my proficiency in Word 2003 and WordPerfect."

When addressing the cover letter, address it to a specific person. This should be the person who is making the hiring decision. Do not address it to a department, the company name, or to whom it may concern. If you have done research and still cannot get a name, use a subject line instead of a salutation. If you have talked to a specific person or with the employer, refer to the previous communication. Make sure you include the specific position you are seeking and how you found out about the job. Request an interview (not the job), include an enclosure notation for your resumé, and close courteously.

Use correct name and title, use spell and grammar check, use left margin justification, and get the employer's permission before sending a letter and resumé. Common mistakes include making typographical or grammar errors, forgetting to including a date, and forgetting to sign the cover letter. Any error communicates a lack of attention to detail. Even minor errors have the potential to eliminate you from any chance of being interviewed.

In chapter 10, you learned how to write a business letter. Be sure you use the proper format for your cover letter. As stated in the resumé section, have someone you trust proofread your letter before sending it to the potential employer. Each paragraph has a purpose. Make sure you have done your research and learned about the position and the company. The cover letter setup in figure 14–7 and sample cover letters in figures 14–8 and 14–9 will help you create your cover letter. The cover letter should be printed on the same type of paper used for your resumé. Make sure you sign your cover letter.

Date of Letter

Employer's Name, Title
Company Name
Address
City, State ZIP

Dear Mr./Ms./Dr.:

First Paragraph. Give the reason for the letter, the position for which you are applying, and how you learned of this position. Note any previous contact you may have had with the employer.

Second Paragraph. Tell why you are interested in the position, the organization, and its products or services. Indicate any research you have done on the position and/or the employer.

Third Paragraph. Refer to the attached resumé and highlight relevant aspects of your resumé. Emphasize the skills mentioned in the advertisement or on the job description. Provide specific reasons why the organization should hire you and what you can do for it.

Last Paragraph. Indicate your desire for an interview, and offer flexibility as to the time and place. Thank the employer for his or her consideration and express anticipation in meeting him or her. Include a telephone number for contact.

Sincerely,

(Do not forget to sign your cover letter.)

Your Name
Your Address
City, State ZIP

Enclosure

◀ **FIGURE 14–7** Cover Letter Setup

September 25, 2007

XYZ Corporation
Attention Rick Raye
435 East Chesny Street
Santa Rosa, CA 91188

Dear Mr. Raye:

As a recent accounting graduate of Fresno City College I was delighted to learn from your web site of the available account clerk position. The purpose of this letter is to express a strong interest in becoming a XYZ Corporation account clerk at your Santa Rosa Facility. In addition to possessing an A.S. degree in Business and a Certificate of Completion in the Account Clerk Program, I am responsible and consider myself a leader.

XYZ sponsors a variety of community services and employee recognition programs, which I have read a great deal about. Your company has earned my respect, as it has from much of the community for your involvement in after-school programs.

As you will see on the attached resumé, XYZ would benefit from the skills I have learned throughout college. These include: general ledger and journal posting; Microsoft Word, Excel, and Access programs; Quickbooks; and accurate ten-key (150 cspm). In addition, I also offer a superior work ethic, strong communicative abilities, attention to detail, and a keen interest in upgrading my skills.

I am confident that my skills and abilities will make me an ideal candidate for a position in this field. I would appreciate an opportunity to meet with you to discuss how my skills can meet the needs of XYZ. I will contact you by phone within the week to discuss the possibility of an interview.

Sincerely,

(Do not forget to sign here.)

Cory Kringle
4 Tolearn Avenue
Fresno, CA 93705

Enclosure

◄ **FIGURE 14–8**   Cover Letter Example 1

◄ **EXERCISE 14–3: List Your References:** *List at least three people you can use as references. Then list at least three people you can ask to write you a letter of recommendation. Include their relationship to you.*

References	Relationship
1.	
2.	
3.	
Letter of Recommendation	Relationship
1.	
2.	
3.	

DENISE S. SHORE

1408 North Ferris, Fresno, CA 93702
559-451-5899   dshore02@yahoo.com

September 21, 2007

Mrs. Lisa Anders
Plenty Office Supplies
1122 Friant Road
Fresno, CA 93725

Dear Mrs. Anders:

I recently spoke with Heidi Johns, an employee at your company; and she recommended that I send you a copy of my resumé. Knowing the requirements for the position and that I am interested in working at this type of establishment, she felt that I would be an ideal candidate for your office assistant position.

My personal goal is to be a part of an organization such as yours that wants to excel in both growth and profit. I would welcome the opportunity to be employed at Plenty Office Supplies since this is the largest and best-known office supply company in the city. Your company has a reputation of excellent products and service.

Plenty Office Supplies would benefit from someone such as I who is accustomed to a fast-paced environment where deadlines are a priority and handling multiple jobs simultaneously is the norm. As you can see on the attached resumé, my previous jobs required me to be well organized, accurate, and friendly. I enjoy a challenge and work hard to attain my goals. Great customer skills are important in a business such as yours.

Nothing would please me more than to be a part of your team. I would like very much to discuss with you how I could contribute to your organization with my office skills and my dependability. I will contact you next week to arrange an interview. In the interim, I can be reached at 559-111-5899.

Sincerely,

(Do not forget to sign here.)

Denise S. Shore

Enclosure

◀ **FIGURE 14–9**   Cover Letter Example 2

► JOB SEARCH PORTFOLIO

As you are conducting your job search, you should begin creating a **job search portfolio.** The job search portfolio is a collection of paperwork you will need for your job search and interviews. The items you collect for your portfolio will be used to keep you organized and prepared while job searching.

It is best to have a binder with tabs to keep this paperwork organized and protected. Because you should not punch holes in your original documents, you should put them into plastic notebook protectors. When you start collecting your paperwork, be sure that you keep your original and at least two copies available at all times while conducting your job search. The copies are for your interviews.

The following is a list of items to keep in your job search portfolio.

ITEM:	IMPORTANCE:
Network list	This is a place to keep it where it is accessible and can be easily updated.
Resumé	Usually asked for by an employer, update once a year.
Cover letter	Usually asked for by an employer, update once a year.
Reference list	Usually asked for by an employer, update once a year.
Letters of recommendation	Usually asked for by an employer, update once a year.
Transcripts	Employers may ask for school transcripts to verify your education. You should have a copy available.
Awards and/or certificates	These are ideal extras you can share with the employer at your interview. Some employers may request certificates for specific skills.
Work samples	These are ideal extras you can share with the employer at your interview. It can prove what you say you can do. Work samples are not necessary in all careers.
Completed application	Although each company will usually have its own application, most of the information requested is the same. By having a completed generic application, you will have most of the information available if you are requested to complete an application while at the job site.
Copy of driver's license	Some employers will ask for this, depending on the job.
Personal commercial	Assists with interview, update at least once a year (chapter 15).
Small calendar, note paper, and pen	Keep track of important dates and use to make notes.
Performance appraisal	Only include if positive.

All items in your portfolio will assist you in your job search and interview process. You will take an **interview portfolio** with you to an interview. The interview portfolio should be a separate folder (such as a paper folder with pockets). Your interview folder should contain copies of the items pertinent to the position for which you are applying. You should bring copies of documents and not your originals. This way you can give them to the employer if necessary. Your resumé, cover letter, and references should be on resumé paper. You will not necessarily take all of the items from your portfolio with you to each job interview. You should have the following for each interview: copies of resumé, cover letter, reference list, application, personal commercial, calendar, note paper, and pen. The other items are included if you want the employer to have a copy because they are relevant to the job. Your folder should remain on your lap while interviewing. If needed, put your personal commercial on the top of the folder in case you get nervous and forget what you have included in this commercial. You can peek at the commercial, but do not read it.

If you are currently working and you start looking for a job, make sure to keep your job search confidential. If you are listing your supervisor as a reference, make sure you let him or her know you are looking and why. Do not quit your current job before being offered a new job. Also, make sure you do not bad-mouth your company or anyone that works for your current or former employer(s).

Even though you now have the experience of being in a career job, you still need to make sure you are prepared when you go on an interview. This means practicing answering interview questions with work-related experiences. Do your homework. Research the company where you will be interviewing, and use that information to let the interviewer know you are interested in working at his or her company.

▶ APPLICATIONS AND PREPARATION

You may be asked to fill out an application to turn in with your resumé packet, or you may be asked to fill out an application after you have been interviewed. If you fill out the application at home, make sure it is typed. If you fill out the application while at the employer's, print neatly and in black ink.

You should have an application filled out in your portfolio so if you are asked to fill one out while at the interviewer's office you have the information needed to complete the application. Make sure you fill out the application completely, but do not list your social security number or birth date. This information should not be given to the prospective employer until you have accepted a job offer.

If you have been convicted of a felony, be honest and check *yes*. Then explain during your interview what you have learned from the mistake. You do not need to reveal any arrests unless you were convicted.

◀ SUMMARY OF KEY CONCEPTS

Professional networking is the act of creating professional relationships. It is an important part of your career process.

- ▶ Almost everyone you know should be a part of your professional network
- ▶ In addition to people you already know, you can develop additional network contacts through various activities
- ▶ You should update your resumé with new skills and accomplishments at least once a year
- ▶ Include both job-specific skills and transferable skills on your resumé
- ▶ Use the correct resumé format for your career time frame
- ▶ A cover letter is most often an employer's first impression of you
- ▶ Make sure your resumé and cover letter are free of typing and grammar errors

◀ KEY TERMS

chronological resumé
   format
cover letter
functional resumé format
informational interview

interview portfolio
job search portfolio
job-specific skills
network list
networking

resumé
soft skills
transferable skills

◀ IF YOU WERE THE BOSS

1. What would you look for first when reviewing a resumé?
2. What would your reaction be if you were reading a cover letter that had several typing and grammar errors?

◀ WEB SITES

http://www.rileyguide.com/network.html#netprep

http://jobsearch.about.com/od/networking

http://www.truecareers.com

http://resume.monster.com

http://jobstar.org/tools/resume/index.htm

◀ WORKPLACE DO'S AND DON'TS

Do keep a network list and keep the people on your list updated	*Don't* be annoying or inconsiderate of your network contacts' time
Do keep your resumé updated with skills and accomplishments	*Don't* wait until the last minute to update your resumé
Do change your resumé format after you have had work experience	*Don't* use outdated reference names and letters
Do use the correct format for your resumé	*Don't* send out a resumé or cover letter that has not been proofread by someone you can trust
Do check your resumé and cover letter for errors before sending them to employers	*Don't* forget to sign your cover letter
Do keep your original job search documents in a portfolio	*Don't* give employers your original documents and expect them to be returned to you

ACTIVITY 14–1

Fill in the following information that will be used to create a resumé.

Skills

JOB-SPECIFIC SKILLS	TRANSFERABLE SKILLS
1.	1.
2.	2.
3.	3.
4.	4.
5.	5.
6.	6.
7.	7.
8.	8.

Education

College Name, City, State

Major information, dates

1. _____

_____

2. _____

_____

Work Experience

Company Name   Dates Worked (month/year)

Job Title

List of duties, not in complete sentence

1. _____

_____

2. _____

_____

ACTIVITY 14–2

Search for a job you would like to have when you graduate and fill in the following information that will be used to create a cover letter.

Paragraph 1

Position for which you are applying	
How you learned about the job	
Any contact you have had with employer or others about the job	

Paragraph 2

Why are you interested in this job?	
Why are you interested in this company?	
What products or services are provided?	

ACTIVITY 14–2 (*Continued*)

Paragraph 3

List relevant skills related to the job description.	
List reasons this company should hire you.	

Paragraph 4

Indicate your desire for an interview.	
Indicate your flexibility for an interview (time and place).	

ACTIVITY 14–3

Create a reference list with at least three names; include the following information.

Reference 1

Name	
Job title	
Place of employment	
Address	
Telephone number	
E-mail address	
Relationship (why is he or she a reference?)	

Reference 2

Name	
Job title	
Place of employment	
Address	
Telephone number	
E-mail address	
Relationship (why is he or she a reference?)	

(*Continued*)

ACTIVITY 14–3 (*Continued*)

Reference 3

Name	
Job title	
Place of employment	
Address	
Telephone number	
E-mail address	
Relationship (why is he or she a reference?)	

ACTIVITY 14–4

Using the following Network Table, develop a networking list. At a minimum, include each contact's name, address, and telephone number.

NETWORK TABLE

Network List

NAME	ADDRESS	TELEPHONE NO.	E-MAIL ADDRESS	LAST DATE OF CONTACT

1. The act of creating professional relationships is referred to as _____.

2. The following people could be included in a professional network: _____, _____, _____, _____, and _____.

3. It is important to update your career resumé at least _____.

4. If you are starting in your career, you should create a resumé using the _____.

5. A/An _____ resumé format emphasizes your related work experience and skills.

6. _____ skills are those that are directly related to a specific job.

7. _____ skills are transferable from one job to the next.

8. Remember to use _____ words whenever possible in your resumé; they describe your accomplishments in a lively and specific way.

CHAPTER 15

JOB SEARCH AND INTERVIEW TECHNIQUES

OBJECTIVES

► Name key steps in a targeted job search

► Identify sources for job leads

► Identify how to tailor a resumé and cover letter for a specific position

► Identify questions to ask when invited to interview

► Identify pre-interview preparation activities

► Identify key responses and cues to look for during an interview

► Explain key areas of employee rights and how to respond to discriminatory questions

► Describe specific statements and behaviors to exhibit at the close of an interview and job offer

All the world's a stage.
William Shakespeare
(1564–1616)

THE TARGETED JOB SEARCH

After you have created a winning resumé, it is time to begin a targeted job search. A targeted job search leads you through the process of identifying open positions for which you are qualified in addition to identifying companies for which you would like to work. The ultimate goal of a job search is to, of course, secure an interview and a job offer.

The first step in a targeted job search is to identify where you want to work. If your job search is limited to your local area, you will be restricted to employers in your community. If you are willing to commute outside of your area, you must determine how far you are willing to drive (both directions) on a daily basis. Finally, if you wish to move out of the area, you need to identify what locations are most appealing.

A job search is work. It takes time and can sometimes be frustrating. Do not get discouraged if you do not get an interview or job offer on your first try. The purpose of this chapter is to give you the skills and confidence to secure a good job in a reasonable time period.

SOURCES OF JOB LEADS

There are many sources for job leads. The first and most obvious job lead is directly from your targeted company. Information regarding open positions within your targeted company can be obtained from the company Web site or from visiting the company's human resource department. This is where you will find a list of open positions. If you do not have a targeted company but have an area where you would like to work, conduct an Internet search. Check message boards and job search sites such as monster.com and hotjobs.com. Other job sources include newspaper advertisements, industry journals, industry associations, and current employees who work in your targeted industry and/or company. Most individuals rely on posted job positions. However, many jobs are unsolicited (not made public). This is why it is important to use your professional network. Inform network members of your desire for a job and ask for potential job leads.

If you are unable to find a job lead, we recommend that you send an unsolicited cover letter and resumé to your target company. When sending an unsolicited resumé, you should send two copies: one to the human resource manager and the other to the manager of your target job. Prior to sending your resumé, call the company to secure the names of both managers. Make sure you have identified the correct spelling and gender for both individuals. Sending two resumés to the same company increases the opportunity for you to secure an interview. The targeted department manager will most likely read and file your resumé for future reference. The human resource manager will also review your resumé and may identify other jobs for which you may be qualified.

TAILORING YOUR RESUMÉ AND COVER LETTER

As mentioned in the resumé chapter, when you have identified a position for which you are qualified, you should tailor your resumé and cover letter specifically to the job and company for which you are applying. Carefully review the job announcement. If possible, secure a copy of the job description from the company's human resource department if it is not available or attached to the job posting. Identify the key job skills that the position requires and highlight the company needs with your skills. Make sure to include your key qualifications in both your cover letter and resumé. In the cover letter, mention the target company by name, how you learned of the job, and your specific qualifications (reflected from the job posting) that make you an excellent candidate to interview.

Make sure your cover letter and resumé include a daytime telephone number. Because most invitations for job interviews occur over the telephone, your telephone voice mail and/or message machine should be professional. Do not include musical introductions or any other greeting that would not make a positive first impression to a potential employer.

Cory's friend Shelby was a practical joker. Cory enjoyed calling Shelby because her voice-mail message started with a joke or had some strange voice and/or music. However, the last time Cory called Shelby, Cory noticed that Shelby's message was normal. The next time Cory saw Shelby, Cory asked Shelby why her voice message was suddenly so serious. Shelby explained that she had recently applied for a job and had been selected to interview. Unfortunately, every time the interviewer called to arrange an appointment, the interviewer kept getting Shelby's unprofessional message machine and did not leave a message, fearing he had dialed the wrong number.

▶ PRIOR TO THE INTERVIEW

When you are invited to interview, find out with whom you will be interviewing. You may be meeting with one person or a group of individuals. Try to find out how much time the company has scheduled for the interview. If possible, find out how many applicants are being called in for interviews. Although this is a lot of information to secure, if you are friendly, respectful, and professional, most people will share this information.

Arrange your interview at a time that puts you at an advantage to be remembered in comparison to the other candidates. Typically, the first and last interviews are the most memorable. If you are given a choice of times to interview, try to schedule your interview in the morning. People are much more alert at that time, and this puts you at an advantage. Ideally, you want to be the first person interviewed or the last person interviewed prior to the lunch break. If this is not possible, try to be the first person interviewed immediately after the lunch break. Be aware that sometimes you will have no say in when your interview is scheduled. Do not make demands. Politely ask the interview scheduler if it is possible for him or her to tell you who will be conducting the interview and/or if the interview can be at a specific time. The goal is to secure as much information as possible prior to the interview so that you can be prepared.

Prior to your interview, conduct research on the company. Many candidates ignore this step thinking it is unnecessary or takes too much time. Doing so better prepares you for your interview, increases your confidence, and provides you a great advantage over the other candidates who will be interviewing for the same job. Learn as much as you can about the company's leadership, strategy, and any current event that may have affected the company. Review the company Web site. Note the key products/services the company produces. Also, identify the company's key competitors. There are many sources for securing company-specific information. Sources include company-produced brochures/literature, industry journals, the Internet, and interviews with current employees and business leaders. The easiest source for securing information will be from a Web search. In your Web search, identify if and why the company has been in the news. Your Web search may reveal how involved the company is in its community. All of this research will assist you during your job interview.

It is important to have a **personal commercial** that sells your skills and ties these skills to the particular job for which you are interviewing. Once you create your personal commercial, you should modify the personal commercial and adapt it to the requirements for your target job. Your personal commercial should take no more than one minute. The personal commercial should include career goals, education, qualifications, and related job skills. The purpose of the commercial is to sell your skills in a brief statement. Your goal is to sell yourself and match your skills to fit the company needs. Do not include personal information such as marital status, hobbies, or other private areas of your life. Use your personal commercial during your interview when instructed, "Tell me about yourself." If you are not given this instruction during the interview, include your personal commercial at the end of the interview.

◀ **EXERCISE 15–1: Targeted Personal Commercials:** *Create your personal commercial for a customer service position for a local department store.*

_____

_____

_____

_____

_____

_____

_____

Another very important activity involved in preparing for the interview is to practice interview questions. Table 15–1 identifies common interview questions, the purpose of each question, and an appropriate answer for each question. Whenever you are answering interview questions, provide examples of your skills and experiences that support your answers.

◀ **TABLE 15–1** Interview Questions

QUESTION	ANSWER	DO NOT
Tell me about yourself.	Use your personal commercial modified to the job description.	Do not divulge personal information or background information on where you were born, personal hobbies, and so on.
What are your strengths? mother").	Include how your strengths meet the job requirements and how they will be an asset to the company.	Do not include strengths that are not related to the job. Do not include personal information (e.g., "I'm a good mother").
Tell me about a time you failed.	Be honest. Use an example that is not too damaging. Include the lesson learned from your mistake.	Do not exclude the lesson learned. Do not place blame on why the failure occurred.
Tell me about a time you were successful.	Be honest. Use an example that relates to the job for which you are applying.	Do not take full credit if it was a team effort.
How do you handle conflict?	Be honest. Use an example that is not too damaging. Including how the conflict was positively resolved. Apply the lesson from chapter 12.	Do not exclude the lesson learned. Do not give specifics on how the conflict occurred and do not use a negative example.
Would you rather work individually or in a team? Why?	State that you prefer one or the other and why, but make sure your answer relates to the job requirements.	Do not state that you will not work one way or the other.
Why do you want this job?	Your answer should convey career goals and how the job supports your current skills. Include company information.	Do not state money or benefits in your response.
How do you deal with stress?	Share positive stress reducers addressed in chapter 4.	Do not state that stress does not affect you. Do not use negative examples.

(Continued)

What is your greatest weakness?	Use a weakness that will not damage your chance of getting the job. Explain how you are minimizing your weakness or are turning it into a strength (e.g., "I'm a perfectionist, but I don't allow it to interfere with getting my job done on time").	Do not state, "I don't have any."
Where do you want to be in five years?	Share the goals you created in chapter 2.	Do not say you want the interviewer's job.
Tell me about a time you displayed leadership.	Use a specific example and try to relate the example to the needed job skills.	Do not appear arrogant.

◀ **EXERCISE 15–2: Formulating Interview Responses:** *Using the preceding table, identify two questions you would find most difficult to answer. Formulate an answer. Then, with a classmate, role-play an interview asking each other the most difficult questions. Constructively critique each others' answers.*

Question	Answer
1.	
2.	

Conduct a practice day prior to the day of your interview. If possible, drive to the interview location. Ideally, you should do this at the same time as your scheduled interview time to identify potential problems including traffic and parking. Park your car and walk to the location of where the interview will be held. This will enable you to become more comfortable and familiar with your surroundings. Do not go into the specific office, just the general area. Make note of the nearest public restroom. You may need it the day of the interview to freshen up prior to your meeting.

Ensuring your interview attire is clean and professional is another important activity to conduct prior to the day of the interview. Chapter 6 addresses professional dress in greater detail. Dress at a level above the position for which you are interviewing. For example, if you are interviewing for a clerk position, dress like you are interviewing for a supervisor position. Make sure your clothes are spotless and fit appropriately. Check your shoes. Ladies, it is a good idea to have an extra pair of nylons available. Check your hair and fingernails to ensure they are professional and appropriate for an interview. Do not overdo your perfume/aftershave or jewelry. Remember that cleanliness is important.

Purchase a package of thank-you notes. The thank-you notes should be simple and professional. The evening before your interview, write a draft thank-you note on a piece of paper.

The thank-you note should be brief (three to four sentences). In the note, thank the interviewer for his or her time. State that you enjoyed learning more about the position, you are very interested in the job, and look forward to hearing from the interviewer soon. This draft note will be used as a foundation for notes you will be writing immediately after your interview. Place the draft note, the package of thank-you notes, and a black pen in your car.

◀ **EXERCISE 15–3: Thank-You Note:** *In preparation for an upcoming interview with a local retailer, write a draft thank-you note.*

Finally, prepare your interview portfolio. Include extra copies of your resumé; a notepad and pen for note taking; your reference list; an extra copy of a most recent performance evaluation, if applicable; and copies of any other documents that pertain to the job. Place your portfolio in your car.

▶ THE DAY OF THE INTERVIEW

Before leaving your home, look in the mirror. Make sure everything fits properly and you project a professional appearance. Practice extending your hand and introducing yourself. The more you practice, the more comfortable you will be. Plan to arrive at your destination fifteen minutes early. This gives you plenty of time to deal with unforeseen traffic and/or parking issues. If there is a public restroom available, go to the restroom and freshen up. Check your hair (and makeup, if applicable). Enter the meeting location five minutes prior to your scheduled interview. This is where your interview unofficially begins. Remember that first impressions matter and that every interaction with every representative of the organization must be professional.

Immediately upon entering the interview location, introduce yourself to the receptionist. Offer a smile and a handshake, then clearly and slowly state your name. For example, "Hi, I'm Cory Kringle, and I am here for a 9:00 a.m. interview with Mr. Wong for the accounting clerk position." If you recognize the receptionist as the same individual who arranged your interview appointment, make an additional statement thanking the individual for his or her assistance. For example, "Mrs. Jones, weren't you the one that I spoke with on the phone? Thank-you for your help in arranging my interview." Be sincere in your conversation, and convey to the receptionist that you appreciate his or her efforts. The receptionist will most likely ask you to have a seat and wait to be called into the interview. Take a seat and relax. While you are waiting, use positive self-talk. Mentally review your personal commercial, qualifications, and the key skills you want to convey to those conducting the interview.

Cory's friend Shelby had finally been asked to interview with one of her target companies. Shelby really wanted the job but was afraid she was not going to do well during her interview. Cory worked with Shelby the evening before the interview by role-playing interview questions and reviewing Shelby's company research. The next day, when Shelby arrived for the interview, she arrived early, thanked the receptionist, and took a seat. As Shelby waited to be called into the interview, she began getting extremely nervous. Remembering Cory's tips, Shelby briefly closed her eyes and used positive self-talk to improve her attitude, increase her confidence, and calm her nerves.

▶ THE INTERVIEW

During the interview, your goal is to communicate confidence. You also need to communicate how your knowledge, skills, and abilities will be an asset to the company. When the appropriate time arrives, you will be invited into a room for your formal interview. When your name is called, stand up and approach the individual who called your name. If it is not the receptionist who called you, extend a smile and a handshake, then clearly and slowly state your name. For example, "Hi, I'm Cory Kringle. It's nice to meet you." Listen carefully to the individual's name. He or she will escort you to an office or conference room where the interview will take place.

The interview may be conducted several ways. It may only involve one person; it may involve several individuals (commonly referred to as a panel interview); or it may include testing. Testing activities may include typing tests, lifting, and demonstrating skills that are included in the job requirements and/or job duties. If you enter a room and there is someone in the room that you have not met, extend a smile and a handshake and introduce yourself. Once again, listen for names. Do not be seated until you are invited to do so. Although you may be offered something to drink, it is best to decline the offer so there is nothing to distract you from the interview. When seated, if possible, write down the names of the individuals you have just met. That way, you can inject the interviewer's name into your conversation.

If the interview is taking place in an office, look around the room to get a sense of the person who is conducting the interview (assuming it is his or her office). This provides useful information for conversation, should it be necessary. Depending on the time available and the skills of the interviewer(s), you may first be asked general questions such as, "Did you have trouble finding our office?" The interviewer is trying to get you to relax. In addition to relaxing, use these questions to connect with your interviewer by including his or her name in your response. For example, if there are family photos or a piece of artwork, ask your interviewer a simple, nonintrusive question such as, "What a nice picture, Mr. Wong. Is this your family?"

During the interview, pay attention to body language—both yours and that of the individual conducting the interview. Sit up straight, sit back in your chair, and try to relax. Be calm but alert. Keep your hands folded on your lap or ready to take notes, depending on the situation. If you are seated near a desk or table, do not lean on the furniture. Do not cross your legs. Remember to make eye contact, but do not stare down the interviewer.

When asked a question, listen carefully. Take a few seconds to think and digest what the interviewer truly wants to know about you. Formulate an answer. All interview answers should relate back to the job qualifications and/or job duties. Your goal is to convey to the interviewer how your skills will assist the company in achieving success. Keep your answers brief but complete. Your job is to sell yourself. Whenever possible, inject information you learned about the company during your research.

Interview questions are either structured or unstructured. Structured questions address specific issues. An example of a structured question is: "How long have you worked in the retail industry?" The purpose of a structured interview question is to secure specific information. An unstructured question is more general. The purpose of an unstructured interview question is to identify if the candidate can appropriately sell his or her skills. An example of an unstructured interview question is: "Tell me about yourself." When you are instructed to "talk about yourself," make sure you state your personal commercial. Whenever possible, pull job samples from your portfolio if you are referring to a specific skill. Relate all answers back to the job for which you are applying.

▶ DISCRIMINATION AND EMPLOYEE RIGHTS

Title VII of the Civil Rights Act was created to protect the rights of employees. It prohibits employment discrimination based on race, color, religion, sex, or national origin. Other laws prohibit pay inequity and discrimination against individuals over forty years of age, individuals with disabilities, and individuals who are pregnant. This does not mean that an employer must hire you if you are a minority, pregnant, over forty, or have a disability. Employers have a legal obligation to provide every qualified candidate equal opportunity to interview. Their job is to hire the most qualified candidate. Unfortunately, some employers often ask interview questions that can be discriminatory. Table 15–2 was taken from the California Department of Fair Employment and Housing to provide acceptable and unacceptable employment inquiries.

◀ **TABLE 15–2**   Illegal Interview Questions

ACCEPTABLE	SUBJECT	UNACCEPTABLE
Name	**Name**	• Maiden name
Place of residence	**Residence**	• Questions regarding owning or renting
Statements that employment is subject to verification if applicant meets legal age requirement	**Age**	• Age • Birth date • Date of attendance/completion of school • Questions that tend to identify applicants over forty
Statements/inquiries regarding verification of legal right to work in the United States	**Birthplace, citizenship**	• Birthplace of applicant or applicant's parents, spouse, or other relatives • Requirements that applicant produce naturalization or alien card prior to employment
Languages applicant reads, speaks, or writes if use of language other than English is relevant to the job for which applicant is applying	**National origin**	• Questions as to nationality, lineage, ancestry, national origin, descent or parentage of applicant, applicant's spouse, parent, or relative
Statement by employer of regular days, hours, or shifts to be worked	**Religion**	• Questions regarding applicant's religion • Religious days observed
Name and address of parent or guardian if applicant is a minor Statement of company policy regarding work assignment of employees who are related	**Sex, marital status, family**	• Questions to indicate applicant's sex, marital status, number/ages of children or dependents • Questions regarding pregnancy, childbirth, or birth control • Name/address of relative, spouse, or children of adult applicant
Job-related questions about convictions, except those convictions that have been sealed, expunged, or statutorily eradicated	**Arrest, criminal record**	• General questions regarding arrest record

If an interviewer asks you a question that is illegal or could be discriminatory, do not directly answer the question; instead, address the issue. For example, if the interviewer states, "You look Hispanic. Are you?" Your response should not just be "yes" or "no." Politely smile and say, "People wonder about my ethnicity. What can I tell you about my qualifications for this job?" Most employers do not realize they are asking illegal questions. However, some employers purposely ask inappropriate questions. In this case, you need to decide if you want to work for an employer that intentionally asks illegal questions. If employers are behaving inappropriately during an interview, one would wonder how they will treat the applicant after he or she is hired.

It is important to protect your rights. Please note that it is inappropriate to disclose personal information. During your interview, avoid making any comment referring to your marital status, children, religion, age, or any other area of protected rights.

◄ **EXERCISE 15–4: Handing Illegal Interview Questions:** *With a classmate, role-play an interview. During the interview, ask one legal question and one illegal question. Practice answering the illegal question with confidence but in a nonoffensive manner.*

Illegal Question	Answer
1.	
2.	

► TOUGH QUESTIONS AND TOUGH ANSWERS

Unfortunately, some job seekers have had negative work-related experiences that they do not want to disclose during an interview. Disclosing such information could be potentially devastating to a job interview if it is not handled properly. Some of these experiences include being fired, having a poor performance evaluation, or knowing that a former manager will not give you a good job reference if called. Perhaps you behaved in a negative manner prior to leaving your old job.

If you did have a difficult situation and are not asked about the situation, you have no need to disclose the unpleasant event. The only exception to this rule is if your current or former boss has the potential to provide a negative reference. If this is the situation, tell the interviewer that you know you will not receive a positive reference from him or her and request that the interviewer contact another manager or coworker who can provide a fair assessment of your performance.

Being honest and factual is the best answer to any difficult question. If you were fired, performed poorly, or left in a negative manner, state the facts. Tell the interviewer that you have matured and realize that you did not handle the situation appropriately. Do not speak poorly of your current or previous employer, boss, or coworker. It is also important to not place blame on who was right or wrong in your negative workplace situation. Remember that every experience, be it positive or negative, is a learning experience.

▶ CLOSING THE INTERVIEW

After the interviewer has completed his or her questioning, you will be asked if you have any questions. Having a question prepared for the close of your interview demonstrates to your prospective employer that you have conducted research on the company. A good question refers to a current event that has occurred within the company. For example, "Mr. Wong, I read about how your company employees donated time to clean up the ABC schoolyard. Is this an annual event?" A statement such as this provides you one last opportunity to personalize your interview and demonstrate that you researched the company. This is also a good time to share any relevant information you have in your portfolio.

Do not ask questions that imply you did not research the company or that you only care about your needs. Inappropriate questions include questions regarding salary, benefits, or vacations. These questions imply that you care more about what the company can do for you than what you can do for the company. However, it is appropriate to ask what the next steps will be in the interview process, including when the hiring decision will be made.

After the interviewer answers your general question, restate your personal commercial and ask for the job. An example of a good closing statement would be: "Once again, thank-you for your time. As I stated at the beginning of our meeting, I feel I am qualified for this job based upon my experience, knowledge, and demonstrated leadership. I would like this job and believe I will be an asset to the XYZ company." The purpose of the job interview is to sell yourself. A sale is useless if you do not close the sale.

After you make your closing statement, the interviewer will signal that the interview is over. He or she will do this either through conversation or through body language (he or she may stand up and walk toward the door). Prior to the close of the interview, ask the interviewer for a business card. As you are handed the card, shake the interviewer's hand and, once again, thank him or her for his or her time and state that you look forward to hearing from him or her. Remember to continue communicating confidence, friendliness, and professionalism to every company employee you encounter on your way out of the building.

When you return to your car, retrieve your draft thank-you note. If necessary, modify your draft thank-you note to include information that was shared during your interview. Then hand-write a personalized thank-you note to each individual who interviewed you. Use your finest handwriting and double-check your spelling and grammar. Refer to the business cards for correct name spelling. After you have written your note, hand deliver it to the reception area and ask the receptionist to deliver the notes. Your goal is to make a positive last impression and stand out from the other candidates.

QUESTIONS YOU *MAY* ASK THE INTERVIEWER

1. Does your company have any plans for expansion?
2. What type of formal training does your company offer?
3. What is the greatest challenge your industry is currently facing?
4. What is the next step in the interview process?
5. What are the hours of the position?
6. When will you be making a hiring decision?

QUESTIONS YOU *SHOULD NOT* ASK DURING AN INTERVIEW!

1. How much does this job pay?
2. How many sick days do I get?
3. What benefits will I get?
4. What does your company do?
5. How long does it take for someone to get fired for poor performance?

► AFTER THE INTERVIEW

After delivering your thank-you notes, return to your car and congratulate yourself! If you did your best, you should have no regrets. Prior to leaving the company, jot down notes regarding specific information you learned about your prospective job and questions you were asked during the interview. Through the excitement of an interview, you may forget parts of your meeting if you do not immediately write notes. Finally, make a mental note of what you did right and areas in which you would like to improve upon next time you need to interview. This information will be helpful in the future. Remember that it may take several interviews to land a job, so do not be disappointed if you do not get a job offer on your first attempt.

► NEGOTIATION

Within a few weeks, you should hear back from the company. At that point, you may be called in for a second interview or may receive a job offer. You may be told that your job offer will be contingent upon your reference checks. This will be a good time to call the individuals on your reference list to give them an update on your job search. This way they will be prepared to respond to the individual conducting your reference check.

If you are a final candidate for the job, the interviewer may ask you about your salary requirements. Prior to stating your salary requirement, you should sell your skills. For example, "Mr. Wong, as I mentioned in my initial interview, I have over five years' experience working in a professional accounting office; therefore, I feel I should earn between $XXX and $XXX." In order to negotiate an acceptable salary, you must first conduct research and compare your research to the salary range that was included in the job posting. Check job postings and conduct online research to determine local and regional salaries. In your search, attempt to match the job description as closely as possible to that of the job for which you are applying. Depending on your experience, start a few thousand dollars higher than your desired starting salary and do not forget to consider your experience and/or lack of experience. Some companies do not offer many benefits but offer higher salaries. Other companies offer higher salaries and fewer benefits. You need to weigh these factors when determining your desired salary. If you are offered a salary that is not acceptable, use silence and wait for the interviewer to respond. This minute of silence may encourage the employer to offer a higher salary.

Cory's friend Shelby was invited to a second interview. Prior to the interview, Cory and Shelby once again prepared for potential questions and situations Shelby might encounter during the interview. In their practice, Cory asked Shelby about her starting salary. Shelby said she did not care; she would just be happy to get a job. Cory reminded Shelby that she needed to sell her skills and go into the interview with a desired target salary. Cory and Shelby then conducted an Internet search of both local and statewide jobs that were similar to the one Shelby wants. Fortunately, the next day, when the interviewer asked Shelby about her desired starting salary, Shelby was prepared to answer.

► WHEN YOU ARE NOT OFFERED THE JOB

As stated at the beginning of the chapter, a job search is like a full-time job. It takes time and can sometimes be discouraging. If you are not called in for an interview or do not get a job offer, do not be discouraged.

If you are not called in for an interview, evaluate your resumé and cover letter. Check for typographical or grammatical errors. Make sure you have listed important skills that reflect the needs of the job for which you are applying. Have someone who knows you and your skills—and whom you trust—review your cover letter and resumé. Many times, a fresh perspective will catch obvious errors or opportunities for improvement.

If you are invited to interviews but do not receive a job offer, do not be discouraged. Remember to make every experience a learning experience. Sit down and carefully review each step in the interview process and grade yourself. Consider your pre-interview preparation, interview day appearance, your interview answers, your ability to interject your company research into each interview answer, and your overall attitude. Any area that did not receive an *A* grade is an area poised for improvement.

There are several steps you can take to increase the probability for success in your next interview. Consider your overall appearance. Reviewing the information in chapter 6, make sure you convey professionalism. Ensure that your clothes are clean and that they fit properly. Have a hairstyle that is flattering and well kept. Make sure your fingernails and jewelry are appropriate and do not deter from your personality and job skills.

Mentally review job interview questions that were asked and the responses you provided. Remember that every answer should communicate how your skills will assist the target company in achieving success. Review the amount of company research you conducted. Did you feel amply prepared or did you just conduct the bare minimum? If you felt you did conduct the appropriate amount of research, assess whether you fully communicated your research to the interviewer.

Assess your body language and attitude. Stand in front of a mirror and practice your answers to difficult and/or illegal questions. If possible, have a friend videotape you and provide a critical evaluation of your appearance, attitude, and body language. Check for nervous gestures, and keep practicing until you are able to control these nervous habits.

Finally, be honest with your overall performance. Did you ask for the job? Did you immediately send a thank-you note to your interviewer(s)? You must sell your skills through your mannerisms, answers, and attitude. Your goal is to stand head and shoulders above the other candidates.

◀ SUMMARY OF KEY CONCEPTS

▶ A targeted job search leads you through the process of identifying open positions for which you are qualified in addition to identifying companies for which you would like to work
▶ There are many sources of job leads, including directly from the company, an advertisement, and a professional network
▶ You should review common interview questions and formulate answers as part of your interview preparation
▶ You should modify your personal commercial and adapt it to the requirements of your target job.
▶ Conduct a dry run prior to the day of your interview
▶ During your interview, communicate how your knowledge, skills, and abilities will be assets to the company
▶ There are laws that protect employees from discrimination
▶ At the close of the interview, you should ask for the job. The purpose of the job interview is to sell yourself

◀ KEY TERM

personal commercial

◀ REFERENCE

State of California Department of Fair Employment and Housing. *Pre-Employment Inquiry Guidelines.* CA, DFEH-161, Sacramento, CA, 2001.

◀ IF YOU WERE THE BOSS

1. What kind of information should you share with your current staff members as they prepare to interview a new employee?
2. How would you handle a prospective employee who disclosed inappropriate information during the job interview?

◀ WEB SITES

http://jobstar.org/electra/question/sal-req.cfm

http://www.collegegrad.com/intv

http://www.careercc.com/interv3.shtml

http://interview.monster.com

http://www.rileyguide.com/interview.html

◀ WORKPLACE DO'S AND DON'TS

Do realize that a targeted job search takes time	*Don't* get discouraged if you do not get an interview or job offer on your first try
Do explore various sources of job leads including your personal network, the Internet, and industry journals	*Don't* limit your job leads to newspaper advertisements
Do tailor your resumé and personal commercial to the needs of your targeted employer	*Don't* have unprofessional introductions on your voice-mail message
Do try to schedule your interview at a time that puts you at an advantage over the other candidates and secure information that better prepares you for the interview	*Don't* make demands with the individual scheduling the interview
Do learn as much as you can about the company, its strategy, and its competition	*Don't* forget to include your research information in your interview answers
Do practice interview questions and formulate answers that highlight your skills and experience	*Don't* show up to an interview unprepared
Do remember that your interview begins the minute you step onto company property	*Don't* let your nerves get the better of you on a job interview
Do know how to handle inappropriate questions that may be discriminatory	*Don't* answer an illegal question. Instead, address the issue

ACTIVITY 15–1

Identify a local company for which you would like to interview. Using the following table, conduct a thorough targeted job search on this company. Answer as many of the questions as possible.

1. Company name	
2. Company address	
3. Job title	
4. To whom should the cover letter be addressed?	
5. What are the job requirements?	
6. What is the duration of the job?	
7. What are the hours/days of work?	
8. What are the working conditions?	
9. Is there room for advancement?	
10. What kind of training is offered?	
11. What other positions at this company match my qualifications?	
12. What are the average starting salaries (benefits)?	
13. Is traveling or relocation required?	
14. Where is the business located (home office, other offices)?	
15. What are the products or services that the employer provides or manufactures?	
16. What is the mission statement?	
17. What kind of reputation does this organization have?	
18. What is the size of the employer's organization relative to the industry?	
19. What is the growth history of the organization for the past five, ten, or fifteen years?	
20. How long has the employer been in business?	
21. Who is the employer's competition?	

ACTIVITY 15–2

Using an Internet job site or other medium, identify four job leads that match your career goals and current qualifications.

JOB LEAD	INTERNET SITE ADDRESS OR MEDIUM NAME AND DATE
1.	
2.	
3.	
4.	

ACTIVITY 15–3

Write out at least two different statements you can use during a telephone conversation when you are invited to interview at a specific time. Make one statement for when you accept the interview time and make the other statement for when you must change the time. Make sure your statements attempt to secure all relevant interview information.

INITIAL STATEMENT	RELEVANT INTERVIEW INFORMATION NEEDED

ACTIVITY 15–4

Using information obtained in your target company research (activity 15–1), write out three common interview questions and answers. Integrate relevant company information in your answers.

QUESTION	ANSWER
1.	
2.	
3.	

ACTIVITY 15–5

Using information gathered in activity 15–2, conduct a salary search. Develop a grid illustrating the highest salaries and lowest salaries for these positions. Using your research data, write out a statement you could use to negotiate a higher salary.

LOWEST SALARY	HIGHEST SALARY

Your Statement of Negotiation

1. The purpose of a/an _____ is to identify _____ and identify companies for which you would like to work.

2. One of the most obvious job sources is utilizing your _____.

3. Your telephone message should be _____.

4. In addition to finding out with whom you will be interviewing, find out how much _____ the company has scheduled and _____ are being called in to _____.

5. Prior to your interview, _____.

6. If possible, prior to the interview day, _____.

7. When asked a difficult question, it is important to be _____ and _____.

16

CHANGES IN EMPLOYMENT STATUS

OBJECTIVES

▶ Define the importance of continual *formal learning* and *informal learning*

▶ Explain the importance of *training* and *development*

▶ Know the various ways your status of employment can change

▶ Define the various types of workplace terminations

▶ Demonstrate how to write a *letter of resignation*

▶ Know the appropriate behavior to exhibit when leaving a position

Real success is finding your lifework in the work that you love.

David McCullough
(1933–)

► TRAINING AND DEVELOPMENT

When you start a new job, your company should train you in your new job. In addition to receiving an orientation to your job, many companies offer additional **training** to help you learn new skills. The teaching of new skills may be used to help promote employees and/or increase their responsibilities. With the increase of technology, employee training is an important part of many companies. Training is usually provided by the company and/or paid for by the company.

As an employee, you should make every effort to attend **development** sessions to enhance or increase your skills. Development sessions will make you more diverse in your knowledge, skills, and abilities, which will give you an advantage when promotional or other opportunities arise in the workplace. Even if you do not think a development session is in your area of expertise, you should continue expanding your knowledge and skills in as many areas as possible. This is especially helpful if you are considering a promotion into a management position.

As an employee who is considering a management position, you should learn not only the areas of your responsibility but also other skills. You should be aware of the key duties within other departments. The development of these skills will increase your knowledge and vision of the company's missions and objectives. When you can see beyond your job, you become even more aware of what you are contributing to the company and how you are making it more successful. This will increase your awareness of how important it is to do your job as best as you can.

The marketing department for Cory's company invited all employees to meet in the conference room during lunch hour to learn more about how to conduct a media interview. Cory did not know a lot about marketing and did not think media interviews would be a part of Cory's job. However, Cory attended because it would be not only a good skill to learn but also a good way to meet people in other departments.

► CONTINUAL LEARNING

In addition to training and development programs offered by your company, there are other ways to improve and increase your skills and knowledge. **Continual learning** is the process of increasing your knowledge in the area of your career. This can be accomplished by formal and/or informal learning.

Formal learning includes going back to college to increase knowledge or to improve your skills in your area of career interest or to receive an additional or advanced degree. This can easily be done while you are working. You can take one or two night classes a semester while you work. You should not take too many classes while working full time because that may stress you to a point that you will perform poorly at both work and school.

Another method of increasing your professional knowledge and skills while working fulltime is to take online classes. Online classes have become increasingly popular for working students. These classes allow you more freedom and flexibility. Instead of having to attend class on a certain day and at a certain time, you can log on to the Internet and do your classes at your convenience around work hours.

In addition to college, there are many seminars and conferences you can attend. Some of these seminars and conferences offer college credit. Many seminars and conferences are offered by vendors or industry experts. Although you may have to pay for the conference, your company may be willing to reimburse you or share the cost with you. Conferences may last one day or may be over a period of several days.

Informal learning includes reading career-related magazines, newsletters, and other articles associated with your job. Another means of informal learning is using the Internet to search career-related information. Make every opportunity a learning opportunity. Remember, informal learning takes place during interviews, in conversations with professionals in your career area, and by attending association meetings.

◀ **EXERCISE 16–1: Additional Career Interests:** *What additional classes may be helpful to you when you start working in your new job? Name at least three classes.*

1. _____

2. _____

3. _____

▶ CHANGES IN EMPLOYMENT STATUS

It is very natural for employees to have a desire to change jobs. When this change occurs and where an individual moves are dependent upon many factors. Throughout this text, we have stressed the importance of personality and goal setting. As you begin meeting your stated goals, it is time to establish new ones. Some reasons for changing jobs are:

▶ Acquired experience for an advanced position
▶ Opportunity for higher salary
▶ Desire for improved work hours
▶ Need for increased responsibility, status, and/or power
▶ A perceived decrease in stress
▶ Need for a different boss or coworker

Other times, you may be forced to change positions. It is common for employees to move within and outside of their company. Changes in employment status include promotions, voluntary terminations, involuntary terminations, lateral transfers, and retirement. This chapter presents and discusses each of these changes in employment status and provides tips on how to handle each situation in a professional manner.

▶ NEW JOB SEARCHES

Some employees determine that they must find a new job immediately while other employees are constantly exploring opportunities. No matter what your situation, you should identify when to share your desire for a new job and when you should keep your job search a secret. If you have recently received a college certification or degree that qualifies you for a higher position, approach your supervisor or human resource department to inform the appropriate individuals of your increased qualifications and desire for additional responsibilities and/or promotion. It is also appropriate to share your need to change jobs if a situation is requiring you to move out of the area. In this instance, your employer may have contacts that can assist you in securing a new job in another city. If you have had good performance evaluations and are leaving voluntarily, ask your immediate supervisor, another superior, or coworkers if they are willing to serve as references for future employers. If they agree to serve as references, secure letters of recommendation written on company letterhead. It is always helpful to write a draft letter for your reference that highlights your accomplishments and favorable work attitude. Finally, if you have mastered your job duties, have had good performance evaluations, and are beginning to feel bored, you should share your desire for increased responsibilities with your boss.

Apart from the previously mentioned circumstances, you should not share your desire to change jobs with anyone at work. This includes coworkers. Oftentimes, sharing secrets at work can be used against you. Therefore, keep your job search private. Conduct your job search during nonwork hours. Job interviews should be scheduled before or after work hours or during your lunch period.

◀ **EXERCISE 16–2: Your Recommendation:** *List at least four key points to include in a draft letter of recommendation for you. Give an example for each key point.*

Key Point (Quality)	Example
1.	
2.	
3.	
4.	

Grace and style are two key words to remember when your desires for a new position are found out by others. When confronted about your job search, be positive. State that you desire a move, be it the need for additional responsibility or the need for more money, but keep your explanation simple. You do not have to share details as to why you want to move on. You also do not have to share details about potential employers or the status of your job search.

▶ PROMOTIONS

A **promotion** is defined as moving to a position higher in the organization with increased responsibility. Oftentimes, an individual wants a promotion but there is not an available position. The first step in securing a future promotion within your company is to begin behaving and dressing for the desired position. If possible, secure a copy of the job description for your desired position. Begin acquiring work experience in the desired area by volunteering for assignments that provide the needed experience. Develop new skills by taking appropriate classes, job training, and other educational experiences to increase your qualifications. Watch and learn from those who are already in the position you desire. Implement this plan and you will gain the necessary qualifications and have the experience when an advanced position does become available.

When you are promoted, always thank your former boss. This can be done verbally or with a simple, handwritten thank-you note. Communicate how your former boss has helped you acquire new skills. Remember to be sincere. Even if your former boss was awful, his or her poor example showed you how not to behave. Keep the note positive and professional. With your promotion, you will see an increase in pay, a new title, and new responsibilities. If your promotion occurred within the same company, never gloat. Remember that there were probably others within the company that also applied for the job. You must behave in a professional manner that reinforces that your company made the right choice in selecting you for the position.

In your new job, do not try to reinvent the wheel. Become familiar with the history of your department or area. Be sensitive to the needs and adjustments of your new employees. Review files and begin networking with people who can assist you in achieving your department goals. Remember, grace and style. You are new to a position and do not know everything. Ask for and accept help from others.

With a history of favorable performance evaluations, Cory wants a promotion. Cory decided to take responsibility and began evaluating potential positions for which Cory might qualify. During Cory's research, Cory created a list of additional knowledge, skills, and abilities to increase Cory's qualifications needed for the promotion. Cory began taking classes, attending training seminars, and watching leaders within the company to prepare for a future promotion.

▶ VOLUNTARY TERMINATIONS

Leaving a job on your own is called a **voluntary termination.** While at times the workplace can be so unbearable that you want to quit without having another job, it is best to not quit your job unless you have another job waiting. No matter what the situation, when voluntarily leaving a job, it is important to be professional and not burn bridges.

You should resign with a formal letter of resignation. A **letter of resignation** is a written notice of your voluntary termination. Unless you are working with a contract of employment that specifies an end date of your employment, you are technically not required to provide advance notice of your voluntary termination. It is, however, considered unprofessional to resign from work and make your last day the same day you resign. Typically, two weeks' notice is acceptable. Make sure you state your last date of employment in your letter of resignation. Include a positive statement about the employer and remember to sign and date your letter.

Following is a sample letter of resignation.

February 1, 2007

Susie Supervisor
ABC Company
123 Avenue 456
Anycity, USA 98765

Re: Notice of Resignation

Dear Ms. Supervisor:

While I have enjoyed working for ABC Company, I have been offered and have accepted a new position with another firm. Therefore, my last day of employment will be February 23, 2007.

In the past two years, I have had the pleasure of learning new skills and of working with extremely talented individuals. I thank you for the opportunities you have provided me and wish everyone at ABC Company continued success.

Sincerely,

Jennie New-Job

Jennie New-Job
123 North Avenue
Anycity, USA 98765

No matter how bad the boss or horrific the work environment, do not speak or behave negatively in your final days of employment. Leave in a manner that would make the company want to rehire you tomorrow. Coworkers may want to share gossip or speak poorly of others, but you must remain professional. You may also be tempted to damage or take property that belongs to the company. Do not behave unethically. Only take your personal belongings and leave your work space clean and organized for whoever assumes your position. It is important to preserve the confidentiality of your coworkers, department, and customers.

Cory had a coworker that had been looking for a job for the past few months. Cory knew this because the coworker not only told everyone but always used the company equipment to update and mail her resumé. Cory often heard the coworker talking to potential employers on the telephone. On the day Cory's coworker finally landed a new job, the coworker proudly announced to everyone in the office that she was "leaving the prison" and that afternoon would be her last day at work. The coworker went on to bad-mouth the company, her boss, and several colleagues. As she was cleaning out her desk, Cory noticed that the coworker started packing items that did not belong to her. When Cory shared this observation, the coworker said she deserved the items and that the company would never miss them. A few weeks later, Cory's former coworker came by the office to say hello. Cory asked her how her new job was going. "Well . . ." said the coworker, "the job fell through." The coworker explained that she was stopping by the office to see if she could have her old position back. Unfortunately, the former coworker left in such a negative manner that the company did not want to rehire her.

On your last day of employment with your company, you will meet with a representative from the human resource department or with your immediate supervisor to receive your final paycheck. This paycheck should include all unpaid wages and accrued vacation. This is when you will formally return all company property including your keys and name badge. You may also receive an **exit interview.** During this interview, a company representative will ask you questions regarding your former position, boss, and work environment. The company's goal is to secure any information that provides constructive input on how to improve the company. You can share opportunities for improvement, but do not turn your comments into personal attacks. While it is tempting to provide a negative interview, remember to remain positive and professional.

▶ INVOLUNTARY TERMINATIONS

Involuntary terminations are when you lose your job against your will. These include **firing**—when you are terminated because of a performance issue; a **layoff**—the company's financial inability to keep your position; or a **restructuring**—when the company has eliminated your position.

If you are fired, you have lost your job as a result of a performance issue. Unless you have done something outrageous (such as blatant theft or harassment), you should have received a poor performance warning prior to the firing. Typically, this progressive discipline includes a verbal and/or written warning prior to termination. If you are totally unaware of why you are being fired, ask for documentation to support the company's decision. Firing based on outrageous behavior will be supported by a policy, while any performance issue should be supported with discipline in writing. When you are told of your firing, you will immediately receive your final paycheck, which should include your accrued vacation. You will also be asked to return all company property on the spot (including keys and name badge). Do not damage company property. Doing so is not only immature but punishable by law. While you may be angry or caught off guard, do not make threats against the company or its employees. Remain calm and professional. If you feel you are being wrongfully terminated, your legal recourse is to seek assistance from your state's labor commission or a private attorney.

◄ **EXERCISE 16–3: How to Handle Being Fired:** *If you were fired, what would be the first three things you would do? Justify your answers.*

Activity	Justification
1.	
2.	
3.	

Many people consider a layoff a form of firing. This is not true. Firing is a result of poor performance. A layoff is a result of the company being unable to financially support the position. Most employees are laid off based upon their seniority with the company. Typically, those who were recently hired are the first to lose their jobs. While some companies lay off employees based upon performance, most do it on seniority. Frequently, when the company's financial situation improves, employees may be recalled. A **work recall** is when employees are called back to work. If you have been laid off, remain positive and ask your employer for a letter of reference and job search assistance. This job search assistance may include support in developing a resumé, job training, and job leads.

In today's competitive environment, it is common for companies to restructure. Restructuring means the company is changing its strategy and reorganizing resources. This commonly results in eliminating unnecessary positions. If yours is a position that has been eliminated, remain positive and inquire about new positions. In a restructuring situation, it is often common for new positions to be created. Once again, do not bad-mouth anyone or openly express your anger or dissatisfaction of the situation. If you have recently acquired new skills, now is the time to communicate and demonstrate your new skills. Keep a record of your workplace accomplishments, and keep your ears open for new positions for which to apply.

► OTHER MOVES WITHIN THE ORGANIZATION

In addition to promotions and terminations, there are several other methods of moving within and outside the company. These include lateral moves, demotions, and retirement. A **lateral move** is when you are transferred to another area of the organization with the same level of responsibility. Lateral moves only involve a change in location. A change in pay is not involved in a lateral move. If you experience a pay increase, it is considered a promotion. If you experience a pay decrease, you have been demoted. While **demotions** are rare, they can occur if one's performance is not acceptable but the employee chooses to not leave the company. Of all the changes an employee can make, a demotion is by far the most difficult. You typically experience not only a decrease in pay but also a decrease in job title and status. If you are demoted, remember to remain professional and be respectful of your new boss.

The final change in employment status is called **retirement.** Retirement means that you are voluntarily leaving your employment but no longer working. Although this text addresses those entering the workforce, it is never too early to start planning for your retirement both mentally and financially. This can be done by establishing career goals and deadlines, in addition to contributing to a retirement fund.

As you can see, there are several means of moving within and out of an organization. Those with healthy careers move and rarely stay in one position their entire career. It is not healthy to move too frequently, nor is it healthy to remain in the same position for a long time. Regardless of your plans to advance in the near future, it is important to always keep your resumé updated. Doing so keeps you motivated to take on additional responsibilities and increase your knowledge, skills, and abilities. You will also be prepared, should some unforeseen opportunity come your way.

◀ SUMMARY OF KEY CONCEPTS

▶ Continue training for new skills and knowledge to help reach your career potential
▶ Formal learning is another way to increase your skills and knowledge
▶ Changes in employment status include promotions, voluntary terminations, involuntary terminations, lateral moves, and retirement
▶ Be cautious about sharing your desire to move away from your current position
▶ There are two types of terminations: voluntary and involuntary
▶ When leaving voluntarily, you should always submit a letter of resignation
▶ When leaving in an involuntary manner, do not burn bridges or behave in an unprofessional or unethical manner
▶ There is a difference between being fired and being laid off
▶ It is never too early to begin planning for your retirement

◀ KEY TERMS

continual learning	informal learning	restructuring
demotion	involuntary termination	retirement
development	lateral move	training
exit interview	layoff	voluntary termination
firing	letter of resignation	work recall
formal learning	promotion	

◀ IF YOU WERE THE BOSS

1. Why would it be important to encourage training and development sessions within your department?
2. You hear through the grapevine that one of your best employees is looking for another job. What should you do?
3. Management has told you that you must lay off four of your employees. How do you determine who to lay off and how best to tell them? How do you defend your decision?

◀ WEB LINKS

http://agelesslearner.com/intros/informal.html
http://careerplanning.about.com/od/quittingyourjob
http://www.insiderreports.com/bizltrs/resign1.htm

◀ WORKPLACE DO'S AND DON'TS

Do update your skills and knowledge through training	*Don't* assume additional skills and knowledge are not necessary for advancement
Do keep an open mind for job advancement opportunities	*Don't* openly share your dissatisfaction for your current job
Do write a formal resignation letter when leaving a company and a thank-you letter to a boss or mentor when receiving a promotion	*Don't* leave your job abruptly without giving adequate notice to your current employer
Do behave professionally when leaving a position	*Don't* take or ruin company property when leaving a position
Do provide valuable feedback and opportunities for improvement during an exit interview	*Don't* turn an exit interview into a personal attack on your former boss or coworkers

ACTIVITY 16–1

Based on your career plan in chapter 2, identify additional training, development, and continual learning you will need for professional success.

TRAINING	DEVELOPMENT	CONTINUAL LEARNING

ACTIVITY 16–2

Identify your ideal job. What continual learning do you need to get there?

JOB MOVE	CONTINUAL LEARNING

ACTIVITY 16–3

Name at least five ways you can begin to develop work experience for a future promotion.

1. _____
2. _____
3. _____
4. _____
5. _____

ACTIVITY 16–4

Throughout this text, you have learned good human relations for the workplace. Name at least three things you can do to decrease your chances of being laid off if that becomes necessary with your company.

1. _____
2. _____
3. _____

ACTIVITY 16–5

Write a draft letter of reference for yourself.

_____

_____

_____

_____

_____

_____

_____

_____

_____

1. To make you more diverse in your skills you should attend _____.

2. The process of increasing knowledge in your career area is referred to as _____ _____.

3. Changes in employment status include promotions, _____ terminations, involuntary _____, lateral moves, and _____ .

4. If you have had good performance evaluations and are leaving voluntarily, secure a _____.

5. A/An _____ is a written notice of your voluntary termination.

6. Your _____ should include all unpaid wages and _____.

7. Employees who are _____ are terminated due to a/an _____ issue.

8. Employees who are _____ are terminated due to the company's _____.

9. A/An _____ is when you are transferred to another area of the organization. A change in pay is not involved.

abusive boss: a boss who is constantly belittling or intimidating his or her employees

accommodating management style: a conflict management style that gives the other party what he or she wants without consideration of your own needs; used when preserving a relationship is a priority

accountability: accepting the responsibility and reporting back to whoever gave you the power

adjourning stage: when team members bring closure to a project

agency shop: employees do not have to join the union after being hired; however, the employee is required to pay a fee to the union because he or she is enjoying the benefits of being represented by the union

aggressive behavior: the behavior of an individual who stands up for his or her rights but does so in a manner that violates others' rights, generally in an offensive manner

appearance: how you look

assertive behavior: the behavior of an individual who stands up for his or her rights without violating the rights of others

assets: tangible items that you own that are worth money

attitude: a strong belief toward people, things, and situations

automatic deduction plan: when money is automatically deducted from an employee's paycheck and placed into a bank account

avoiding management style: a passive conflict management style used when one does not want to deal with the conflict

bargaining issues: workplace topics that will be addressed in a new union contract

board of directors: a group of individuals responsible for developing the company's overall strategy and major policies

budget: a detailed financial plan for a specific time period; a plan used to allocate money

burnout: the desire to no longer work

business memos: written communication sent within an organization (also called *interoffice memorandums*)

capital budget: a financial plan used for long-term investments including land and large pieces of equipment

casual workdays: workdays when companies relax the dress code policy

charismatic power: a type of personal power that makes people attracted to you

chronological resumé format: a resumé format that emphasizes related work experience and skills

coercive power: power that uses threats and punishment

collaborating management style: a conflict management style in which both parties work together to arrive at a solution without having to give up something of value

communication: the process of a sender sending a message to an individual (receiver) with the purpose of creating mutual understanding

company resources: financial (fiscal), human (employees), and capital (long-term investments) resources that the company can utilize to achieve its goals

competent: knowing the product(s) a company offers

compromising management style: a conflict management style that is used when both parties give up something of importance to arrive at a mutually agreeable solution to the conflict

confidential: matters that should be kept private

conflict: a disagreement or tension between two or more parties (individuals or groups)

conflict of interest: when someone influences a decision that directly or indirectly benefits him or her

connection power: based on using someone else's legitimate power

continual learning: the process of increasing your knowledge in the area of your career

corporate culture (organizational culture): values, expectations, and behavior of people at work; the company's personality being reflected through employees' behavior

courtesy: exercising manners, respect, and consideration toward others

cover letter: a letter that introduces your resumé

credit report: a detailed credit history on an individual

culture: different behavior patterns of various groups

customer: one who buys a service or product

customer service: the treatment an employee provides the customer

debt: money owed

decoding: when the receiver interprets a message

demotion: when an employee is moved to a lower position with less responsibility and a decrease in pay

dental benefits: insurance coverage for dental care

departments: subareas of divisions that carry out specific functions respective of their division

dependable: capable and honest when assisting a customer

development: sessions to enhance or increase your skills

direct benefits: monetary employee benefits

directional statements: a company's mission, vision, and values statements; these statements are the foundation of a strategic plan

diversity statements: corporate statements that remind employees that diversity in the workplace should be an asset and not a form of prejudice and stereotyping

diversity training: company training designed to teach employees how to eliminate workplace discrimination and harassment

divisions: how companies arrange their major business functions

dress code: an organization's policy regarding appropriate workplace attire

employee assistance program (EAP): an employee benefit that typically provides free and confidential psychological, financial, and legal advice

employee handbook: a formal document provided by the company that outlines an employee's agreement with the employer regarding work conditions, policies, and benefits

employee loyalty: an employee's obligation to consistently support a company and its mission

employee morale: the attitude employees have toward the company

employee orientation: a time when a company provides new employees important information including the company's purpose, its structure, major policies, procedures, benefits, and other important matters

employment-at-will: a legal term for noncontract employees that states that an employee can quit any time he or she wishes

empowerment: pushing power and decision making to the individuals who are closest to the customer in an effort to increase quality; customer satisfaction; and, ultimately, profits

encoding: identifying how a message will be sent (verbally, written, or nonverbally)

ethics: a moral standard of right and wrong

ethics statement: a formal corporate policy that addresses the issue of ethical behavior and punishment should someone behave inappropriately

etiquette: a standard of social behavior

executive presence: having the attitude of an executive

exit interview: a situation in which a company representative interviews an employee who is leaving the organization; topics include questions regarding the former position, boss, and work environment

expenses: money going out

expert power: power that is earned by one's knowledge

extrinsic rewards: rewards that come from external sources including such things as money and praise

feedback: when a receiver responds to a sender's message based upon the receiver's interpretation of the original message

finance and accounting: a department that is responsible for the securing, distribution, and growth of the company's financial assets

firing: when an employee is terminated because of a performance issue

fixed expenses: expenses that do not change from month to month

flexible expenses: expenses that change from month to month

forcing management style: a conflict management style that deals with the issues directly and head-on

formal communication: workplace communication that occurs through memos, meetings, or lines of authority

formal learning: going back to college to increase knowledge or skills in your area of career interest or to receive an additional or advanced degree

formal teams: developed within the formal organizational structure and may include functional teams or cross-functional teams

forming stage: when team members first get to know each other and form initial opinions about other members

full-time employee: an employment status for employees who work forty or more hours per week

functional resumé format: a resumé format that emphasizes relevant skills when work experience is lacking

glass ceiling: invisible barrier that frequently makes executive positions off limits to females and minorities, thus prohibiting them from advancing up the corporate ladder through promotions

glass wall: invisible barrier that frequently makes certain work areas such as a golf course off limits to females and minorities, thus prohibiting them from advancing up the corporate ladder through promotions

goal: a broad, long-term target or aim

good boss: a boss who is respectful and fair

grievance procedure: formal steps taken in resolving a conflict between the union and an employer

gross total income: the amount of money on a paycheck before taxes or other deductions are made

group: two or more people who share a common goal and have one leader

hostile behavior harassment: any behavior of a sexual nature by another employee that someone finds offensive including verbal slurs, physical contact, offensive photos, jokes, or any other offensive behavior of a sexual nature

human relations: interactions occurring with and through people

human resource department: a department responsible for hiring, training, compensation, benefits, performance evaluations, complaints, promotions, and changes in your work status

human resource management: a business function that deals with recruiting, hiring, training, evaluating, compensating, promoting, and terminating employees

impasse: when a union and an employer cannot come to an agreement in contract negotiations

implied confidentiality: an obligation to not share information with individuals with whom the business is of no concern

income: money coming in

incompetent boss: a bad boss who does not know how to do his or her job

indirect benefits: nonmonetary employee benefits such as health care and paid vacations

informal communication: workplace communication that occurs among individuals without regard to the formal lines of authority

informal learning: reading career-related magazines, newsletters, and other articles associated with your job

informal teams: group of individuals who get together outside of the formal organizational structure to accomplish a goal

information power: power based upon an individual's ability to obtain and share information

information systems: a business function that deals with the management of computer-based information within the organization

informational interview: an interview of a professional to find out about a company or specific career field

interest: the cost of borrowing money

interview portfolio: a folder that contains photocopies of documents and items pertinent to a position

intrinsic rewards: internal rewards that include such things as self-satisfaction and pride of accomplishment

introductory employee: newly hired employee who has not yet successfully passed his or her introductory period

involuntary termination: when an employee loses his or her job against his or her will

job description: a document that outlines specific job duties and responsibilities for a specific position

job search portfolio: a collection of paperwork needed for a job search and/or interview

job-specific skills: skills that are directly related to a specific job

labeling: when one describes an individual or group of individuals based upon past experience

lateral move: when an employee is transferred to another area (department) of an organization

layoff: when a company releases employees from their jobs due to financial problems

leadership: a process of one person guiding one or more individuals toward a specific goal

learning style: the method of how you best take in information and/or learn new ideas

legal counsel: a function within a business that handles all legal matters relating to the company

legitimate power: the power that is given to an employee from the company

letter: a written form of communication

letter of resignation: a written notice of your voluntary termination

letterhead: paper that has the company logo, mailing address, and telephone numbers imprinted on quality paper

levels of ethical decision making: the first level is the law; the second level is fairness; the third level is one's conscience

liability: money that is owed

lockout: when an employer does not allow union employees to work until a contract is approved

locus of control: identifies who you believe controls your future

long-term goals: broad targets that are anywhere from five to ten years

mandatory time off: time off that is required by law including jury duty, voting, military leave, domestic violence issues, and crime victim related issues

marketing: responsible for creating, pricing, selling, distributing, and promoting the company's product or service

mediator: a neutral third party whose objective is to assist two conflicting parties in coming to a mutually agreeable solution

medical benefits: insurance coverage for physician and hospital visits

mentor: someone who can help an employee learn more about his or her present position, provide support, and help develop the employee's career

middle managers: typically have the title of *director* or *manager;* these individuals work on tactical issues

mission statement: a company's statement of purpose

money wasters: small expenditures that actually use up a portion of one's income

motivation: an internal drive that causes people to behave a certain way to meet a need

negative stress: an unproductive stress that affects your mental and/or physical health including becoming emotional or illogical or losing your temper

negotiation: working with another party to create a situation (resolution) that is fair to all involved parties

net worth: the amount of money that is yours after paying off debt

network list: a list of individuals included in a person's professional network

networking: meeting and developing relationships with individuals outside one's immediate work area; the act of creating professional relationships

noise: anything that interrupts or interferes with the communication process

norming stage: when team members accept other members for who they are

objectives: short-term goals; must occur within one year's time and be measurable

open shop: employees do not have to join the union; nor are they required to pay a fee for union representation

open-door policy: a management philosophy the purpose of which is to communicate to employees that management and the human resource department are always available to listen should the employees have a concern or complaint

operational budget: a financial plan used for short-term items including payroll and the day-to-day costs associated with running a business

operational issues: issues that occur on a daily basis and/or for no longer than one year

operations: a business function that deals with the production and distribution of a company's product or service

operations managers: first-line managers who are typically named *supervisors* or *assistant managers*

organizational chart: a graphic visual display of how a company organizes its resources; identifies key functions within the company and shows the formal lines of authority for employees

organizational structure: the way a company is organized

part-time employee: an employment status for employees who work less than forty hours a week

passive behavior: the behavior exhibited when an individual does not stand up for his or her rights

perception: one's understanding or interpretation of reality

performance evaluation: a formal appraisal that measures an employee's performance

performing stage: when team members begin working on their task

personal commercial: a statement that sells your skills and ties these skills to a particular job

personal financial management: the process of controlling one's income

personality: a stable set of traits that assist in explaining and predicting an individual's behavior

physiological needs: an individual's need for basic wages to obtain food, shelter, and other basic needs

picketing: when union employees stand outside the workplace and inform others of a current disagreement between the employer and the union

politics: obtaining and utilizing power

positive stress: productive stress that provides strength to accomplish a task

power: one's ability to influence another's behavior

prejudice: a favorable or unfavorable judgment or opinion toward an individual or group based on one's perception (or understanding) of a group, individual, or situation

president or chief executive officer (CEO): the individual responsible for operating the company; this individual takes his or her direction from the board of directors

priority: determines what needs to be done and in what order

product: a tangible item or something that one can physically see or touch

productivity: to perform a function that adds value to a company

profit: revenue (money coming in from sales) minus expenses (the costs involved in running the business)

projection: the way you feel about yourself is reflected in how you treat others

promotion: moving to a position higher in the organization with increased pay and responsibility

quality: a predetermined standard that defines how a product is to be produced or a service is to be provided

quid pro quo harassment: a form of sexual harassing behavior that is construed as reciprocity or payback for a sexual favor

race: a group of individuals with certain physical traits

reciprocity: creating debts and obligations for doing something

respect: holding someone in high regard

responsibility: accepting the power that is being given

responsive: being aware of a customer's needs often before the customer

restructuring: when a company changes its strategy and reorganizes its human resources

resumé: a formal document that presents a person's knowledge, skills, and abilities to potential employers

retirement: when an employee voluntarily leaves the company to no longer work

retirement plan: a savings plan for retirement purposes

reward power: the ability to influence someone with something of value

right to revise: a statement contained in many employee handbooks that provides an employer the opportunity to change or revise existing policies

safety needs: an individual's need for a safe working environment and job security

self-actualization: when an employee has successfully had his or her needs met and desires to assist others in meeting their needs

self-esteem: how you view yourself

self-esteem needs: an individual's need for workplace titles, degrees, and awards

self-image: how an individual thinks others views him or her

sender: an individual wanting to convey a message

senior managers or executives: individuals who work with the president in identifying and implementing the company strategy

service: an intangible product that one cannot touch or see

sexual harassment: unwanted advances of a sexual nature

shop steward: a coworker who assists others with union-related issues and procedures

short-term goals: goals that can be reached within a year's time (also called *objectives*)

social needs: an individual's need for positive workplace relationships

soft skills: people skills that are needed to get along with others

stereotyping: making a generalized image of a particular group or situation

storming stage: when team members have conflict with each other

strategic issues: major company goals that typically range from three to five years or more

strategic plan: a formal document that is developed by senior management; the strategic plan identifies how the company secures, organizes, utilizes, and monitors its resources

strategy: a company's road map for success that outlines major goals and objectives

stress: a body's reaction to tense situations

strike: when union employees walk off the job

supervisors: first-level managers that concern themselves with operational issues

synergy: extra excitement that occurs when people are truly working together as a team

tactical issues: business issues that identify how to link the corporate strategy into the reality of day-to-day operations; the time line for tactical issues is one to three years

teams: two or more people who share a common goal and share responsibility and leadership

temporary employee: an employee who is hired only for a specified period of time, typically to assist with busy work periods or to temporarily replace an employee on leave

time management: how you manage your time

trade-off: giving up something to do something else

training: the process of learning new job skills for the purpose of an employee promotion and/or increased responsibility

transferable skills: skills that can be transferred from one job to another

union: a third-party organization that protects the rights of employees and represents employee interests to an employer

union contract: the formal document that addresses specific employment issues including the handling of grievances, holidays, vacations, and other issues

union shop: an employee does not have to be a member of the union to secure employment; however, after a specified time period, employees are required to join the union

value: getting a good deal for the price paid for a product or service

values: ideas that are important to an individual

values statement: part of a company strategic plan that defines what is important to (or what the priorities are for) the company

vision benefits: insurance coverage for vision (eye) care

vision statement: part of a company's strategic plan that describes the company's viable view of the future

voluntary termination: leaving a job on your own

whistle-blower law: a law that protects employees who inform authorities of an employer's illegal conduct

work recall: when employees are called back to work after a layoff

work slowdown: when employees work but significantly decrease their output until the employer meets union contract objectives

work wardrobe: clothes that are primarily worn only to work and work-related functions

workplace bullies: employees who are intentionally rude and unprofessional to coworkers

workplace discrimination: acting negatively toward someone based on race, age, gender, religion, disability, or other areas

workplace diversity: differences among coworkers; primarily cultural and racial differences

INDEX